Accessing Higher Education: Footprints of Marginalised Groups

Accessing Higher Education: Footprints of Marginalised Groups

Edited by

Govardhan Wankhede
Ivan Reid

AAKAR

ACCESSING HIGHER EDUCATION: Footprints of Marginalised Groups
Edited by Govardhan Wankhede and Ivan Reid

First Published 2017

ISBN 978-93-5002-485-0

Published by
AAKAR BOOKS
28 E Pocket IV, Mayur Vihar Phase I, Delhi 110 091
Phones: 011 2279 5505, 2279 5641
aakarbooks@gmail.com

Type set
Arpit Printographers, Delhi 110 0032

Printed at
Saurabh Printers Pvt. Ltd., Greater Noida

Contents

Acknowledgements

This book is a compilation of papers presented at a national seminar themed *'Higher Education and the Marginalized: A Critique to Access and Quality in the Global Context'*, held on 03-04, March 2014, at the Tata Institute of Social Sciences (TISS), Mumbai, organized by the Centre for Higher Education, School of Education.

I take this opportunity to thank the seminar sponsor, the Indian Council of Social Science Research (ICSSR), New Delhi, without whose support the seminar would not have been possible. I thank Prof Sukhadeo Thorat (Chairman, ICSSR) for encouraging me to go ahead with such a large scale seminar. I also thank Prof S. Parasuraman (Director, TISS) for granting the required permissions and providing his continuous guidance and support. My special thanks to Prof Ivan Reid (York St John University, UK) for delivering the Valedictory Speech at very short notice, to Prof Jandhyala B.G. Tilak (NUEPA) and Prof N. Jayaram (TISS) for addressing the plenary sessions, and to my guide Prof Karuna Chanana (formerly with JNU). Lastly, I thank all the contributors and participants, my team—Ankit Saraf, Pratima Zore, the staff of School of Education and TISS, the rapporteurs Maansi Parpiani and Vikrant Wankhede all of whom worked tirelessly to make this Seminar a success. I sincerely hope that this book too would be well received.

Govardhan Wankhede

Foreword

Education has become the main source of economic and social mobility, and therefore for the government it is a critical policy issue. For the people, particularly the marginalized and the poor access to education has become an investment, insofar as it gives return through gainful employment. However, the history of education, particularly Higher Education has not been smooth with respect to its access to the poor and marginalised communities who were denied the right to education till public education was initiated by the British. During much of the British period, education was remained confined to the so-called high caste, urban males. After independence, the Government of India was required to provide access to all, particularly the marginalised sections like the Scheduled Castes (SCs), Scheduled Tribes (STs), Persons with Disabilities (PWDs), religions minorities (especially Muslims) and the Other Backward Classes (OBCs). Altogether, these sections form the majority of India's population. Due to the expansion of higher education institutions, the access to education has expanded significantly. The enrolment rate in higher education which was less than one per cent in 1950, now touch about two fifth. Beside increasingly the sections which were kept away from access to higher education began to enter into higher education. The increase in the enrolment for higher education has been marked by noteworthy diversity. From 'high caste' urban mates, the composition of the students has shifted to women, 'low castes', and minorities from urban area. Even the relatively poorer sections began to get access to higher education. Expansion of government and the private aided institutions which run institutions similar to public ones have been instrumental in providing access to relatively poor and socially marginalised sections. This has also resulted in economic mobility among them. Thus public higher education has acted as a so called leveller and an instrument of minimising inequalities in their economic lives.

However, there has been a paradigm shift in the pattern of higher education since the 1980s. Under the pretext of financial tightening since the mid-1980s, there has been a move towards the privatisation of higher education.

In undergraduate courses of education, particularly in the areas of professional higher education, like engineering, medicine, management, and similar courses; there was a move from the 1990s towards privatisation of universities, the so-called deemed universities and State-level private universities, including the self-financing courses in public universities and colleges. The magnitude of the self-financing private sector has enhanced quite significantly. In 1995/96 about 7 per cent of the students were in self finance private institutes. This ratio has increased to almost 25 per cent. It is about 70 per cent in professional courses. What is disturbing is that the ratio of the poor going to self-financing private institute has been much lower compared to the non-poor due to the high costs. Besides this the access of SC/ST groups to higher education has been much lower. Therefore the present higher education system being increasingly dominated by self-financing institutions has led to unequal access to higher education. The unequal access particularly in professional education has created the inequalities in capabilities and employability. This has affected the economic and social mobility of the poor and the socially marginalised groups like SC and ST. Unlike in Europe the inequality in the access to education has become the source of economic and social inequality.

This book has come as a timely reminder to the Government and policy making bodies: contains papers on higher education that were presented at a seminar by distinguished scholars who have been engaged in teaching and researching in their respective areas of interest. In the present context of privatisation of education in India and the global scenario, this collection provides a fresh approach, new ideas and discusses issues that need to be taken up for further study. I am sure, the book will be useful for planners, policy-makers and scholars besides general readers.

Prof Sukhadeo Thorat
Chairman
Indian Council of Social Science Research
New Delhi

1

Introduction and Overview: Setting the Scene of this Book

Govardhan Wankhede and Ivan Reid

Education has been globally accepted as an effective and efficient means to upward development. This has come to be especially true post-the-1990s-era of globalisation. In case of India, the relevance of Higher Education (HE) is incomparable owing to the rising demands of knowledge, skills and techniques. However, another important role of HE that seems to have been more or less neglected is the need of HE for individual, communitarian and social welfare. This book attempts to depart from the debate that revolves around the need of HE for polishing skills as demanded directly and/or indirectly by the market forces. It instead tries to understand the importance of HE, the role it plays in relation to the process of marginalisation and its limited and fractured availability to the marginalised.

In the Indian context, the role of HE has been increasingly observed to be dual, and therefore contradictory. India has been heavily dependent on education as an agent of change and development in a situation where it has been monopolised by a small urban elite middle/upper class and upper castes. Despite constitutional provisions, commitments and several measures, the monopoly further extends in a rather complex manner by excluding communities such as the Scheduled Castes (SCs), Scheduled Tribes (STs), Other Backward Castes (OBCs), religious minorities and women. These groups continue to face difficulties to access, perform and utilize HE in a relevant and appropriate manner. One finds differences all across and within different marginalised groups in terms of rural-urban divide, caste, tribe, gender, religion and region when it comes to HE. These communities continue to remain largely excluded from the educational scenario as a result of the complex and hierarchical structure of the Indian society, a society which relies heavily on social constructs. The case of exclusion has only gotten curious with a myriad of biases and technicalities against the marginalised in terms of the Reservation Policy, its features and implementation. The reasons for this vary from ignorance, biases, discrimination, to plain lack of information and motivation. Lately, opposition to the Reservation Policy can be observed to have a 'materialistic' aspect to it—the non-marginalised or the privileged missing out on seats in institutions which grant them a freeway to high paying opportunities in multinationals. The concomitant arguments of merit can also be seen from this very prism. Alternatively, the rise and mushrooming of private universities throughout the urban and semi-urban pockets of the country have further only added to the problem; Reservation Policy not being applicable in the private arena, the majority of the marginalised sections have been excluded and discriminated against because of high fee structures, lack of grievance redressal mechanisms and other forms of material/non-material support mechanisms.

Acknowledging that HE has been a vital constituent of inclusive growth, it is equally pertinent to understand the existence of HE as a system that is part of a larger societal structure. The positioning of the HE system has made it furthermore susceptible to external hierarchical influences, thereby structurally excluding the weaker sections. In other words, the indispensable nature of HE makes it a must for scholars, academicians and policy-makers to continuously analyse and review HE in terms of access, equity, quality, availability of resources, schemes, policies, support, pedagogic practices, content, scope and practices.

The chapters in this book also examine the range of varied issues pertaining to higher education in the global context. The issue of commonality here lies in the structured practice of exclusion and discrimination in various forms and manifestations. The matter of higher education as an agent of change therefore needs an intense, critical and a renewed approach with special attention to the ground realities and practice.

This book can be seen to fall into three parts:

Part I [Chapters 1 and 2]

This provides a discursive tour of the epistemological landscape of the terms of equality, equity, access and participation and an extensive review of the Indian empirical data.

Part II [Chapters 3 through 6]

This presents a set of contemporary accounts of the experiences of the marginalised minorities in Indian universities.

Part III [Chapters 7 through 11]

This is concerned with the academic institutional and disciplinary roles and issues in widening participation for the marginalised

Part I

Chapter 2 : 'Issues of Equality, Equity and Quality in Widening Access to, and Participation in Universities', by Ivan Reid, adopts a discursive manner to address some of the global underlying cultural and philosophical assumptions of widening participation in higher education. It provides a tour of the epistemological landscape of the terms of equality, equity, access and it aims to stimulate thinking and conversation, so it is of a challenging, if not controversial in nature. It is based on his experience of having had the opportunity to engage with the educational systems of a number of countries over several years and recognising the persistent and global nature of issues, such as: what is meant by equality, equity and quality in higher education? The chapter reviews: economic, cultural, individual purposes of education systems and the functions of social control, engineering and justice, together with the basis of competition or competency. The implications of access from a stratified society to a stratified education system are discussed and looks at the extent to which the result is integration or isolation. Further aspects looked at are: selection and segregation by disability, social class/caste, ethnicity, religion, age and gender—the primacy of socio-economic background and hierarchies of higher education institutions and disciplines and their selection procedures. It poses the question: is the widening participation about assimilation, multiculturalism or can it be transformative?

Part II

Chapter 3: 'How Inclusive is Higher Education in India?' by Jandhyala B.G. Tilak, in the broad context of inclusive growth policies in India, and the rich data available from the National Sample Survey 1983 and 2009-10, examines the growth and inequalities in higher education in India. It is primarily concerned with inequalities by gender; by social groups—caste and religion; by region—rural and urban; and by economic groups of population—population classified by monthly per capita household expenditure. Using two important indicators on higher education, gross enrolment ratio and higher education attainment [percentage of adult population having completed higher education] the chapter examines whether inequalities in higher education have increased or declined overtime. It also throws light on which groups have improved most over the years in their higher education status and whether inequalities between which groups have declined or increased.

Chapter 4: 'Cultural Capital and Social Exclusion and the Marginalised Groups' by Prashant Bansode Abstra utilises Bourdieu's concept of cultural capital in the Indian context. It focuses on how caste inequalities are reproduced in higher education, and how reservation policy has played an important role for inclusion (though not as expected) of SC/ST in higher education. The chapters points out that the reasons for these inequalities are: a lack of cultural capital and the persistent caste discrimination/exclusion in higher education and a lack of will on the part of implementers/institutions for efficient implementation of the benefits of reservation policy.

Chapter 5: 'Discourses of Caste in the Classroom: Reflections from Undergraduate Teaching in a Delhi University College' by Smriti Singh, argues that while excluding structured practices of institutions captured before, the more fluid aspect of public opinion within classrooms remains an uncharted issue. Based on participatory observation in a first year undergraduate classroom it uses the discussions to explore the assumptions and character of popular discourse.

Chapter 6: 'Aiming High: Higher Education among the Kunchikorves of Dharavi' by Pradeep Shinde explores the relationship between social construction, state policies, and higher education vis-à-vis a Denotified Tribe (the Kunchikorves) in a Mumbai slum. It argues that the recognition of a Denotified Tribe as a discriminated category is contingent upon the State and not upon their social claim that they have been the victims of social stigma. As a result, today most Kunchikorves do not possess their caste certificates and are therefore deprived of securing access to reservation benefits and higher education.

Part III

Chapter 7: 'Higher Education, Conflict Resolution and Peace Building in Rural Areas of Jammu and Kashmir State' by Renu Nanda proposes a delivery model whereby educational interventions could enhance income and employment avenues among the educated strata that are located on the international border of the state. The chapter suggests that if appropriate, location-specific, institutional interventions are made operational, it could help in building a climate of peace and tranquility in otherwise conflict affected regions in the country.

Chapter 8: 'Access to Higher Education: Issues and Challenges of Students with Disability' by Vaishali Kolhe states that the problems of students with disabilities in higher education are multifaced and need an interactive communication technology to bridge all the learning gaps.

Inclusion can be done at the structural and the social levels. The Information and Communication Technologies and use of mobile technologies and Social Networking technologies can play a key role. It examines the core issues of postgraduate students with disabilities in a qualitative study using the narrative analysis with thematic enquiries. Students with visual and locomotor disabilities were included in the study.

The last two chapters are concerned with the academic institutional and disciplinary roles and issues in widening participation for the marginalised.

Chapter 9: 'Counter-Hegemonic Assertions of Marginalised Students on University Campuses in India' by Gaurav J. Pathania argues that Indian universities are in a transitional phase, on which student activism is based - the issue of privatisation, globalisation and liberalisation are deeply affecting university campuses, while issues of equity, quality, inclusion and employment are the most serious concerns. Data from qualitative studies from 2009 to 2013 in four major institutions, in the limelight for their student activism has been examined. One finding is that student activism offers a "counter-culture" to the dominant ideological activism of both left and right wing student politics.

Chapter 10: 'Exclusion of Dalit Issues in Social Sciences' by Vivek Kumar argues that Indian social sciences have been exclusionary in nature with respect to 'Dalit' issues by neglecting the extential and experiential realities of Dalits. Their icons, movements, labour, worldview etc. have been ignored or discussed partially, according to him. Vivek Kumar gives a few evidences of such exclusionary treatment by social sciences in India and further argues that how social sciences are being used to maintian the hegemony in Indian academics.

Chapter 11: 'The "Coming Crisis" of Social Science Education in India: Issues and Challenges' by Avinash Kumar Singh highlights that the coming crisis of social science education lies at the subordination of the state to market forces, increasing withdrawal of State resources from the education system in general, the social-order-based university system in particular and the growing disenchantment among the educated towards the efficacy of their own thoughts and paradigms. It argues that the rising social problems are linked to the eroding social base of individuals reflected in the ineffective social science education in India.

2

Issues of Equality, Equity and Quality in Widening Access to, and Participation in Universities

Ivan Reid

Introduction

This chapter adopts a discursive manner to address some of the global underlying cultural and philosophical assumptions of widening participation in higher education. It aims to stimulate thinking and conversation, so it is of a challenging, if not controversial nature. It is based on my experience of having had the opportunity to engage with the educational systems of a number of countries over several years and recognising the persistent and global nature of issues, such as:

What is meant by equality, equity and quality in higher education?

The economic, cultural, individual purposes of education systems and the functions of social control, engineering and justice, and the basis of competition or competency.

The implications of access from a stratified society to a stratified education system—integration or isolation?

Selection and segregation by disability, social class/caste, ethnicity, religion, age and gender—the primacy of socio-economic background.

Hierarchies of higher education institutions and disciplines and their selection procedures.

Is widening participation about assimilation and

multiculturalism or can it be transformative?

An initial concern is the definition of words or terms of concern used. Here these are straightforward dictionary definitions:

Equality. The state of being identical, in terms of social status/rights/services. In respect to some aspects of social life and perhaps especially education, equal or identical treatment would be, and is, unfair, since individuals and groups display wide and diverse variations. A simple example is the disabled. Consequently the next term below is more apt.

Equity. An impartial, or fair, act, or decision.

Quality. A degree, or standard, of excellence, especially a high standard.

Access. The right, or privilege, to make use of something.

Participate. To take part, to become actively involved. This definition raises the questions of the ease and level of participation.

Formal and Informal, or Institutional and Non-institutional education

It is important to appreciate that most learning, if not teaching goes on outside school and/or Formal Education/Higher Education institutions—before, during and after.

Though all societies educate their young to take their place as adults, only at a certain stage of development does this become institutionalised—when a political decision is made that what is necessary in terms of knowledge and skills is beyond the capacity of the family and other informal agencies.

Education for what, or why Education for all?

Economic

Industrial development has been seen as requiring a population with basic levels of literacy and numeracy. The evidence for higher education is less clear, though there is a profound belief in the West that the future economic wellbeing of the country depends on the increasing educational attainment of the population.

Social/cultural

For a peaceful society there is a need for adults to understand aspects of citizenship, to develop a moral code, to understand and obey the legal system, and to participate in politics within whatever form of democracy or political system that exists.

Individual/personal

To develop the capacity for, if not the love of, learning, to enable individuals to adopt roles in a family, community and to be able to cope with changing circumstances and opportunities, including those of occupation. In the West most people can expect to change jobs and therefore be required to learn new skills. Even where women do not participate in paid employment, their education is important—as it is said to educate a woman as opposed to a man is to educate a family.

Education Systems

Globally most societies have adopted what is essentially a Western model of higher education. However, it is clear that education is culturally specific and a one size fits all approach will not work. Adapting existing patterns and practices of education to fit particular societies is not necessarily straightforward and calls for sensitive and well researched policy making. This is often missing and I could give many examples from schooling in the UK. In these examples, ideas have been lifted from other educational systems and resulted in severely limited, or unexpected, impact and outcomes. I have also observed this in the so-called developing countries. In what follows I outline some of the considerations that need to be taken into account in order to maximise equity, quality and access in respect to higher education wherever it occurs.

There appears to be near universal agreement that all children should receive some schooling. However, both its provision and its take-up vary, both within and across societies. Actually the costs of education, both direct and indirect, affect take-up in many, if not all countries, as do some cultural beliefs concerning the need for, or the desirability of, schooling for girls.

Most societies see education as being part of being a child or young person rather than a lifelong undertaking. Often this amounts to, or has amounted to, if a person does not take advantage of schooling or higher education then there is/was no second chance. Yet in those societies that have seen the need to provide life-time opportunities at all levels of education, uptake has been generally good. It is interesting to note that learning is a normal, continual and spontaneous activity of humans, and only when learning is institutionalised does it become seen as artificial, difficult and tiresome. There may be some lessons to be learnt about how institutionalised learning could be made more normal and generally acceptable to pupils and students.

The Functions of Education

Social Control

Of course education is also about social control and order. Sunday Schools in England were started to keep troublesome children off the streets on Sundays as well as having Christian purposes. As soon as child labour became uneconomic in Britain, around the 1980s, compulsory elementary schooling was introduced and it is arguable that subsequent rises in the school leaving age and expansion of further and higher education addresses youth unemployment and social control issues as well as those of the educational needs. Pupils entering secondary school this year in England will have to stay until they are seventeen years old.

Part of schooling is about learning to obey rules and adopting values which are not necessarily those of the families, or the community, to which the pupils belong, but are deemed necessary for them to have in order to take on adult roles in society.

For many education also 'legitimises' the unequal nature of society in providing what is seen as a neutral field in which all have the opportunity to succeed. In essence this belief appears to be based on Young's idea on meritocracy in which IQ [or let's say ability] + effort equals merit. Young wrote his book as a satirical futurist comment, but meritocracy has become an internalised value or belief in many societies which clearly includes the UK as well as the USA. This leads to the belief that the individual, having had educational opportunity, is responsible for their own lifestyle and success, as these are due to their efforts. Hence inequality is justified. However, this is to overlook the basics in inequalities both in education, the job market and society.

Social Engineering

It is clear, at least on reflection that education is about social engineering. Through education society produces its workforce and its citizens. Political decisions are made about the educational system and these determine almost every aspect—from who gets what, through what they get, to how they receive it. Typically this results in the best education for those who have political power and/or are wealthy. Further it maintains, or even heightens, existing inequality. In effect education reinforces the existing social structure, albeit usually with some limited social mobility. This mobility allows the more able and motivated members of the disadvantaged to be recruited into higher status occupations and hence change social class. The latter arguments are often used as a defence along the lines of, "well if some of disadvantaged succeed then the system is fine" because it allows, or enables, such.

Social Justice

Yet for many who work in education, or who are concerned about, educational opportunity and widening participation, education should be about social justice. That for example a student's background should not determine, or markedly affect, their attainment. In other words that education should compensate for society. This can be seen in two ways. The first is generally accepted, at least as an objective, that pupils from poor homes and with uneducated or lowly educated parents should not be disadvantaged and should have the opportunity to succeed. The effort and resources put into this varies considerably across societies. The second, which argues that in order to redistribute opportunity it is necessary to limit the advantaged, is typically rejected. The current debate concerning widening participation in higher education in the UK, where institutions are encouraged to recruit students from disadvantaged backgrounds and schools is often rejected on the ground that it is unfair to those from, for example, private schools.

The Characteristics of Education Systems

The educational systems of all societies are intimately related to, and reflect, the forms of social stratification of that society. This feature appears to account for the lack of equity and the variation in quality and access to education. Consequently it forms the major part of my lecture.

There are five global forms of social stratification

Social Class [Socio-economic status/Educational background and/or support]

Gender.

Ethnicity. [Culture and religion].

Age. [Chronological and seasonal].

Disability, [Physical and/or mental disability, or handicap].

It is important to appreciate that both the forms of social stratification are intimately inter-related and that social class is the fundamental form. This is because most aspects of social life are directly, or indirectly, affected by economic circumstances. It seems obvious and, indeed, is true, that if a society is stratified hierarchically then its educational institutions will be similarly stratified.

Quality.

No society claims that all its universities or schools are equal in quality and that therefore its students are treated to equity in respect to their education. As is argued below, in general terms, the quality of schools, and higher education institutions can often be intimately linked to the social stratification composition of their pupils and students.

Many societies see the quality and outcomes of education as being related to physical plants and resources. However it has been my experience that one can observe good teaching and learning in the some most impoverished of schools and poor teaching and learning in the finest and best equipped schools. The obvious and critical resource is of course the teachers.

It is perhaps surprising that few university staff in most societies are qualified teachers and are therefore ill-equipped to service the learning styles of diverse groups of students. I have a profound belief in the necessity to educate rather than to train teachers. This belief is in contrast to the marked shift away from educating to training in teacher preparation current in the UK and elsewhere. There is a clear need for university staff to have more knowledge of how students learn, more about students' backgrounds and cultures, an understanding of the institutions and systems in which they work, together with the knowledge of how to be reflective practitioners – in short, they need educating in the psychology, sociology, history and philosophy of education.

It appears to be a global assumption that the status of teachers is based on the age and ability of those that they teach, so teachers of infants are not as highly regarded as those who teach seniors let alone university students. There are several assumptions here. The major consideration is that it is the early years of education that are critical—the foundation on which all else is built. If the political objective is, raise the standards of attainment of the population, then there needs to be a concentration on the sector where access is universal or nearly so in order to provide the best learning opportunities for all. This applies not only to teachers but also to expenditure, and includes class size. What we typically find is that more is expended on secondary than primary pupils, more on those above the legal school-leaving age and even more on those in higher education, a pattern followed by class size. In the 1980s I posed the suggestion that a revolution in attainment would likely follow the adoption of a simple formula in which class size was simply a doubling of the children's age, so that at age five they would be taught in classes of ten, at six in 12s and so on up to 16 when the class would be 32.

Competition, or Competition-based Education?

Education is typically delivered in a competitive manner, yet its objective is to achieve the levels of competence required to adequately undertake adult roles in society. Students are expected to compete to get higher scores than the others in their class, and higher level degrees in order to compete for jobs. Yet in other fields a different approach is used, for example, the driving test. In this the only requirement is to display driving competence. More importantly, failure is both relatively private and the normal reaction to it is to prepare for and take the test again. Test takers are not judged by their age, background or the number of lessons they have taken or the number of their previous test failures, only on their performance. In some, contrast students typically experience both informal and formal assessment. While some are encouraged and motivated by relative success, others perhaps in equal or larger numbers, internalise failure and/or are demotivated. Put as simply as possible, failure is as much a product of education as success. Educational outcomes are often the result of self-fulfilling prophecies often innocently made by university staff and their institutions.

Comprehensive or Segregated Education Institutions?

Personally I have a profound belief in the comprehensive principle both in respect to education and society. Partly this based on my observations that wherever segregation occurs and particularly where it reflects inequality the result is the maintenance, or extension of inequity and lack of social cohesion and possible conflict. It is also based on my belief that since there is one God, and there is one world, so there must be one people, and hence one type of education institution. Social cohesion and the lack of hostilities between social groups is obviously a global concern and it becomes more so as societies become more mixed and complex and relationships between and across societies more common. The concept of the global village maybe somewhat far-fetched at present but would seem to be on its way. If we hope for it to be a peaceful village we need to take steps to ensure just that and education will have a significant role to play in achieving it. My experience within such enterprises has led me to be sceptical about multi-cultural education and indeed the concept of a multi-cultural society. It has led me to believe that the only way forward is through experiential-learning, [learning through experience] —only meeting through people of different social strata and sharing their culture can real understanding and acceptance be achieved. Schooling and higher education could provide the opportunity for such experience and learning, but their organisation often works in the opposite direction.

Some segregation appears inevitable for so long as there is residential segregation along social stratification lines. For example, attempts in the USA and in Bradford to balance ethnicity in schools by busing pupils from their neighbourhoods have been declared illegal. Similarly in most cases there is economic residential segregation and hence poor and rich districts. This is not to deny the possibility of tackling such segregation by way of suitably planned housing policies and the positioning of schools.

Such considerations lead to the obvious conclusion that many educational problems cannot be tackled or solved through educational change as they are social, economic and political problems and require solutions from those spheres. However, this is not to deny that those of us within education should not consider and act when and where we can to at least challenge segregation. The following outlines some considerations in respect to segregation by social strata within education.

Segregation by Physical and or Mental Disability or Handicap. Such segregation of pupils with Special Educational Needs can be seen as undesirable both for the SEN-child and the others in that it denies each both common experiences, and the knowledge and understanding of each other. Obviously a balance has to be achieved; some SEN pupils need specialist care and facilities that can only be provided in special schools. The aim should be to integrate as many of such pupils as can benefit from the experience and can be provided for in an ordinary school. This is, of course, not to deny the additional costs involved in providing for such children in 'normal schools'.

Segregation by Social Class. The clearest form of segregation here is in terms of the state and private education provision, though selection by achievement often has results in similar fashion. Apart from declaring private educational institutions illegal—which few if any societies could afford either economically or politically—the only way to tackle the inequity involved would be to make state institutions equal or better than the private ones.

Segregation by Ethnicity. I could well be on dangerous ground in expressing my views on this topic, especially perhaps in India with its complexity and variation of ethnic groups of which I have had limited experience. My views are based mainly on my experiences and observations when staying in a range of communities in several countries that I have spent some time studying or researching in. I am not sure of the theological arguments but I find it difficult to believe that any religion requires segregation of its followers from the rest of mankind, or that it would. Consequently I do not believe that schools and particularly universities should be segregated along ethnic or religious lines. Rather as suggested above potentially they could serve to build real understanding of, and peaceful relationships between, groups in societies where they are presently divided.

Segregation by Age. It is interesting to note that the majority of school systems segregate by chronological age, so that classes are formed and progression is made by age rather than by grade. One consequence that has been tracked since the 1930s in the UK is that summer-born children as a group do less well at school all through their careers there than do autumn-borns, mainly on account of being up to a year younger.

Segregation by Gender. Most societies have some or all educational institutions that are single sex. There is considerable debate as whether, or the extent to which such segregation affects attainment. While this debate remains unresolved, it can be argued as the two sexes live together in society their segregation during education is as questionable as segregation along the other forms of social stratification.

Multiple-segregation. There is a danger in treating the forms of segregation separately that the reality of multiple-segregation is overlooked. Consider, for example, the experience of those educated in a single sex, private, faith education institutions compared with those educated in a state comprehensive ones.

Gender Aspects

In most, if not all societies there are educational achievement differences between males and females, usually in favour of males. This issue is a significant one from a range of concerns and warrants a fuller consideration. Interestingly enough in Britain we have moved from the situation of superior academic performance of males to one of superior academic performance of females at all levels of education. While some explanation for this change can be made in terms of social and political change, there would be educational factors which have had effects and that may hold the key to other systems seeking for change, and, indeed for the possible balancing of gender performance in Britain.

It is apparent that the genders have preferences in terms of which aspects of the curriculum subjects that they prefer to study. This is clearly indicated wherever choice is available and hence the subjects offered are liable to affect the relative achievement of the two genders.

There is evidence that the form of assessment used might favour one gender over the other. In the UK, both in schools and higher education there has been a marked shift in formative and summative assessment away from timed examinations to continuous assessment. This change has coincided with the marked improvement in female performance and attainment. It is suggested that female pupils and students are 'by nature' better suited than males to this form of assessment and that males prefer examinations. I suspect that in the same way as students learn in different ways they would be best assessed by methods that they find most comfortable and which enable them to display the learning and understanding best. The questions then arise as to whether students should be able to choose how they are assessed, and/or whether mixed forms, including E=–assessment should be used.

Stratification within Education

Since all societies are stratified it therefore follows that all education systems are stratified. Here only two of the consequences are viewed.

The Hierarchy of Subjects

Curriculum subjects are ordered, or structured, in much the same way as social strata. For example the sciences and mathematics are generally held in higher esteem than arts subjects. Often this is seen as being caused by the former subjects being easier, though it is also worth noting that they are male dominated subjects, while the arts are seen as more feminine. However Einstein claimed that there was not a scientific principle that could not be explained to a person of normal intelligence by another person who properly understood the principle. It is also worth noting that the sciences and mathematics are seen as being more important in respect to the economy and that even taking into account their intrinsic additional need for resources—laboratories, etc— they often receive more generous resourcing and support. For example in the UK Universities, physics and other science departments have been subsidised for a long time because of their assumed importance, while the same has not been true of other disciplines including teacher education.

A further typical clear divide is between subjects or courses that are seen as either academic or vocational. The general higher status of the 'academic' is interesting in that certainly at university level degrees in medicine and the law for example are held in very high regard, yet are very clearly vocational. This is probably because of their association with high status professions, their social significance and the high costs to students and their families in pursuing such courses.

The Hierarchy of Educational Institutions

Schools and higher education institutions are typically ranked. While the justification for such ranking is typically their outputs in terms of the quality of attainment of pupils or students, it is easy to see that there are three other factors involved in the ranking. Often two of these factors are the age of the institution —the older the higher rank, for example, Oxford and Cambridge, and whether they are state or private. However, the most important and generic factor is the social status of those who attend the institution. In other words educational institutions are ranked by the forms of social stratification within a society. Overall it is also typically true that the higher status educational institutions have superior resources.

A common major dimension is between state provided institutions the use of which is either free or low fee and private ones which invariably charge high fees and are therefore often well beyond the means of ordinary citizens. While there is a considerable range in terms of both pupil and student attainments and resources within both types, private institutions typically have smaller class sizes and better facilities that state ones.

Selection for University

In the UK, the Robbins Report of 1963 included what I regard as an excellent principle. Courses of higher education should be available for all those who are qualified by ability and attainment to pursue them and wish to do so. Generally speaking, higher education and particularly university entry is limited and this gives rise to competition. While few would argue for open entry to higher education, let alone higher education for all, the manner in which it is achieved is open to question. Leaving aside the considerable direct and indirect costs involved for the students and their families, entry is usually on the basis of prior examination results. This is justified on the grounds that higher education should be for the most able, and examination results are an objective way of distributing a scarce resource. However the correlation between school leaving results and final degree classifications is not high, and where the less well qualified have been admitted many have performed as well or even better than the rest. In the 1980s I set up a part-time degree at the University of Bradford which was open to all, with examinations at the end of the first term. Regardless of prior qualifications those who passed continued and those who did not had to leave. There were examples of entrants without prior qualifications who in five years achieved an honours degree.

A final observation here is that selection may be based on the unwillingness of higher education staff to teach at levels that they see as outside their scope. This could be because few higher education lecturers in most societies are trained as teachers, or recognise teaching as the major aspect of their profession, or believe that their subject can only be taught to those who have attained a high prior attainment within the discipline. Willingness to teach is as important as willingness to learn in all forms of higher education.

Philosophies of Inclusion and Integration

It is fairly obvious that apart from acquiring knowledge students entering higher education are supposedly being prepared for life and employment in what are essentially diverse societies. It seems clear therefore that higher education has a duty to provide opportunities for inclusion and integration. Only in this way will we achieve a community of scholars and appropriately prepare young people for their place in society. Their situation and their needs as well of those of society have/can/should give rise to consideration of the following social philosophies.

Assimilation

This philosophy is based on the assumption is that new entrants should adopt the existing culture and roles within an institution or society. This was seen as entirely acceptable when the proportion of entrants or migrants was small. As the proportions and their variety grew it was and is challenged, but remains evident in both institutional and social belief and practice.

Assimilation is precisely what my family as immigrants both wanted and expected when entering the UK, and was also true of me as a first generation higher education student.

Acceptable or unquestioned assimilation is more prevalent in some societies and higher education institutions than in others, and is probably more apparent in the latter in respect to vocational and professional higher education courses, than to academic ones.

Multiculturalism

This is a policy, or practice, of maintaining a diversity of ethnic and other groups and cultures within a society or a higher education institution. It requires provision for diversity, sometimes involving law. In higher education it is evidenced, for example, by special curricula, learning support, student societies and facilities. Simply it is about maintaining, or allowing for, cultural differences between and among members of the community of scholars. In other words it is a provision for diversity. There were, and are, hopes that this provision would lead to enhanced understanding and integration of cultures. Such hopes have shown a range of outcomes, some positive and others that have reinforced the original divisions.

Hopes of Cultural Transformation

Here it is argued there is focus on the broader interests of both the underrepresented and the majority. Non-traditional students are not viewed as being deficient, but able to inform the institutional change process. All institutional activities are underpinned and informed by positive view of diversity. The hoped for outcome is then a transformation into a new culture developed out of and from those brought to the social situation by memebers of the higher education institution or society.

Moral Questions

Here the term moral is used in the sociological rather than the theological sense. Among the several philosophies of inclusion and integration which underline widening participation outlined above, the transformative one is arguably the most attractive though at the same time by far the most challenging. As can be appreciated, the implications of such a philosophy are considerable and raise a number of moral questions in respect to widening participation in higher education, such as:

The extent to which individuals and groups should, or can be made to participate inclusively and to integrate.

The duty of higher education institutions and their staff to provide opportunities for participation, and provide opportunities for integration. Alongside these duties will be the realisation and acceptance that such action will result in fairly dramatic changes and challenges for students, staff and the institution.

Clearly a balance has to be found between individual freedom and duty to provide for inclusion and integration, the implication for which is a change in the institution and among all its participants.

3

How Inclusive is Higher Education in India?*

Jandhyala B.G. Tilak

Inclusive growth is the modern day m*antra* of development. Inclusive growth is defined as a concept that advances equitable opportunities to every section of society. The concept is becoming increasingly important against a background of widening inequalities in the society which are associated with globalisation and related economic reform policies. For a long time, the term 'equity' has been popular in policy discourses; 'Growth with distribution' 'growth with equity', 'growth with a human face', 'integrating growth with development' and 'pro-poor growth' have been some of the important and popular slogans in development policy discourses. Now these terms are being replaced by 'inclusive growth.' Inclusive growth might mean either progression in our thinking and approach (we have already achieved equity and we may have to go beyond), as Abhijit Sen (2010) felt, or retrogression as equity and other terms described above are viewed as representing much larger strategies of development and as concepts more desirable than inclusiveness, which could be narrowly interpreted as ensuring representation of every group of population, but not necessarily equal or equitable representation. However, it is widely and

* This paper is an edited version of the article that was published in *Social Change*, 2015, 45(2), published by Sage Publications India Pvt. Ltd., New Delhi

generally felt that inclusive growth might mean all of these and much more. The Commission on Growth and Development (2008) defines inclusiveness as a concept that encompasses equity, equality of opportunity, and protection of the people mainly the weaker sections in market and employment transitions; it is an essential ingredient of any successful growth strategy. It is a growth strategy 'with emphasis not only on the distribution of economic gains but also on the security, vulnerability, empowerment, and sense of full participation that people may enjoy in social life' (World Bank 2006).

Inclusive growth refers to both the pace and the pattern/distribution of growth, which are considered interlinked, and therefore need to be addressed together. The inclusive growth approach takes a longer term perspective and is supposed to be inherently sustainable as distinct from the mechanism of income distribution schemes which can, in short run, reduce the inequalities between the poorest and the richest, but the reduction in inequalities might not be sustainable over a long period (Ianchovichina and Lundstrom 2009). It is a growth process which yields broad-based benefits and ensures equality of opportunity for all (Planning Commission 2007). It is regarded as 'the only sure means for correcting the deeply ingrained regional imbalances, inequities and for consolidating economic gains' (World Bank 2006).

Inclusive growth policies are expected to aim at creation of a 'society for all.' They are viewed as affirmative policies that aim at empowering the marginalised people and the involuntarily excluded, ensuring equal access to markets, services and economic, political and social spaces to all, and in short, make all effective partners in the processes of socioeconomic and political development. Accordingly, inclusive growth is meant to focus on the poor, the marginalised, the disadvantaged strata of the society, and those living in backward regions. It is concerned with overall equity, not excluding any section of the society. A major part of any strategy for increasing the 'inclusivity' part of 'inclusive growth' must be to improve the capabilities of persons of all vulnerable and weaker sections of the society (Basu 2001). This involves increasing their endowment of assets, including human capital endowments.

In the famous *Theory of Justice*, Rawls (1971) proposed two principles of justice: the first principle implies 'fair equality of opportunity' meaning equal claim by all to basic rights and liberties, and the second principle ('difference' principle) means that 'greatest benefit to the least-advantaged members of society' (p. 47). On similar, but not exact lines, Ianchovichina and Lundstrom (2009) argue that inclusive growth should be defined and measured in two ways: first, in line with the absolute definition of pro-poor growth, it is to be defined as growth for all—all sections including the poor and the excluded and marginalised groups benefit. Secondly, it needs to be defined in relative terms: while all sections of the society benefit, the rate of growth in levels of living of the poor would be expected to be higher than the non-poor. So according to the later part of the definition, relative growth has to be measured. If the relative definition is not considered, inclusive growth might mean growth or even growth for all with static or even increasing inequalities.

The approach of the Government of India in favour of inclusive growth has been clearly articulated in the Eleventh Five Year Plan (2007-12) and later the Twelfth Five Year Plan (2012-17). Given that caste, religion, gender, region and poverty have been the main basis for exclusion in India, it is intended that these groups form the main focus of attention while formulating policies and plans for inclusive growth.

The contribution of education to development is widely recognised. Direct and indirect benefits education produces to the individuals and externalities are indeed large in quantum (see McMahon 1999). Abundant literature is available that highlights the contribution of education to economic growth, poverty reduction and reduction in inequalities (e.g., Psacharopoulos and Woodhall 1985; Tilak 1994). To break the cyclical chain of inequalities—where inequalities in education contribute to inequalities in labour market information, which lead to inequalities in employment, which further causes inequalities in earnings that result in social political inequalities, which in turn cause inequalities in participation in education—education is considered as a very effective strategy. In fact, education is found to be a better and more sustainable option, and a more effective measure than other measures to reduce inequalities in society (Carnoy 1993). It is more so in democratic societies like India where other approaches may not be practicable. Given all this, the role of education in inclusive growth and also the relationship between education and inclusive growth need no emphasis. After all, education is a constituent of inclusive growth; as an instrument, it contributes to inclusive growth and its development is also influenced by inclusive growth. As the World Bank (2006) notes, inclusive growth process is intricately linked with attempts to improve markedly the quality of basic services such as education (healthcare, power and water supply) for every one across the country.

Inclusive growth process and its outcomes get seriously influenced by the level and kind of education development. Inclusive growth requires inclusive education. It is rightly noted that 'the inclusive nature of the growth itself will be conditioned by the progress that is made in the areas of education' (Ministry of Finance 2007, p. 16). It is also recognised that 'a strategy of inclusiveness and broad based participation in the development process calls for new emphasis on education, health and other basic facilities' (Planning Commission 2007; emphasis added).

For education to promote inclusive growth, it has to be necessarily inclusive. A system of education characterised by exclusiveness or by a high degree of inequalities, cannot contribute to inclusive growth. It has to be qualitatively good and widely accessible to all sections of the society in an equitable way. Inequality in education or unequal access to education is costly, as it results in loss in individual welfare, and loss in social welfare as well (Birdsall and Sabot 1996). Unequal education reproduces social inequality (Velaskar 1990). As Salmi and Bassett (2014, p. 363) observed, 'Given the extensive social and private benefits that result from tertiary education, inclusive access and success are essential for achieving social justice and ensuring the realisation of the full potential of all young people.' Even from a narrow perspective of the education sector, inequalities mean loss to the education sector, in terms of lack of or low 'diversity' (UNESCO 2009).

This paper examines how inclusive is education in India? Acknowledging that inequalities in primary and secondary education will produce unequal participation in higher education and hence they need to be studied together, the paper nevertheless proposes to focus on higher education, as higher education is regarded as an engine for equitable economic and social progress, and inequalities in higher education are also reflective of cumulative inequalities in school education.

Higher education in India expanded at a very fast rate during the last quarter century or so. Does the rapid expansion automatically lead to reduction in inequalities in education? While some strongly argue that the benefits of expansion have percolated to the lower strata of the society, some (e g, Deshpande 2006) view that higher education is inherently an exclusive field and hence its elitism is an integral aspect of its nature; and that modes of exclusion are built into its fundamental structure as a matter of principle. Hence it cannot be expected that growth in higher education will necessarily percolate to the downtrodden strata of the society. Some (Raftery and Hout 1993) even argue that the principle of 'maximally maintained inequality' would hold, according to which educational inequality remains unchanged until enrolment ratio at a given level reaches the saturation point, estimated at around 95 per cent. Many also feel that inequalities would be higher at lower levels of education, and they become less at higher levels of education, as only the better-abled would survive up to higher level of education. However, one might note higher degree of inequalities in higher education, as the costs of participation in higher education are much higher than costs of school education.

How inclusive is higher education in India? The National Sample Surveys (NSS) provide some rich empirical data that help in unravelling some of these dimensions of growth and inequalities in higher education in India. Based on an analysis of data of several rounds of the National Sample Surveys over the period 1983 to 2009-10 [38th (1983), 43rd (1987-88), 50th (1993-94), 55th (1999-2000), 61st (2004-05), 64th (2007-08), 66th (2009-10) Rounds; and also the special rounds devoted to education, viz., 42nd, 52nd and 64th rounds], supplemented by official statistics of the Ministry of Human Resource Development (MHRD) and University Grants Commission (UGC), and other studies that analysed these data and even provided estimates, growth and inequalities in higher education are examined here. For the period 1983-84 to 2004-05, the estimates on different indicators used in this paper are drawn from Azam and Blom (2009), [1] Dubey (2008), Raju (2008), Sinha and Srivastava (2008) and Srivastava and Sinha (2008).[2]

Gross enrolment ratios, transition rates and higher education attainments are drawn from Azam and Blom (2009); estimates on eligible enrolment ratios and net enrolment ratios are drawn from Raju (2008); other estimates for 2005-05 and for earlier years are drawn from other sources mentioned above. Comparable estimates are made by the present author for 2007-08 and 2009-10 using NSS data of the concerned rounds.[3]

Looking at the two dimensions of inclusive growth that are described above—the absolute and relative, the paper examines the evidence on a few select indicators of higher education development, and tries to answer the question, how inclusive is higher education in India. Inequalities in education are examined by several characteristics, such as gender, caste, religion, economic conditions and between several regions. Inequalities in education are often examined by social groups —by caste (scheduled caste, scheduled tribes, other backward castes, and non-scheduled/non-backward castes), and by religion (Hindus, Muslims, Christians and others), and by gender—between women and men. These dimensions are widely considered as important inequalities that need to be addressed and accordingly receive serious attention of the policy makers. Other equally, if not more important dimensions of inequalities refer to inter-state inequalities and inequalities between rural and urban population, and inequalities by economic groups—between the rich and the poor. These categories are not mutually exclusive; the principal dimensions of inequalities often overlap; they even mutually reinforce each other. For example, Scheduled Caste population may be predominantly economically poor; the relatively economically poor may be living in rural areas; Scheduled Tribe population may be predominantly living in rural areas; gender categorisation cuts across all other categories; and so on. Further, scheduled castes may be generally worse off; but in some states they may be much better off than non-Scheduled population. As Shariff and Sharma (2013) have shown, a Dalit or Muslim in South India, though from the most disadvantaged among communities, would have better access to higher education than even upper caste Hindus in many other regions.

It is widely recognised that economic and social factors such as class, gender or race, that contribute to inequalities, do not function in isolation but are interlinked; and the 'mutual reinforcement of inequalities' (Drèze and Sen 2013, p. 214) gets further strengthened with addition of every new dimension of inequality, which of course is uneven across the whole country, the degree of reinforcement being higher in northern regions than in other parts of India. Hence in order to understand one form of inequality, other forms of inequalities involved should also be taken simultaneously into consideration. The manner in which one source of inequality functioned had a direct or indirect bearing on how the other sources fashioned inequality (Gita Sen 2008). Acknowledging all this, the paper examines the extent of inequalities in education between different broad social, gender, regional and economic groups of population and finds out which groups did improve/worsen in terms of inequalities.[4]

Without going into semantics, women, scheduled castes, scheduled tribes, 'other backward castes', rural population and bottom expenditure quintiles are referred in this paper as weaker/deprived/marginalised sections of the society.

Equity in higher education does not only mean providing

entry for the disadvantaged sections into higher education institutions; it is also about their continuation in higher education and successful completion of higher education. Equity in labour market outcomes—employment and earnings is yet another important issue.[5] Ignoring these labour market dimensions, growth and inequalities in higher education are examined here considering two important indicators—gross enrolment ratios, and higher education attainments. Available estimates for a few years drawn from others' studies on net enrolment ratios, 'eligible enrolment ratios,' and transition rates are also referred to in this context.

Inequalities in enrolment ratios refer to inequalities in access to higher education. Gross enrolment ratios—students enrolled in higher education as a percentage of population of the age-group 18-23—may also capture, to some extent, accumulated inequalities, particularly inequalities at school level. They and net enrolment ratios reflect levels of representation of population in higher education. 'Transition rates' refer to the entrants in higher education, as a proportion of senior/upper secondary school graduates. Thirdly, 'eligible enrolment ratios' refer to students enrolled in higher education as a percentage of high school graduates (people who are eligible for entry into higher education). As the base for computation of such a ratio is those students, who have already crossed barriers into entry into senior secondary school education,[6] inequalities in eligible enrolment ratio reflect the actual barriers into entry into higher education, faced by those who have crossed hurdles at earlier stages of education.

The other indicator considered is 'higher education attainment,' which is measured as a percentage of adult population who completed higher education over the years. While the enrolment ratios are flow variables, 'higher education attainment'—percentage of population who completed higher education over the years is a stock variable, reflecting the accumulated progress or the lack of it. Estimates could be made for different age-groups among the adult population – 25-34 (youth population), 15-64 (working adults) and 15+ (adults) for certain years. Improvements in this take generally more time than improvements in flow variables like enrolments and enrolment ratios. For the same reason, inequalities in higher education attainment do not get narrowed as fast as those in enrolments.

Simple measures of inequality are estimated to examine the trends in inequality. The coefficient of inequality is measured here simply as a ratio of the status of the concerned group in relation to the most privileged group. For example, the coefficient of inequality (C) in gross enrolment ratio (GER) is defined as = GERm/GER i

m is the most privileged group and *i*-the relevant group. *m* and *i* refer to men and women respectively in case of gender inequalities.

In case of inequalities by economic groups, the coefficient is defined as

$$c\ q1 = GERq5/GER\ q1$$
$$c\ q2 = GERq5/GER\ q2$$

where *qi* refer to the quintile groups.

Inequalities by caste and religion are also estimated in the same way. In case of regional inequalities between rural and urban regions, the Sopher's (1974) index of regional disparity[7] is estimated.

The estimates presented here are constrained by the nature and quality of data available, and methodologies and definitions adopted by other scholars when their estimates are used. All rounds of NSS are not strictly comparable: some are based on large samples, and some on thin samples; some are special surveys on education and some on employment-unemployment and other aspects, which adopted different definitions and methods of estimation. Hence caution is suggested in making strict comparisons over time.

Growth in Higher Education in India

The growth in higher education during the post-independence period has been remarkable, in terms of the number of universities, colleges, students, and teachers. Compared to a small number of 20 universities at the time of independence, presently there are more than 700 universities, including institutions deemed to be universities and university level institutions. The number of colleges has increased from less than 500 to more than 37,000 during the same period, and the enrolments have increased to nearly 21 million from less than two lakh in 1947-48. Presently there are nearly one million teachers in higher education. The gross enrolment ratio in higher education stands at 21.1 per cent in 2012-13, compared to 1.5 per cent in 1960-61.

With the phenomenal growth, higher education system in India emerged as the second largest in the world after China, producing the second or the third largest stock of scientific and technical manpower. The spectacular growth has also helped the nation in achieving self-reliance in manpower needs and even to 'export' manpower to the advanced countries. The number of graduates produced in the system is so large that the emigration of graduates to other countries is no more regarded as brain drain and as a problem. The massive expansion of higher education has also helped in democratising the higher education system to some extent, which was highly elitist and restricted to the high income groups at the time of independence. Today about forty per cent of the students in higher education are women, and about one-third are from the weaker socioeconomic strata of the society. The growth in higher education also made a significant contribution to socioeconomic and political development of the nation. Its contribution in strengthening democracy and ensuring political stability is also significant.

However, the growth in higher education has not been problem-free, nor is it even. Certain aspects of the growth are quite marked. But for the first two decades of development planning in India, the growth rates in higher education were modest until the beginning of the last decade of the last century. The rate of growth in enrolments was nearly doubled between 1990-91 and 2000-11. In fact, much of the growth took place between 1995-96 and 2010-11. The sudden rise in demand for higher education caused setting up of new colleges and universities. The rates of growth in the number of colleges and universities have doubled in the present decade compared to the previous decade. Most of the new institutions that came up during the last two decades have been in the private sector, which itself has had an effect on equitable access to higher education. The growth in the enrolments experienced in the earlier decade could not be sustained in the present decade. Growth in teachers has never kept pace with the growth in enrolments, resulting in a steady increase in pupil-teacher ratios in higher education, which has had its own effect on the instructional process and the overall quality of higher education. Further, except for the decade of 1960-61 to 1970-71, the growth in teachers was below the rate of growth of number of colleges and universities. Similarly, except for the two recent decades, growth in the number of higher education institutions—universities and colleges, has been below the growth in enrolments also, reducing the overall accessibility of higher education. However, during the present decade, increasingly more and more colleges and universities were set up, and the rate of growth far exceeds the rate of growth in enrolments and teachers. But that the number of teachers has not proportionately increased suggests that average number of teachers per university/college has declined. Growth in public expenditure has also not kept with pace with growth in student numbers or with the growth in the number of higher education institutions, resulting in sparse distribution of financial and physical resources.

Further, the growth has been uneven across different social and economic groups of population, between rural and regions and between several states. Though some progress has been made, inequalities in higher education are persistently high.

According to the gross enrolment ratios estimated based on NSS reports, compared to the ten per cent of the 18-23 age-group attending higher education in 1983-84, 23.1 per cent attended in 2009-10: in about twenty-six years, the ratio increased by three times. In contrast, net enrolment ratio increases at a slower pace; it increased very modestly from 8 per cent in 1999-2000 to 10.2 per cent by 2004-05 by about 2 points in 5 years.

The eligible enrolment ratio is a better ratio than gross or net enrolment ratio, as it refers to the students enrolled in higher education as a percentage of those who have successfully graduated from schools. On an average, according to available estimates, 53 per cent of the high school graduates were found to be entering higher education institutions in 2004-05. The remaining half might opt for different choices, might go to labour market for work, might not like to go to higher education (like women getting married), might not be really eligible for higher education having graduated with very poor (just minimum pass) scores, or might find higher education costly, or there were other supply constraints. In general, one can state that, as only half the school graduates go in for higher education, there is much scope to improve the eligible enrolment ratio.

Estimates on a slightly different indicator, transition rates are also worth examining. Generally transition rates are defined as enrolments in the first year of higher education as a proportion of enrolments in the final year of school level education. Constrained by unavailability of required data, Azam and Blom (2009) have redefined transition rate as total population in the age-group 18-23 who either attend or have completed higher education as a proportion of population in the age-group 18-23 who have completed higher secondary education. This is, thus, not confined to fresh entrants in higher education in the numerator or to just those who were in the final grade of secondary education in the last year in the denominator; it includes a small part of the stock of school/higher education graduates. The thus defined transition rate is estimated to be fairly high, higher than eligible enrolment ratio. This ratio was 67.4 per cent for in 1993-94, which increased to 71 per cent by 2004-05, after a marginal decline to 65.2 per cent in 1999-2000. These rates suggest that a high proportion like 70 per cent of the high school graduates take admission in higher education institutions. This is seemingly very high. A more accurate estimate is made here based on enrolment of age 18 enrolled in first grade of higher education as a proportion of total population in the age-group of 18-23 who have completed higher secondary education. This is better than the way Azam and Blom (2009) have measured, but this is also not perfect (see Tilak and Biswal 2013). But given the constraints on data, this can be treated as more reliable. Unless otherwise mentioned, the thus estimated transition rates are analysed here; but they refer to 2009-10. We refer to the estimates of Azam and Blom also as no other estimates are available for earlier periods. For the total population, this ratio is found to be very small: 19.4 per cent in 2009-10.[8]

Progress in enrolments finally gets reflected in the stock of higher educated people in the country. This is considered as the most reliable indicator to describe the status of higher education in any society. Hardly eight per cent of the population of the age-group 15-64 in the country in 2009-10 was found to be educated at higher level. The corresponding ratio was 2. 6 per cent in 1983.

All these numbers mean improvement over the years, but small improvements.

Is the Growth in Higher Education Adequate?

Despite huge numbers and their growth, the system of higher education is believed to be highly inadequate, as some ratios described above already clearly suggest.

Not only with respect to the stock of educated population, evidence on the flow variable also shows that the higher education system is highly inadequate. The gross enrolment ratio in higher education is around 20 per cent according to estimates of the Government of India, Ministry of Human Resource Development. Alternative estimates based on NSS data also more or less correspond to these and Census-based estimates, if we ignore differences by one or two points.[9]

The enrolment ratio in higher education in many other countries is much higher: it is above 75 per cent in developed/ high income countries; the average for the developing countries is 24 per cent and the world average is 31 per cent in 2011 (UIS

2014). It can be noted that in no developed country the enrolment ratio is below 40 per cent. Based on the examination of the international evidence, it can be observed that an enrolment ratio like 40 per cent forms a threshold level for a country to cross the stage of the 'developing countries' and a ratio of above 40 per cent consistently might be an essential condition for sustainable high rates of growth and even to become and more importantly to remain as a developed country.

With a three-time increase between 1983 and 2009-10, the percentage of adults (15+) who had higher education stands at 8.2 per cent. This is also found to be highly inadequate for a fast developing country that aims at becoming a knowledge economy. In the United States, 42 per cent of all 25-64 year-olds have tertiary education in 2010. The corresponding rates in other advanced countries are: 54 per cent in Russian Federation, 51 per cent in Canada, 46 per cent in Israel and 45 per cent in Japan, the OCED average being 31 per cent (OECD 2012, p. 36).

An equally, if not a more important problem of higher education in India refers to the quality of education. It is widely held that though there are a few pockets of excellence, many institutions of higher education in India are indeed substandard in their quality, producing unemployable graduates. That no Indian higher education institution figures among the top 200 in global rankings of universities is also widely felt (Tilak 2014). The need to improve the quality of infrastructure and teachers in higher education and thereby in the quality of the graduates is obvious.

While the above figures refer to all groups of population on average, there are wide differences between several groups; certain groups of population fare much worse than others.

On the whole, the quantity and quality of the system of higher education in India reflected in huge numbers are highly inadequate for rapid economic growth, to face global challenges, to reap gains from policies of globalisation and international competition, for reducing inequalities—regional, social, and economic, for sustainable high levels of human development, and for building an equitable system of higher education that ensures opportunities for all and helps in the creation of a knowledge society.

Persistence of Inequalities in Access to Higher Education

Probably the most important problem faced by the higher education system in India is the persistence of inequalities in access to higher education. Inequalities in access to higher education result in socio-economic inequalities in the society, which in turn accentuate inequalities in education. In fact, it is a cyclic chain of inequalities: inequalities in access to higher education result in inequities in access to labour market information, which will result in inequalities in employment and participation in labour market, resulting in inequalities in earnings, which in turn contribute to socio-economic and political inequalities. The socio-economic and political inequalities will again get translated into the education sector, resulting in inequalities in education. Inequalities in access to education reflect loss in individual as well as social welfare. That economic returns to investment in education of the weaker sections are estimated to be higher than returns to their counterparts (Tilak 1987), implies that inequalities in education would cause huge losses in national output; and that inclusive strategies that contribute to equity should be viewed favourably not only from the point of view of social justice, but also even in terms of economic wellbeing, as the total equity gains might surpass the losses in efficiency if any (Patnaik 2012).

Gender Inequalities in Higher Education

One of the most important dimensions of inequality is between men and women. Women are generally found to be lagging behind men in every sector, including in higher education in India, as in many countries, though of late reverse trends could be observed in a good number of countries.

During the post-independence period, there is significant improvement in women's participation in higher education. Women constitute 43 per cent of the total enrolments in higher education in 2011-12, while there were only 14 women per every

100 men in higher education in 1950-51, according to the available UGC statistics (UGC 2013). Thus, compared to the earlier decades, this marks a significant improvement. While this 43 per cent is an all-India average across all disciplines of study, there are wide variations between different states and also across disciplines. Women students constitute 11 per cent in engineering/technology, four per cent in medicine and less than five per cent in education. Nevertheless, the overall level of participation of women in higher education has improved remarkably and the current overall level is quite impressive. Further, research studies (e.g., Basant and Sen 2012) have also shown that "after controlling for other factors, the chances of women participating in higher education are higher than that of men," meaning the generally observed inequalities by gender in higher education need to be interpreted with caution.

The gross enrolment ratio among men increased from 10. 9 per cent in 1983-84 to 27 per cent in 2009-10—it increased by 2.5 times in about two decades and a half. In contrast, only 19 per cent of the women in the relevant age-group are enrolled in higher education in 2009-10. But what is strikingly clear is: there has been a rapid progress in the enrolment ratio among women, compared to men. The gross enrolment ratio for women increased by more than four times. As a result, gender inequalities in gross enrolment ratio have come down very significantly during this period. A simple coefficient of inequality (ratio of male enrolment ratio over female enrolment ratio) declined from 2.4 in 1983-84 to 1.4 in 2009-10.

The available estimates on net enrolment ratios, however, indicate that between 1999-2000 and 2004-05, the increase in enrolment ratios is very small in case of both men and women; hardly it increased by two per cent points in either case, and the level of inequality remained the same. The male-female differences are much less in case of eligible enrolment ratios. While 49 per cent of eligible girls join higher education institutions, the corresponding ratio is marginally higher for men, 56 per cent, a difference of about seven per cent points. Gender variations are the least in transition rates—the rate being

19 per cent in case of women and 20 per cent in case of men in 2009-10.

Percentage of adults (15+) with higher education reflects the cumulative growth. Absolute rates of higher education attainment have increased in case of both men and women, but there has been faster growth in case of women. Compared to the enrolment ratios, a higher degree of inequality is reflected in the rate of higher education attainment (among the population of the age-group 15-64, a stock indicator, though inequality with respect to this rate has declined over time. Among men 3.7 per cent of adults had higher education in 1983-84; the ratio rose to 9.9 per cent by 2009-10—3.7 times increase in a period of 26 years. In contrast, the ratio of women who had higher education increased by 4.5 times during this period, reaching a level of 6.3 in 2009-10, showing a sharp decline in gender inequality over the years—the difference declined from 2.6 per cent to 1.6 per cent.

The rapid improvement in women's status in higher education and thereby the remarkable decline in gender inequality might be attributed to several factors, including specific public policy measures that aimed at promoting women's education. Many states provide free higher education (at least up to first degree level), and scholarships to women. There are also colleges exclusively meant for women in a majority of states; they constitute 12 per cent of all colleges in the country in 2011-12; and there are also a few universities for only women. A few states offer reservations for women in admission in higher education institutions. Special measures and special thrust on girls' education at school level also helped in increasing the participation of women in higher education. On the whole, overall policy environment is generally favourable to women's education during the post-independence period.

Inequalities by Social Groups

It is widely recognised that inequalities across social groups are multi-dimensional and difficult to capture empirically.

Inequality by caste is a major phenomenon in India, and is also subject to extensive rigorous research, policy making and policy analysis. Caste is considered as one of the most important determinants of perceived social status in India (Bros 2014), and is 'too strong to be suppressed permanently' (Deshpande 2012). Scheduled Castes and Scheduled Tribes are traditionally regarded as the most backward sections of the Indian society. They were also subject to discrimination in social, political and economic spheres for a long time and to correct some of these historical disadvantages, reservations are provided to them in education and employment. Some more castes are recognised as 'Other Backward Castes.' Following the Mandal Commission Report (Government of India 1980), adopted by the Government of India, reservation policy was extended to a few 'Other' Backward Castes. Some of the minority religious groups like the Muslims have been lagging far behind others in education development. The report of the Sachar Committee (Government of India 2006) has highlighted this in the recent years. This has also become an important issue of research, and also an important policy issue (Hasan 2012). It is often quoted that Scheduled Castes constitute only 12 per cent of the total enrolments in higher education, and Scheduled Tribes 4.5 per cent (2011-12); or Muslims constitute such a small proportion. But a more meaningful analysis can be based on enrolment ratios and the rates of higher education attainment. This is attempted below.

Inequalities by Caste

The enrolment ratios of Scheduled castes and scheduled tribes have been consistently very much below those of non-Scheduled population or the total population on average. But both Scheduled Castes and Scheduled Tribes have made significant advancement, by increasing the enrolment ratios of the respective population groups by 4-5 times in about two decades and a half between 1983-84 and 2009-10. The growth was relatively faster in case of Scheduled Tribes, though in absolute terms their enrolment ratio is less than that of the scheduled castes; and as a result, the differences between Scheduled Castes and Scheduled Tribes have come down; and also the differences between the Scheduled population and non-Scheduled population declined. However, it must be added that (a) the enrolment ratios among both the Scheduled Castes and Scheduled Tribes are low, and (b) still significant inequalities persist between Scheduled and non-Scheduled population groups. The enrolment ratio in 2009-10 was nearly 12 per cent among the Scheduled Tribes and 15 per cent among the Scheduled Castes, compared to 23 per cent for all.

Quite interestingly, there is no much variation in the eligible enrolment ratio between several caste groups. While it ranges between 50 per cent and 54 per cent for Scheduled Castes, other Backward Castes and others (non-Backward sections), the ratio is much higher, 62 per cent in case of Scheduled Tribes. Between various caste-groups the transition rate ranges between 14 per cent (for Scheduled Tribes) and 22 per cent (Scheduled Castes). Scheduled Castes are ahead of all others.

As the rates of higher education attainment are only a stock indicator of the progress made over the years, these also show a high degree of inequality but rapid progress at the same time. Less than three per cent of the Scheduled Tribes and just four per cent among the Scheduled Castes had completed levels of higher education in 2009-10. These data in 2009-10 mark 5 times and 6.5 times increases between 1983-84 and 2009-10.

Data on 'other Backward Castes' are not available for all the years. Available data indicate that they are generally ahead of Scheduled Castes and Scheduled Tribes. For example, in 2004-05 nearly four in every one hundred adults had higher education among the other Backward Castes, compared to two per cent and less than three per cent among Scheduled Tribes and Scheduled Castes respectively. Similar was the situation in 1999.

While the improvement in the status of education of Scheduled Castes, Tribes and other Backward Castes and in inequality between the Scheduled population and non-Scheduled population is impressive, still the absolute levels of educational status of the Scheduled population are far below the status of their counterparts. As many (e g, Weisskopf 2004) have found, the reservation policies, financial incentives and other measures have made a significant impact on improving the rates of participation of the Scheduled population in higher education, but still there is a long way to go. A few (e g, Desai and Kulkarni 2008) also noted no improvement and even mild deterioration in college graduation rates for dalits, casting doubt on the effectiveness of these policies.

Inequalities between Religious Groups

Inequalities in the gross enrolment ratio between various religious groups are much higher. Estimates on gross enrolment ratio are available for Hindus, Muslims, Christians and 'others.' Enrolment ratio among Muslims was only 14 per cent in 2009-10, while it was 24.2 per cent among Hindus and 37 per cent among Christians. The enrolment ratio among 'Others' that includes Jains, Sikhs, etc., is also high 28 per cent in 2009-10. The enrolment ratio is the highest among the Christians and the least among the Muslims. This is the same situation consistently throughout the period between 1983-84 and 2009-10. While there has been improvement in case of all the four groups between 1983-84 and 2009-10, the inter-group inequalities by religion did not decline much. In fact, the gap seemed to have widened.

According to the estimates by Azam and Blom (2009), one does not find much inequality between Hindus and Muslims, with the transition ratio being around 70 per cent in 2004-05. Christians are, of course, far ahead with a ratio of about 80 per cent. Among both Christians and Hindus, out of every 100 secondary school graduates, 71 per cent go for higher education. The ratio was 80 per cent among Christians. But overall refined estimates of transition rates in 2009-10 are very low—about 20 per cent among Hindus and Christians, 16 per cent among Muslims and 11 per cent among others.

Despite reasonably high and comparable transition rates, because of low gross enrolment ratio, Muslims do not fare comparably with Hindus or Christians with respect to the rate of higher education attainment. In 2009-10 while there are 12.5 per cent adult Christians who had higher education, the corresponding figures are 8.6 per cent and among Hindus and 3.8 per cent among Muslims. 'Others' also had a high proportion of population—11 per cent with higher education. Further, inequalities seem to have widened between Muslims and Christians and to a lesser extent between Muslims and Hindus.

Rural-Urban Disparities

Now, spatial inequalities. There are wide inequalities between different states in India in higher education in terms of the number of universities and colleges, infrastructure in those institutions, student enrolment, and even public expenditure. The gross enrolment ratio in higher education varies among major states between less than or around 10 per cent in Jharkhand and Chhattisgarh on the one side and above or around 40 per cent in Chandigarh and Tamil Nadu on the other side (MHRD 2014). Moreover the inequality between the states seems to have increased over the years, the coefficient of variation increasing from 0.13 to 0. 27 between 1986-87 and 2009-10.

There exist not only inter-state disparities, but there also exists a high degree inequality between rural and urban areas in each state. Based on NSS data, rural-urban disparities at all-India level are analysed here. In contrast to inequalities by gender, caste and religion, rural-urban disparities seem to be very high in the enrolment ratios. While 39 per cent of the relevant age-group population in urban areas attended colleges/universities in 2009-10, it is only 16.5 per cent population who attended in rural areas. The ratio in urban areas was nearly 4.5 times higher than the ratio in rural areas in 1983. In 2009-10, this came down to 2.3 times, suggesting a narrowing down of rural-urban disparities. As the Sopher's index of regional disparity (1974) shows, the degree of inequality between rural and urban areas declined over the years, but inequality is still quite high. The decline in inequality can be noted in net enrolment ratio as well, though net enrolment ratios, by definition, are much smaller than gross enrolment ratios both in urban and urban areas. Between 1999-2000 and 2004-05 the urban-rural differences in net enrolment ratio declined from nearly four times to three times. The eligible enrolment ratio is also less in case of rural population, compared to urban population. But it only differs by less than 10 per cent points: 48 in case of rural population and 57 per cent in case of urban population in 2004-05.

Systematically high rural-urban inequalities could also be noted in case of the rate of higher education attainment. The rate increased from one per cent in rural areas in 1983 to 3.6 per cent in 2009-10, while in urban areas it increased from 7.4 per cent to 19.1 per cent during the same period. Though the rural-urban gap is getting reduced in terms of rate of increase, in terms of absolute differences they seem to be widening. In general, the rate of improvement is very slow; and more importantly, the absolute levels of higher education attainment are very low in rural areas.

Inequalities by Economic Classes

Estimates of various indicators of higher education development (and other indicators) based on the NSS data are available by household expenditure quintiles/deciles. A few scholars have used alternative indicators like assets (or asset index) to consider the economic levels of the households. But the monthly per capita expenditure, on which NSS provides rich data, is used extensively in this regard. We analyse the same NSS data by quintiles, the Q1 or the bottom quintile (0-20 per cent population) being the poorest and Q5, the top quintile (80-100 per cnet) referring to the richest 20 per cent of the population.

The gross enrolment ratios are the lowest among the bottom (poorest) quintile and highest among the top (richest) quintile. One finds a very a systematic pattern of increasing enrolment ratios by every increase in the expenditure level of the households, with no single exception. In other words, the enrolment ratio among the second quintile (from bottom) has been higher than the bottom quintile; the ratio among the third (middle) quintile is consistently higher than the ratio among the second quintile; and so on. The population belonging to the top income quintile has the highest ratio. This pattern did not change at any point of time that we study between 1993-94 and 2009-10. We do not find any intersection of the lines!

More importantly, inequalities in enrolment ratios between the poorest and the richest quintiles have increased over the years, as the enrolment ratio among the poorest quintile declined between 1993-94 and 2004-05, while the same has increased in case of all other quintiles, and at a disproportionate rate in case of the richest quintile. The ratio in case of the richest group increased from 26 per cent in 1993-94 to 37 per cent by 2004-05, while the ratio for the poorest declined from a bare two per cent to 1.8 per cent during this period. In 2009-10, however, the ratio for the richest quintile increased to as high as 62 per cent, which is comparable to the ratio in some advanced countries. The ratio between top quintile and bottom quintile, which can be considered as a coefficient of inequality in gross enrolment ratio has increased from 12.8 in 1993-94 to 20.4 in 2004-05. However, this simple indicator of inequality in 2009-10 is somewhat close to the level of 1993-94, meaning thereby inequalities have not declined over the years. In fact, as shown above, it increased between some years. Gross enrolment ratio between 1999-2000 (or 1993-94) and 2004-05 and transition rates for the poorest group have fallen, while for other quintiles they have increased (except the third quintile where the rate has fallen by less than one per cent point.)

Unlike in case of social groups—by caste, religion and gender, the differences in transition rates by expenditure quintiles are much larger. While as high as 80 per cent of the richest expenditure quintile who completed secondary education go to higher education, it is only 52 per cent in case of the poorest quintile, in 2004-05, according to the estimates of Azam and Blom (2009). Further, we find a decline in transition rate among the bottom quintile from 54 per cent in 1993 to 52 per cent in 2004-05. We also find a systematic pattern of increasing transition rates by increasing expenditure quintiles.

According to the redefined rate of transition, it varied between 14 per cent among the bottom quintile and 21 per cent among the op quintile in 2009-10.

The percentage of adult population (15+) who complete higher education also increases systematically by increasing levels of expenditure quintiles. In the bottom quintile 11 out of every one thousand had completed higher education in 2009-10, an increase from 4.7 per thousand in 1983-84. The bottom quintile or even the two bottom quintiles (bottom 40 per cent population) had made very little progress. In comparison, the progress in the richest quintile was by 3.7 times during this period, from 6. 6 per cent in 1983 to 24.2 per cent in 2009-10. In other words, the gap between the bottom quintile and the richest quintile got further widened. In 1983 the difference between the two was of the order of 14 times; while it became 22 times by 2009-10. A similar increase in the gap is found even when we look at the progress made by the bottom 40 per cent population and top 40 per cent.

The systematic pattern of increasing rates of higher education attainment by household expenditure deciles is clearly pronounced both in rural and urban areas. If we further classify the same by gender and have a disaggregated look, we find very systematic pattern of increasing rates of higher education attainment by increasing levels of expenditure in every sub-category, with no single exception. Further we also notice and over all clear and persistent hierarchy in higher education attainment: urban males at every economic category being at the top, followed by urban female, rural male and rural female.

Summary and Conclusions

Inequalities in education not only emanate from social and economic inequalities, but also they contribute to further accentuation of social and economic inequalities. In the broad context of inclusive growth policies in India, with the help of valuable NSS data on several rounds between 1983 and 2009-10, an examination is attempted in this paper, of the growth and inequalities in higher education in India. The NSS data are supplemented by available data from the Ministry of Human Resource Development, Government of India, University Grants Commission and estimates made by other researchers in this regard. The paper is mainly concerned with inequalities in higher education by gender, by social groups— caste and religion, by region—rural and urban, and by economic groups of population—population classified by monthly per capita household expenditure, each separately, though it is acknowledged that there is mutual reinforcement of inequalities among them. We have also concentrated on two important indicators on higher education: gross enrolment ratios (net and eligible enrolment ratios, and transition rates are also referred to), and higher education attainment— percentage of adult population having completed higher education, while examining whether inequalities in higher education have increased or declined overtime. But for minor differences, evidence on all indicators yields similar conclusions and somewhat consistent patterns can be observed both in terms of growth and inequalities. The paper also throws light on which groups have improved most over the years in their higher education status and inequalities between which groups have declined or increased. However, the paper concentrates on formal access to higher education, and has not examined dimensions relating to substantive access, except examining transition rates and rates of higher education attainment which capture partly these aspects.

From the long array of tables and graphs presented above, the following can be described as the main features and trends in growth and inequality in higher education in India:

There has been a rapid growth in higher education in India. But the experienced growth is inadequate. The overall gross enrolment ratio is around 21 per cent in 2012-13, which is much less than the world average and even the average of the developing countries; and less than what is needed for sustainable high economic growth and for transforming the Indian economy into a 'knowledge economy' and into an advanced or semi-advanced society. It may also be reiterated that it is not just higher education, but quality higher education is what is important.

The eligible enrolment ratios, and also the transition rates are found to be reasonably high, but there is scope for improvement in these ratios as well. That eligible enrolment ratio was about 50 per cent, while the transition rates were about 70 per cent, both in 2004-05, Transition rates that are referred here are the estimates made by Azam and Blom (2009) using a definition, which is not strictly in conformity with the standard definition used in the literature on educational planning. A more reliable estimate of transition rate seems to be only around 20 per cent. The seemingly high eligible enrolment rates, and wide differences between estimates of transition rates based on alternative definitions, may suggest the need for proper definitions and measurement of these ratios.

In terms of the stock of the higher educated people in the country—the higher education attainment rate, the absolute levels achieved are low, and the progress made over the years is also low. Overall, only 8 per cent of the adult population (age-group: 15-64) had completed levels of higher education in India in 2009-10. Many advanced countries have above 40 per cent of their adult (25-64) population with higher education.

Growth in higher education does not seem to have resulted in reduction in inequalities in a significant way. Every group of population has registered modest to significant levels of progress in case enrolment ratios and the rate of higher education attainment; but inequalities in higher education seem to be persisting—by social groups (caste and religion), by gender, by region (rural and urban) and between the rich and the poor. In case of both gross enrolment ratio and higher education attainment the direction of the progress—increase/ decrease in inequalities is similar.

Comparison of the rates of higher education attainment for the population of the age-group 25-34 with that corresponding to the population of 15-64, may indicate changes over generations to some extent. Comparable estimates for 2004-05 show that out of the younger population (25-34) a higher proportion of people had higher education, compared to the total active adult (15-64) population. This is true with respect to every sub group of population. That younger age-group has higher rates of higher education attainment than the total adult population would suggest improvement over the years for all groups of population. It is also clear that inequality between different groups tends to decline, though not very significantly.

Despite overall rapid growth in higher education, inequalities seem to be persisting. The reasons, inter alia, could be much of the growth in higher education has been in private sector which is not much bothered about inequalities. Secondly, reduction in public subsidies and high rates of cost recovery rates also may also account for slow improvement in inequalities. Moreover, it may be observed that even when we note improvement, it is only with respect to simple or formal access, but not substantive access, provision of which requires a variety of innovative measures that enable the weaker sections to fully and meaningfully benefit from the state policies and provisions. The paper has not sufficiently dealt with this dimension at all.

Who Improved Most?

According to the relative definition of inclusive growth that we described in the first section, inclusive growth requires that not only all sections of the society improve over the years, but the rate of improvement has to be faster in case of weaker sections than their counterparts. We have noted that all sections of the society have improved their relative status both with respect to gross enrolment ratio in higher education and higher education attainment over the years.

Simple rates of growth in the gross enrolment ratio and in higher education attainment between 1983-84 and 2009-10 are estimated here. They are simply based on the figures relating to the base and final years. They are also simple average rates of growth. The growth of any particular group of population is not smooth during the period. There are ups and downs and the rates of growth are

First, with respect to gross enrolment ratio women improved at a rate of growth of 12.2 per cent per annum, compared to men who experienced a rate of growth of only 5.7 per cent during the same period. Among the different caste groups, 'Other Backward Castes' experienced the highest rate of growth between 1999-2000 and 2009-10. Keeping the Other Backward Castes aside for a moment, one can find that Scheduled Tribes and Scheduled Castes had a very impressive growth of 12-15 per cent compared to a petty 3 per cent growth among non-Scheduled population. There are no significant differences in rates of growth in enrolment ratios among Muslims and Hindus. Both groups progressed at a rate of growth of about nine per cent, Muslims experiencing marginally a higher rate of growth. Similarly the rural population have registered a much higher rate of growth compared to the urban population. In a sense, these rates of growth suggest that there has been pro-poor growth, the rates of growth of marginalised sections being higher than their counterparts. The same cannot be stated about the economic groups of population. The third quintile has progressed faster than the other quintiles. The middle 60 per cent of the population experienced higher rates of growth than the bottom and even the richest quintile.

We find more or less a similar pattern with respect to the rate of growth in higher education attainment, a stock variable. Except the economically weaker sections, and marginalised religious groups, all other weaker sections of the society, viz., women, Scheduled Castes and Scheduled Tribes and rural population registered higher rates of growth than their respective counterparts. Among the religious groups, Hindus and Christians are much ahead of all others; and Muslims are ahead of 'other' religions. The more notable exception is by economic groups of population. While the middle quintile experienced the highest rates of growth in higher education attainment, the bottom quintile did the least. The top quintile enjoyed a rate of growth of above 10 per cent between 1993-94 and 2009-10, compared to about 5 per cent by the bottom quintile, showing widening of inequalities between the poorest and the richest.

Thus based on both indicators—the gross enrolment ratio and higher education attainment, we note that the economically weaker sections have not progressed much, nor has the inequality between the bottom and top quintiles reduced significantly. Muslims are yet to catch up significantly with Christians and Hindus. The growth in higher education has been favouring the other weaker sections, but not as much as in the case of economically weaker sections.

That in general, weaker sections experienced higher rates of growth than non-weaker sections either in the case of gross enrolment ratio or in the case of higher education attainment should not be taken as if convergence is taking place rapidly. The extent of inequalities is still very high, as already noted.

Which Group Experienced Higher Fall in Inequalities More than Others?

Changes in inequality in higher education attainment between different groups show some interesting trends between different groups of population: Gender inequalities have declined significantly; and the degree of gender inequalities can be interpreted as 'minimum.'

Inequalities by caste and religion also declined, though not as significantly as gender inequalities. Differences between Scheduled Castes/Tribes and non-Scheduled population have declined. In fact, Scheduled Tribes have picked up fast, and have progressed, indeed faster than other groups of population, with respect to quite a few indicators of development of higher education. In terms of transition rates in higher education and eligible enrolment ratios, Scheduled Tribes are faring better than all other groups and all groups as a whole. On the whole, one finds, as Desai and Kulkarni (2008) also found, that the gap between 'others' or upper caste Hindus/others and Dalits/Adivasis diminished.

Inequalities between different religious groups of population are marked, though they have not significantly declined over the years. In case of gross enrolment ratios, there has been a significant decline, the ratio between the Muslims and all others improving from 0. 34 in 1993-94 to 0. 6 in 2009-10. But in terms of higher education attainment, in which case reduction in inequalities normally takes a long time, inter-religious group inequalities between Muslims and others got widened. Desai and Kulkarni (2008) also found that the educational gap between Hindus and Muslims continued and sometimes expanded. On the whole, Christians are much ahead of all other religious groups and Muslims are at the far end on the other side. While Hindus are ahead of Muslims, they are behind Christians and 'others'. In terms of hierarchy by religious groups in higher education development, thus, the order is as follows: Christians first, 'others' come next, followed by Hindus and then by Muslims.

Compared to the gender and social groups, inequalities by region—rural and urban, are very high, population in rural areas falling much behind their counterparts in urban areas. Rural-urban inequalities have narrowed down only marginally over the years.

An analysis of inequalities by economic classes, yields more disturbing results. Inequalities in higher education between the poor and the rich have been most significant. In fact, there is a decline in the gross enrolment ratio and also the transition rate among the poorest group of population over the years, in contrast to the very significant improvement in case of the other income groups. As a result, we find widening of inequalities between the poorest and the rich. The estimates on higher education attainment show a consistent increase in the gap between the top and the bottom quintiles.

To sum up, among inequalities between different groups of population, inequalities by economic levels of households are found to be higher than inequalities by other characteristics of population—gender, caste, religion and region. Moreover, inequalities by gender, caste/religion and between rural and urban are decreasing and inequalities by economic levels do not show such a decreasing trend; in fact they are getting widened between several points of time.

Among the various indicators, one finds a high degree of inequality in the gross enrolment ratio. The coefficients of inequality are the highest in case of higher education attainment. Eligible enrolment ratios or the transition rates show the least amount of variation between different groups of population, particularly by social groups, and by gender. Other Backward Castes are found to be ahead of Scheduled Castes and Scheduled Tribes with respect to stock variables, and higher education attainment, but not necessarily and consistently with respect to enrolment ratios, particularly the eligible enrolment ratios.

The paper is concerned with the question: how inclusive has been the growth in higher education in India? While answering this question, it has been examined whether all sections of the society including specifically the weaker sections benefited from growth in higher education, and whether all sections benefited equally or unequally. Rather the attempt has been to examine whether there has been pro-poor growth — whether the rate of growth in the educational status of the weaker sections is higher than the non-weaker sections. The evidence analysed yielded answers which are clearly affirmative in case of gender groups and social groups, somewhat affirmative in case of rural-urban inequalities and are not clearly affirmative in case of inequalities between the rich and the poor, classified by household expenditure levels. Even with respect to social and spatial groups of population, inclusive growth in 'relative' terms has not taken place as much as absolute improvement. With respect to economic groups absolute improvement is also very small, if not negative.

What are the Implications?

As noted earlier, the various groups that we considered for analysing growth and inequalities are not mutually exclusive. The extent of inequalities would be very sharp and clear, when sub-categories are also considered by gender, caste/religion, economic levels and regional. For example, the rate of higher education attainment varies between 2.5 per cent in rural areas and 14 per cent in urban areas in 2004-05. But the corresponding proportion is infinitesimally small—0.03 per cent among the poorest population living in rural areas, while it is 52 per cent among the richest population in urban areas. The difference would be much bigger if we consider Scheduled Castes or Tribes among the poorest quintile living in rural areas vis-à-vis the non-Scheduled population of the top expenditure quintile living in urban areas. In other words, no broad category like Scheduled Castes, or rural population or women, is a homogenous category.

The Constitution provides for reservations for Scheduled Castes/Tribes and Other Backward Classes in student admissions and also in recruitment of faculty in higher education institutions. These affirmative policies formulated considering the broader social situation, are an important instrument for not just formal equality, but substantive equality and they became very controversial. Quite a few studies (e g, Sundram 2006; Basant and Sen 2010) have concluded that there was no need for extension of reservations to 'Other' Backward Castes. Many also raised the question: do the benefits of affirmative action, if any, percolate to the most down-trodden groups, or are they limited to the 'creamy layers' of the Dalit and Adivasi populations? The illegitimate use of the affirmative action programmes by upper-income Dalit and Adivasi families remains a running theme in the Indian discourse on affirmative action. Basant and Sen (2012) argue in favour of parental education as a criterion for affirmative action in place of caste and religion. Ideally, as Roemer (1998) argues, policies may aim at distribution of education that varies along with individual's level of effort instead of family background and other characteristics for which they cannot be held responsible. Family background and other characteristics include not only social but also economic factors. Mehta and Hasan (2006) find that lower completion rates at secondary level of education and economic status are more important factors that need to be addressed in this context than providing reservations based on social identity. Some (e g, Higham and Shah 2013) have argued that affirmative action policies in India have been conceived as a 'contradictory resource' — while on one hand, weaker sections benefit from these policies in securing admission in schools, they nevertheless do not address the deep-seated and historical inequalities; after all the weaker sections, even through these policies, do not necessarily get admission in high quality institutions; besides they result in a division amongst the weaker sections between those who benefit from these policies and those who do not, and remain locked in the vicious circle of exclusion. On the whole it is widely felt that given the structural nature of caste, religion, ethnicity and class inequalities in contemporary India, the extent to which affirmative action policies can fundamentally redress highly structured patterns of inequality remains doubtful (Syed et al 213, p. 715). All this calls for a different approach to policies relating to targeting, focusing not only on formal access, but also to ensure substantive access. In general, it is important to see that these policies do not allow either 'unfair inclusions' or 'unfair exclusions', to use Sen's (2010) terminology.

In public discourses, the issue of inequality is equated to the problems of women and those of Scheduled Castes, Scheduled Tribes and Other Backward Castes. Having received some serious attention of the policy makers during the post-independence period, inequalities by gender and inequalities by caste have declined somewhat significantly and some modest to impressive progress could be noted. Nowadays the religious minorities particularly Muslims began getting attention. Other variants of inequality are yet to receive serious public attention. Of all, inequalities by economic groups of population have not received as much attention as they should have. As a result, inequalities between the rich and the poor seem to have not declined, but have in fact, increased, over the years. Inequalities in education between economic groups of population cut across religious, caste and gender groups, and even regions, and hence they deserve serious attention. But space in policy discourses is taken away by caste and gender inequalities. Promotion of caste and gender based equality should not entail compromising and curtailing the equality of other under privileged groups to augment access to higher education. Regional inequalities are still very large, though some attention has been paid to this issue in the past. They deserve more attention than what is paid. It is important to pay serious attention to reducing inequalities in access to higher education between different income groups of population.

Unequal family incomes translate into unequal access to higher education. A major reason for low participation of low income groups in higher education is the lack of finances to meet household costs of higher education or the need to supplement household income by work. Literature is also abundant that shows a strong correlation between participation in higher education and students' family backgrounds that include socio-economic factors. Hence it is necessary to address the socio-economic factors. While there are some schemes/ subsidies for the socially backward sections and also for women, no such schemes are offered to rural youth, and to economically weaker sections. General public subsidies plus specific targeted subsidies are needed. Sound and carefully thought-out measures are required to reduce the exclusive nature of higher education.

Among the reasons for students dropping out or discontinuing studies after senior secondary education, economic factors figure to be the most important ones, accounting for about two-thirds of all the factors (45 per cent was accounted by 'to supplement household income' and another 20 per cent 'to attend to domestic chores'). Hence the need to ease economic constraints of the poor households. Further, only a tiny fraction (1. 2 per cent) accounts for the factor, 'institution too far.' If this is the case, policies of expansion of higher education, particularly setting up of a large number of colleges and universities may have to be re-examined.

In fact, quite interestingly, the eligible enrolment ratios—which are around 50 per cent for every social group and regional group, suggest that once the students graduate form secondary education, all have more or less equal chances of getting into higher education institutions. This also stresses the need to reduce inequalities in access to secondary education to improve participation in higher education. Large expansion of higher education—in terms of increasing enrolment ratios (it is envisaged to increase the gross enrolment ratio to the level of 30 per cent by 2030), is not possible, unless school education, particularly secondary education is expanded and strengthened, in such a way that transition rates are further raised. It is not adequate to focus on admissions into higher education. Effective measures are needed to ensure continuation of students admitted in higher education and the completion of their studies with high levels of attainment. Strong support mechanisms are to be devised for all weaker sections in this regard.

Lastly, it needs to be noted that goals of inclusive growth in higher education contradict with some of the strategies that are being adopted for the growth in higher education. Heavy reliance on private sector and cost recovery measures may not help in ensuring inclusive growth in higher education; they may actually work in the negative direction. Sustainable inclusive growth may be possible only with strong and vibrant public higher education systems with liberal public funding.

REFERENCES

Azam, M. and Blom, A. 2009. Progress in Participation in Tertiary Education in India from 1983 to 2004, *Journal of Educational Planning and Administration* 23(2) (April): 125-167.

Basant, Rakesh and Gitanjali Sen. 2010. Who Participates in Higher Education in India? Rethinking the Role of Affirmative Action, *Economic and Political Weekly* 45(39) (25 September). 62-70

Basant, Rakesh and Gitanjali Sen. 2012. Parental Education as a Criterion for Affirmative Action in Higher Education: A Preliminary Analysis. Working Paper. Ahmedabad: Indian Institute of Management. http://www. iimahd. ernet. in/ assets/snippets/workingpaperpdf/685170902012-01-01. pdf.

Basu, Kaushik. 2001. On the Goals of Development, in G.M. Meier and J.E. Stiglitz, eds., *Frontiers of Development Economics: The Future in Perspective.* New York: Oxford University Press, pp. 61–86

Birdsall, Nancy and Richard H. Sabot, eds. 1996. *Opportunity Foregone: Education in Brazil*. Washington DC: Inter-American Development Bank.

Bros, Catherine. 2014. The Burden of Caste on Social Identity in India, *Journal of Development Studies* 50 (10) (Oct.): 1411-29.

Carnoy, M. 1993. *The Case for Basic Education*. New York: UNICEF.

Commission on Growth & Development. 2008. *Growth Report: Strategies for Sustained Growth and Inclusive Development.*

Desai, Sonalde and Veena Kulkarni. 2008. Changing Educational Inequalities in India in the Context of Affirmative Action, *Demography* 45 (2) (May): 245-70. http://www. ncbi. nlm. nih. gov/pmc/articles/PMC2474466/ [retrieved on 1 August 2014].

Deshpande, Ashwin. 2012. *The Grammar of Caste: Economic Discrimination in Contemporary India*. Oxford: Oxford University Press.

Deshpande, Satish. 2006. Exclusive Inequalities: Merit, Caste and Discrimination in Higher Education Today, *Economic and Political Weekly* 41(24) (17 June): 2438-44.

Drèze, Jean and Amartya Sen. 2013. *An Uncertain Glory: India and its Contradictions*. London: Allen Lane/Penguin.

Dubey, Amaresh. 2008. Determinants of Post-Higher Secondary Enrolment in India, in *Higher Education in India: Issues Related to Expansion, Inclusiveness, Quality and Finance*. New Delhi: University Grants Commission, pp. 139-98.

Government of India. 1980. *Report of the Backward Classes Commission* (Mandal Commission Report). New Delhi: Government of India. http://www. ncbc. nic. in/Writereaddata/Mandal%20 Commission%20Report%20of%20the%201st%20Part%20 English635228715105764974. pdf [retrieved on 1 August 2014].

Government of India. 2006. *The Social and Economic Status of the Muslim Community in India.* [Sachar Committee Report] New Delhi: Cabinet Secretariat. http://www. minorityaffairs. gov. in/sites/upload_files/moma/files/pdfs/sachar_comm. pdf [retrieved on 1 August 2014].

Hasan, Zoya. 2012. Trapped in an Invisible Present: Muslims and Disparities in Higher Education, in Zoya Hasan and Martha C Nussbaum, eds. *Equalizing Access*. New Delhi: Oxford University Press, pp. 239-55.

Higham, Rob and Alpa Shah. 2013. Conservative Force or Contradictory Resource? Education and Affirmative Action in Jharkhand, India, *Compare* 43 (6) (December): 718-39.

Ianchovichina, Elena and Susanna Lundstrom. 2009. Inclusive Growth Analytics Framework and Application Policy Research Working Paper 4851. World Bank: Washington DC.

McMahon, Walter W. 1999. *Education and Development*. New York: Oxford University Press.

Mehta, Aashish and Rana Hasan. 2006. Under-representation of Disadvantaged Classes in Colleges: What do the Data Tell Us? *Economic and Political Weekly* 41(35) (2 Sept): 3731-96.

MHRD. 2014. *Statistics of Higher & Technical Education 2009-10*. New Delhi: Ministry of Human Resource Development, Government of India. http://mhrd. gov. in/sites/ upload_files/mhrd/files/statistics/Abstract2009-10_0. pdf [retrieved on 10 April 2014].

Ministry of Finance. 2007. *Economic Survey 2006-07*. New Delhi: Government of India.

National Sample Survey Organisation. 38th (1983), 43rd (1987-88), 50th (1993-94), 55th (1999-2000), 61st (2004-05), 64th (2007-08), 66th (2009-10) Rounds. New Delhi.

OECD. 2012. *Education at a Glance 2013: OECD Indicators*. Paris [also available at: http://www. oecd. org/edu/EAG%202012_e-book_EN_200912. pdf] [retrieved on 1 August 2014].

Patnaik, Prabhat. 2012. Affirmative Action and the 'Efficiency Argument', in Zoya Hasan and Martha C Nussbaum, eds. *Equalizing Access*. New Delhi: Oxford, pp. 89-99.

Planning Commission. 2007. *Towards Faster and More Inclusive Growth: An Approach to the 11th Five Year Plan*. New Delhi: Government of India.

Planning Commission. 2013. *Twelfth Five Year Plan (2012–2017): Faster, More Inclusive and Sustainable Growth*. New Delhi: Government of India.

Psacharopoulos, George and Maureen Woodhall. 1985. *Education for Development*. New York: Oxford University Press/World Bank.

Raftery, Adrian E. and Michael Hout 1993. Maximally Maintained Inequality: Expansion, Reform and Opportunity in Irish

Education, 1921-75. *Sociology of Education* 66 (1) (January): 41-62.

Raju, Saraswati. 2008. Gender Differentials in Access to Higher Education, in *Higher Education in India: Issues Related to Expansion, Inclusiveness, Quality and Finance*. New Delhi: University Grants Commission, pp. 79-102

Rawls, John. 1971. *A Theory of Justice*. Oxford: Oxford University Press. [revised edition]

Roemer, John. E. 1998. *Equality of Opportunity*. Cambridge: Harvard University Press.

Salmi, Jamil and Roberta Malee Bassett. 2014. The Equity Imperative in Tertiary Education: Promoting Fairness and Efficiency, *International Review of Education* 60 (3): 361-77.

Sen, Abhijit (2010). Inclusive Growth. Professor L S Venkatramanan Memorial Lecture-9. Bangalore: Institute for Social and Economic Change.

Sen, Amartya. (2010). Social Exclusion: Concept, Application, and Scrutiny. Social Development Paper No. 1 (Working Paper Series). Manila: Asian Development Bank.

Sen, Gita. 2008. Intersecting Inequalities. Second B.G. Kumar Endowment Lecture, Trivandrum: Centre for Development Studies.

Shariff, Abusale and Amit Sharma 2013. Intergenerational and Regional Differentials in Higher Education in India. Working Paper. Washington DC:US-India Policy Institute.

Sinha, Sachidanand and Ravi S Srivastava. 2008. Inclusiveness and Access of Social Groups in Higher Education, in *Higher Education in India: Issues Related to Expansion, Inclusiveness, Quality and Finance*. New Delhi: University Grants Commission, pp. 111-38.

Sopher, David E. 1974. A Measure of Disparity, *Professional Geographers*, 26(4): 389-92.

Srivastava, Ravi and Sachindanand Sinha. 2008. Inter-Social Groups Disparities in Access to Higher Education, in *Higher Education in India: Issues Related to Expansion, Inclusiveness, Quality and Finance*. New Delhi: University Grants Commission, pp. 103-10.

Sundram, K. 2006. On Backwardness and Fair Access to Higher

Education: Results from NSS Survey 55th Round: 1999-2000, *Economic and Political Weekly* 41(50) (16 Dec): 5173-82 OBCs Do Not Need Reservations.

Syed, Yusuf, Paul Morros and Nitya Rao. 2013. Equity and Education Change: Editorial, *Compare* 43 (6) (December): 715-17.

Tilak, Jandhyala BG. 1987. *Economics of Inequality in Education*. New Delhi: Sage.

Tilak, Jandhyala BG. 1994. *Education for Development in Asia*. New Delhi: Sage.

Tilak, Jandhyala BG. 2014. Global Rankings, World-Class Universities and Dilemma in Higher Education Policy in India. Krishna University Public Lecture Series 2014. Machilipatnam: Krishna University

Tilak, Jandhyala BG. and K Biswal. 2013. Transition to Higher Education in India, *IASSI Quarterly: Contributions to Indian Stoical Science* 32 (4) (October-December).

UGC. 2013. Higher Education in India at a Glance. June 2013. New Delhi. http://www. ugc. ac. in/page/Other-Publications. aspx#publication [retrieved on 1 Novemebr 2014].

UIS 2014. *Education:* Gross enrolment ratio by level of education. Montreal. *http://data. uis. unesco. org/index. aspx?queryid=142& lang=en.* [retrieved on 1 August 2014].

UNESCO. 2009. *Report of the UNESCO 2009 World Conference on Higher Education*. Paris.

Velaskar, Padma. 1990. Unequal Schooling as a Factor in the Reproduction of Social Inequality in India. *Sociological Bulletin 39* (1 & 2): 131-45.

Weisskopf, Thomas E. 2004. Impact of Reservation on Admissions to Higher Education in India, *Economic and Political Weekly* 39(39) (25 Sept): 4339-49.

World Bank. 2006. *World Bank India Development Policy Review 2006.* Washington DC.

NOTES

1. This was originally published as a staff working paper of the World Bank.
2. These papers were commissioned and published by the

University Grants Commission.

3. Unless otherwise mentioned, all tables and figures are based on NSS data (various rounds).
4. Without going into semantics, women, Scheduled Castes, Scheduled Tribes, 'Other Backward Castes', rural population and bottom expenditure quintiles are referred in this paper as weaker/deprived/marginalised sections of the society.
5. See Tilak (1979) who highlights the relationship between discrimination in education, employment and earnings.
6. Some scholars (Mehta and Hasan 2006) have used 'eligible population' and 'minimally qualified population' as the base in such a context. Since they used different groups and also measured in different ways, they are not comparable with the estimates given here.
7. If X1 an d X2 represent the respective percentage of the variable so f groups 1 and 2, then the Sopher's Index of inequality. D is written as follows:

   D= log (X2 / X1) -I- Iog (Q- X1)/(Q-X2)

   where Q = 100.
8. The estimates of Azam and Blom for different groups of population are given in the Table A.1 in the Appendix. Temporal comparisons should not be made between these estimates and our estimates for 2009-10.
9. See Sinha and Srivastava (2008), Raju (2008), Dubey (2008) for estimates based on alternative sources of data for 2004-05 which differ from each other quite significantly.

4

Cultural Capital, Social Exclusion and the Marginalised Groups

Prashant Bansode

The literature on sociology of education has largely been focused on the influence of dominant social forces of the society on educational institutions. Rather it has highlighted how educational institutions are deeply embedded in the social structure. For Louis Althusser, educational institutions are a powerful medium of ideological apparatus to maintain control over the masses; thereby the ruling class exercises its control over it for maintaining their class rule. Davies (1973) conceives educational institutions as structured with power relations in a society such that it is a ritual for the dominant elite to initiate its members into the ambit of dominant elites (Davies, 1973: 334). Bourdieu has enhanced the understanding of educational institutions as he conceives that educational institutions are not only a medium of exercising control over society but are a field of power that reproduces the social realm due to differences in endowment in the form of 'cultural capital'.

The important sociological analysis on the complex relationship of education and social structure is explained by Pierre Bourdieu. He criticises that the classical theory had overlooked the aspect of educational system as a means of social reproduction (Bourdieu, 1973). Bourdieu in his analysis integrates the field of power, inequality and social order. He questions the neutrality of the educational institutions as he argues that it transmits power and privileges which in turn reproduce the structure of class relations. Further, he in his analysis uses two important and interrelated institutions which reproduce inequalities a) family and b) educational institutions. In *The Inheritors* he argues that the choice of education and the attitude towards education are produced by the family background. Further he affirms that the connections between family and educational institutions reproduce class inequalities in educational achievement.

Bourdieu further states that the pedagogic actions carried out by families from different social classes as well as that which is practised by schools work in harmonious relationship to transmit the cultural heritage. This cultural heritage is transferred to its inheritors, such that, it gets translated into merit. Therefore, he further argues that those members who are endowed with cultural privileges at home have a legitimate heritage of higher education while others have to struggle for it. For Bourdieu, therefore, educational system is a system of social transformation and social reproduction. This takes place as the education system legitimises the uneven distribution of cultural capital and hierarchies in a society. For him, cultural capital is socially designated and it corresponds to the structure of distribution with reference to the hierarchy of economic capital and power. Therefore, for Bourdieu, those who have cultural privilege (capital) are successful in higher education while those who do not have it automatically get excluded.

The concept of 'cultural capital' becomes important as developed by Bourdieu in *The Forms of Capital* (1986). For him, cultural capital is the accumulated cultural knowledge within the family which is transmitted to its members as part of socialisation process. He has categorised three sub-types of cultural capital a) embodied, b) objectified and c) institutionalised. For him, the embodied cultural capital is consciously acquired and the passively inherited properties by its new members of family are acquired over a period of time. More specifically, cultural capital is linguistic capital embodied by members. Linguistic capabilities provide an effective means of communication and self-presentation which are acquired by its members from one's surrounding culture. Objectified cultural capital means physical objects that are owned, such as scientific instruments or works of art which can be transmitted both for economic profit and for symbolic value whose acquisition they enjoy as part of their family heritage. Institutionalised cultural capital means institutional recognition ie academic qualification or credentials acquired by an individual. This has prominence as far as it can be translated into the labour market for acquiring economic capital.

Bourdieu has linked the concept of cultural capital with his other concepts i.e. 'field' and 'habitus'. He argues that the type of cultural capital acquired would be legitimate in the field in which it is located, which is arbitrary, therefore, it becomes symbolic capital in which it is operationalised. For him habitus is dispositions that are inculcated in the family but manifest themselves in different ways ie the class to which the individual belongs; hence, cultural capital is also derived from its habitus.

Bourdieu's Criticism and Operationalization of the Concept of Cultural Capital

Bourdieu's concept of cultural capital has been severely criticised. One of the important criticisms is that the difficulty to operationalise the concept in various societies (other than France). Another important criticism has come from the Oxford Social Mobility Project in which it was argued that considering cultural capital as a handicap for the disprivileged disregards the importance of the social mobility as it is encouraged by the state education system. Jenkins (2003) acknowledges the criticism offered by Halsey and his colleagues that Bourdieu's model is too rigid and deterministic as he holds that there is hardly any empirical evidence of any link between class and education, but, he also points out that Halsey and his colleagues have emphasised discrimination of cultural capital rather than its hierarchical reproduction.

Michele Lamont and Annette Lareau (1988) had disentangled themselves from Bourdieu and Passeron's original concept of cultural capital and had expanded on it proposing a new definintion of cultural capital which focuses on cultural capital and social exclusion. This can be applicable in the Indian context. As per Lamont and Lareau, the concept of cultural capital helps to analyse the framework of exclusion and how social stratification is maintained or rather reproduced. For this they take cognizance of the work of Bourdieu and Passeron (1977). Bourdieu and Passeron had pointed out that for success in education social and cultural resources play an important role. They point out that an individual's social status and family background transfers social and cultural resources to them such that they become 'investment' for success in education; this may be limited to those who make a proper investment of it. Thus, cultural capital as a concept helps to understand the social exclusion process in education by Lamont and Lareau by expanding Bourdieu and Passeron's original concept.

For Lamont and Lareau schools are not neutral to dominant forces of society; rather they represent the worldview of dominant sections. The members belonging to dominant sections that enter into the education system come with inherited social and cultural codes while those belonging to lower classes are deprived of such social and cultural codes. For members belonging to dominant sections the codes are natural while for lower classes they are devoid of it, which adversely affects their performance in schools. This becomes punishment to the lower classes. The inequalities in educational achievements are explained in terms of the ability rather than on the basis of accumulated cultural benefits enjoyed by members (of dominant class). To ignore it, is to privilege the dominant class. The educational institutions that claim non-biasness and consider it as neutral in fact nurtures reproduction of social stratification. This analysis remains ignored. Bourdieu and Passeron consider it as an institutional process rather than an individual one. Lamont and Lareau argue that Bourdieu and Passeron have added to the understanding of social exclusion in education. Social exclusion happens in four ways as a) self-elimination, b) over selection, c) relegation and d) direct selection.

For Bourdieu and Passeron, social exclusion is a form of

exclusion from power. The use of cultural capital for social exclusion and symbolic imposition by dominant sections is its ability to determine people's life. The cultural values and behaviour are considered as superior which get legitimised as 'superior' such that it becomes institutionalised is the crux of imposing power by cultural capital. Such values and behaviour become acceptable by society. Therefore these become criteria for evaluating the individual. Thus dominant class imposes symbolic violence through cultural capital. Thus selection ie inclusion one's social origin benefits is explained by concept of cultural capital (by Bourdieu and Passeron, 1977).

This modified approach of Lamont and Lareau can help understand centuries-old social exclusion based on complex caste-class line and how educational institutions 'anchors' to reproduce these inequalities in India. There are multiple inequalities within complex caste-class systems and also cultural capital varies with religion, region and gender. But the focus of the present study is to understand the cultural capital and systemic exclusion at the macro-sociological level. The study takes into consideration the two classes who are beneficiaries of cultural capital i.e. the open category students and the reserved category students those who are deprived of it but are beneficiaries of the affirmative action policy.

Caste and Social Exclusion

Indian society is a complex caste-class structure and therefore educational disparities cannot be alone explained on the basis of caste nor class. In fact, caste-class exclusion is systemic. For instance, the movements of the marginalised groups have given new references to caste and origin based inequalities. Dalit, Adivasi, Bahujan, non-Brahmin terminologies have emerged out of systemic fights against both caste and class oppression. These terminologies are based on broader supra-class basis. Scheduled Castes, Scheduled Tribes and Other Backward Classes are also supra-class categories for grant of affirmative action policy.

The unequal division of power, prestige and wealth is not only the reality of social structure in India but the deliberate exclusion of the ex-untouchable castes from access to resources. This structure is hierarchical and rigid such that privileges are conferred as per the hierarchy. The structure was justified by religion. For centuries, the identity of the person was based on birth in the caste which would invite restrictions based on caste. For untouchable castes the severity of inequality was high. Menial and filthy occupations were imposed on them and therefore they were regarded as impure. Not only their touch was polluting but even falling of their shadow on a 'touchable' was also considered as impure by the 'touchable' castes. For Schedule Tribes their exclusion is due to social and geographical isolation.

The history of ancient times in India suggests that the field of knowledge in the *Chaturvarna* system was the domain of Brahmins. The Kshatriya class was allowed to take *Vedic* knowledge but they were not allowed to teach. Vaishya and Shudras were not allowed to have *Vedic* knowledge. A repressive normative system was put in place to disallow access to *Vedic* knowledge. If the knowledge of *Vedas* was imparted by the Kshatriya then their clan was excluded from *The Varna* hierarchy. For the Shudras and Ati-Shudras penal punishments were imposed if they were initiated in accessing the *Vedic* knowledge. For instance, there is evidence that if they listened to the chanting of Vedas then boiling lead was to be poured in their ears and when they chanted the *Vedas* their tongues were to be cut off. The idea behind excluding the Shudras and Ati-Shudras from *Vedic* education was not only to discriminate against them but also to impose slavery on them. Also by keeping them away from knowledge would not only demoralize but also repress their self-esteem. Such a culture of exclusivity and exclusion has diffused into the well-known folk consciousness in Maharashtra, as rightly pointed out by Gopal Guru (2002) and many others in the ditty:

> *Brahmna ghari lihina* (at the brahmin's house you write and learn)
> *Kunbaya ghari dana* (at the tiller's house you thresh)
> *Mahara ghari gana* (at the Dalit's house you sing).

With such a background of the social structure in the past and the continuance of exclusion of the Shudra and Ati-Shudra castes and tribes from education for centuries it would be important to understand how inequalities are structured.

Representation of Scheduled Castes and Scheduled Tribes in Higher Education

In the colonial times though some of the princely states encouraged education of Shudra and Ati-Shudra castes but the colonial education benefited mostly the Brahmin and upper castes. Phule and Dr. Ambedkar published a critique of British Educational Policies and pointed out that it benefited the Brahmin and upper castes and excluded the Shudra and Ati-Shudra castes (Thorat and Kumar, 2008). In independent India, the affirmative action policy was first implemented in 1950. Over the decades due to the implementation of this policy there has been definite increase in enrolment of Scheduled Castes and Scheduled Tribes but it has lagged behind the general enrolment rate. As per Weisskopf (2004) the Scheduled Castes and Scheduled Tribes representation had reached approximately one-half and one-third respectively. Further he has shown the faculty wise representation where he has pointed out that the enrolment in arts faculties of Scheduled Castes and Scheduled Tribes is higher while in engineering, law and medicine it is meagre and there is underrepresentation in masters' and PhD programmes (Weisskopf, 2004: 4399).

Sukhdeo Thorat (2006) made important observations with reference to inter-group disparities in higher education. He points out that the attainment rate at the graduate and diploma level was 4.19 for Scheduled Castes, 3.81 for Scheduled Tribes, 4.55 for OBCs while it was high for general category with 13.37. As per his observations, equally stark was the share seen in intermediate and below, agriculture, engineering/technology and medicine of general and reserved category students.

Further Satish Deshpande and Yogendra Yadav (2006) pointed out that the disparities are linked with caste, class, gender and region. They pointed out that 1 per cent of Scheduled Castes and Scheduled Tribes are graduates in rural India while upper castes Hindus graduates are 5 per cent. They argue that in elite educational institutions the dominance of upper castes Hindus is prevalent. The real inequalities between Scheduled Castes and Scheduled Tribes, Other Backward Classes, Muslims and caste Hindus are in urban India. The upper castes Hindus and Christians are over-represented while Scheduled Castes, Scheduled Tribes, Other Backward Classes and Muslims are under-represented (Deshpande and Yadav; 2006: 2421). The gender disparities are stark and worsen as we go down the hierarchy of caste and class.

The exclusion of Scheduled Castes, Scheduled Tribes and Other Backward Classes from higher education is evident despite the implementation of the affirmative action policy in India. Though it is mandatory for the government and government aided higher and professional educational institutions to fill the quota of seats but in elite educational institutions still the quotas are not filled. The reservation is as per the population percentage of the above-mentioned categories. The latest figures of representation of reserved category as per the Annual Report of SJE (2012-13) the share of Scheduled Castes and Scheduled Tribes in IITs is 13.1 per cent and 4.6 per cent respectively while in IIMs it is 11 per cent and 4.7 per cent respectively. The share of reserved category though is evident due to affirmative action policy but it lowers in higher and professional education.

Educational and Economic Inequalities Amongst Students

The research undertaken in 2008 was to understand the social, economic and education disparities between open and reserved category students. The reserved category students are the beneficiaries of the affirmative action policy while the open category students are the beneficiaries of the traditional privileged class. One of the important objectives of the research was to find out the occupational and educational inequality for three generations of the open and reserved category students. The respondent students were chosen from the D.Y. Patil Medical College, Nerul, Navi Mumbai; Jamnalal Bajaj Institute of Management Studies (University of Mumbai); Bachelor of Mass Media, Sophia College; Department of Mass Communication, University of Mumbai and Social Science Departments of University of Mumbai and Pune. The exclusive group discussion of reserved category students was conducted to understand their families' economic and educational backgrounds. The study has brought out important facts.

Educational Background of Respondent Students

Most of the students did not reveal the educational level of their grandparents but from the responses it was clear that the educational status of grandparents of open category students was far better than reserved category students. It was found on an average that approximately 30 per cent grandfathers (both paternal and maternal) of open category were graduates and 7 per cent grandmothers (both paternal and maternal) were graduates. On the contrary, it was found that 8 per cent grandfathers (both paternal and maternal) were graduates of reserved category students and 3 per cent grandmothers (both paternal and maternal) were graduates. It is clear that across category gender disparity is evident. See Following Boxes 1 and 2.

Box 1: Educational Background of Grandparents of Open Category Students

Level of Education	*Paternal*				*Maternal*			
	Grand-father	*%*	*Grand-mother*	*%*	*Grand-father*	*%*	*Grand-mother*	*%*
Below SSC	3	2	2	1	1	1	2	1
SSC	13	10	15	11	13	10	10	7
HSC	9	7	7	5	9	7	11	8
Graduation	43	32	10	7	39	29	10	7
Post-Grad	2	1	0	0	0	0	0	0
Not Given	66	49	102	75	74	54	103	76
Total	136	100	136	100	136	100	136	100

Source: Questionnaire Survey, 2008

Box 2: Educational Background of Grandparents of

Reserved Category Students

Level of Education	*Paternal* Grand-father	%	Grand-mother	%	*Maternal* Grand-father	%	Grand-mother	%
Illiterate	1	3	2	6	1	3	2	6
Below SSC	3	10	4	13	1	3	1	3
SSC	5	16	4	13	4	13	4	13
HSC	2	6	2	6	2	6	0	0
Graduation	3	10	0	0	2	6	1	3
Post-Grad	0	0	0	0	0	0	0	0
Not Given	17	55	19	61	21	68	23	74
Total	31	100	31	100	31	100	31	100

Source: Questionnaire Survey, 2008.

With reference to the educational qualifications of the parents of the students it was important to know the medium of instruction and types of schools attended by their parents at SSC and HSC level. The medium of instruction matters as far as higher and professional educational education is concerned. Also parents who had studied in English are in a position to groom their children in English and put them in English schools. They are in a better position to nurture amongst their children the habits and behaviour to learn the English language. It was found that the majority (approximately 60 per cent) of the parents of open category students had studied in English medium schools at SSC level and this percentage increased with HSC and graduation levels. The majority of the parents of the students were from the same discipline as their children, for instance, from the Patil Medical College, Mumbai 74 per cent fathers and 34 per cent mothers of the students of open category were in the medical profession i.e. they were doctors. But it is critical that most of them had given donations for getting admission for their children in this private college. The performance of the open category students was low when compared with the open merit in government colleges. The open category students were in an advantageous position with reference to their educational and economic backgrounds for getting admission in such private colleges. There was no student belonging to Scheduled Castes and Scheduled Tribes category found during survey in this college but some OBC students were present.

In general it is true that the quality of government schools at SSC level is lower than private or aided schools. It was found that the majority (more than 60 per cent) of the parents of open category students did their schooling from private schools. When compared with parents of reserved category students, hardly 30 per cent were graduates (fathers 30 per cent and mothers 2 per cent) while the majority were educated till SSC. Most (more than 80 per cent) had studied in government schools and no parent was found to have studied in English medium schools. The educational status of the parents of students of the reserved category of Management Institute was low ie they were either below SSC or SSC passed. Amongst all members of the reserved category only one father of the student was an engineering graduate whereas all the remaining graduates were from arts and commerce faculties.

Thus stark inequalities between the open and reserved categories is seen with reference to their educational backgrounds of their respective families. The open category students definitely have the best educational background in their families as most of their parents have undergone good quality education. Moreover most of the parents of open category students were from the same disciplines as their children.

As far as the occupation of parents is concerned the categories given were private, government, self-employed and agriculture. Within these categories their classification was asked e. g. manager, middle management, working class, etc. In general it was found that parents of open category students were either MDs or CEOs of private companies or doctors and engineers. For instance, of the parents of open category students of medical colleges 20 per cent were MDs/CEOs of private companies with incomes above Rs. 150,000 pm while more than 50 per cent were doctors. The rest did not respond to the question. The same trend was seen in Management and Mass Communication faculties. When compared with parents of reserved category students they were Class IV employees in government offices or peons in private companies while most of their mothers were maidservants. It was found that only the father of one student was a civil servant and another was a manager in a private company. Thus economic disparities are significant between open and reserved category students.

Quality of Schooling

As far as the type and medium of instruction of schools attended by students go it was found that 85 per cent open category students studied in English medium schools and 61 per cent were from private schools. It was found that 65 per cent of reserved category students studied in English medium schools and 32 were from private schools. Thus, there is significant disparity as far as the quality of schooling is concerned when it comes to the medium of instruction and the type of school attended.

Therefore it is clear that the family and school backgrounds differ. The open category students are in an advantageous position economically and educationally when it comes to participation in higher and professional education. On the other hand, the reserved category student's economic and educational background is not conducive to any advantage especially for success in higher and professional education.

In order to generalise, a reference to the national level study also brings out the same facts on similar lines as discussed above. The Planning Commission, Government of India had commissioned the Centre for Research, Planning and Action (CERPA), New Delhi for a study on 'Career Perceptions of SC/ST Students in Institutions of Higher Learning'. The study was carried out in five states across various disciplines to ascertain the perceptions and identify disparities among students who were studying in the final year of graduate and post-graduate courses. The sample size of the students was 4,426 of which 2,947 were SC/ST students, 740 OBC and 739 general category students. The study has brought out important facts with reference to socio-economic conditions, school background, performance, career choice of SC/ST, OBC and general category students. Also it had focused on attitudes and perceptions of teachers, heads of institutions and general category students about reservation policy.

With reference to education status of the parents, the report pointed out that the students belonging to SC/ST category were the sole members of their families who were educated while this was not the case with the general category students as one third of students had their fathers as the highest educated members in their families.

The study found that very few belonged to below the poverty line while most of the students belonged to the middle class. The share of general category students who were middle class was slightly higher than students from reserved category background. But it is worth noting that farming was the main and most common occupation of parents of reserved category students.

As far as the school background of the students was concerned, the study found that for middle school/post-primary levels that most of OBC and SC students came from government and government aided schools followed by ST category students. General category students were from private schools and public schools. At the secondary education level, the shares of those going to government and government aided schools were slightly more than average for SC/OBC students. For senior secondary education, the share of OBC students in government and government aided students was 68 per cent, SC was 64 per cent and ST was 60 per cent. General category students passed out from public schools. The share of SC and OBC students was very low in private schools.

With reference to the medium of instruction at middle school level it was found that 60 per cent general category students had English medium and SC/ST and OBC were much lower than them. On the contrary, Hindi as the medium of instruction was the most common amongst OBC and SC students and regional language was most common amongst ST students. At secondary level of education, regional language as the medium of instruction is more popular amongst STs followed by SC and OBC students. At graduation level English is more popular amongst general category students followed by ST while Hindi is popular amongst SC and OBC students.

The study by CERPA stated that social status has influenced choice of course among SC/ST and OBC students. Those who indicated that they could not secure the course of their choice stated that lack of knowledge was responsible for it. Not being able to qualify for the course of their choice was mostly stated by SC/ST and OBC students than open category students. The reasons for that as given by them were insufficient effort and lack of knowledge.

About the performance in college those who said that SC/ST and OBC students whose level of performance was low possessed insufficient knowledge about the fundamentals of their subjects. Also students, especially SC, stated that the social background was responsible for their not being able to cope with the subjects and attain a satisfactory level of performance. Therefore additional training for improving fundamentals was recommended by students themselves.

Parents as the source of information for career options was projected to a greater extent by open category students than reserved category students. Teachers were the most common source of information for career options and also for influencing changes in their career plans. Also the institution was a factor in the change of career plans for SC/ST and OBC students.

It was revealed that more than 50 per cent of teachers believed that the level of performance of reserved category students was inferior to that of the open category students. Most of them mentioned that mainly the lack of understanding of the fundamentals followed by the lack of ability for comprehension and retention and some added the lack of facilities were the reasons for the low performance of reserved category students. It was clarified by the majority of teachers that most of the students were able to overcome their difficulties but a sizeable number of teachers believed that they were not capable of overcoming the difficulties due to their lack of interest as also financial constraints.

The report has strongly recommended that special guidance, training in the fundamentals, English and pre-entrance coaching should be strengthened.

Discrimination and Exclusion in Professional Educational Institutions

The exclusion of Scheduled Castes and Scheduled Tribes is evident in higher and professional educational institutions as discussed earlier. It is not intended to make a sweeping generalisations that exclusion and discrimination happen in all educational institutions. There are some institutions that can be role models as far as positive representation and imparting quality education to Scheduled Castes, Scheduled Tribes and Other Backward Classes are concerned.

Though the educational institutions appear unbiased and neutral, in practice they are the opposite. The actual execution of affirmative action had to be carried out by these institutions in the true spirit with filling up of the quota while showing sensitively to provide relaxations, concessions and conducting programmes to remove the cultural lag of Scheduled Castes and Scheduled Tribes students for ensuring their success. As per the affirmative action policy the reservation for Scheduled Castes is 15 per cent and for Scheduled Tribes is 7. 5 per cent which is proportionate to their population size. The relaxation of marks and age limits is to ensure that not only their quota gets filled but they should have a fair chance to make it to good educational institutions in the absence of proper guidance and the appropriate family background. Also focused programmes and schemes are meant to remove the barriers to access to higher and professional education. But the implementation of schemes and programmes is fraught with biases and prejudices.

The Vikas Adhyayan Kendra reveals that in educational institutions the Scheduled Castes and Scheduled Tribes students are stereotyped and looked at with prejudice; they have to face insults and humiliations due to the circumstances of their birth. The Vikas Adhyayan Kendra's *Fact Sheet*, January 2007, points out that the Scheduled Castes and Scheduled Tribes students are mistreated by the upper caste teachers, especially the scheduled tribes students are treated as primitive and uncultured persons.

While receiving aid from government the Scheduled Castes and Scheduled Tribes students face discrimination and therefore it leads to their exclusion. Wankhede (2008) presents a comprehensive picture of the implementation of the Post-Matric scheme. He points out that there is not sufficient awareness amongst the Scheduled Castes and Scheduled Tribes about the support scheme, the amount is inadequate and has many bureaucratic hassles and stringent condition of eligibility. The important fact which he highlights is that the social prejudices and biases of the implementers delay its implementation. Therefore he suggests that the scheme intended for accessing higher education for the Scheduled Castes and Scheduled Tribes students needs to be revamped in a big way for effective implementation. Since the implementers are biased and prejudiced this amounts to humiliation and discrimination against Scheduled Caste and Scheduled Tribes students.

Cases of overt discrimination are also reported. The caste discrimination in medical institutions like the AIIMS is indicative of such treatment. The Thorat Committee Report revealed that the caste-based discrimination is still prevalent in this premier institution. The Committee found that there was discrimination by the upper castes as there was no cell established to redress the SC/ST complaints which is mandatory as per rules. The Committee also found that the attitude of teachers was indifferent towards SC/ST students as they were directly addressed by their caste names. They also faced discrimination from the upper caste students as they felt isolated in social and cultural events. Moreover the reserved seats of the faculty were also not filled and the post-based roaster was not followed (Thorat Committee Report, 2007).

In 2011, the reserved category students with the help of the

RTI Act found that 24 students were continuously failing in physiology paper in their medical college in Bihar from 2004 till 2009. All of these students were SC/ST and from other reserved categories. They moved the court when they identified that it was easy that their identity was revealed to teachers who evaluated the papers as the University allotted roll numbers to the reserved category in a serial order and the collection of the answer sheets and coding was done in such a way that the candidates were easily identifiable (ie the identity of reserved category students). The High Court of Bihar under its supervision conducted examinations for these students and all of them were declared passed. Even after the court's direction they were not allowed to take their mid-November examinations. Also stereotyping and humiliation of these students was going on (*The Hindu*, 24 November 2011).

Conclusion

The share of the marginalised groups in higher and professional education is low when compared with that of the open category. The general trend of representation shows that their share decreases in those educational institutions that are highly competitive and are professional educational institutions. Despite implementation of the affirmative action policy for more than six decades, the quota of marginalised groups was not filled in premier professional educational institutions. The exclusion of marginalised groups can be explained using Lamont and Lareau's modified approach to understand cultural capital and its reproduction.

The survey undertaken of students reveals that the educational and economic background of reserved category students was very low when compared with that of the open category. In general, it was found that the economic status of reserved category students was low when compared with that of the open category students. When it came to education of grandparents the educational status of grandparents of open category students was much higher than those of reserved category students. The majority of the parents of open category students were from the same profession as their children's disciplines. This is particularly true for private colleges and the percentage of this was very high ie 75 per cent. Approximately 60 per cent of parents of open category studied in English medium schools and this percentage increased with the level of education ie at HSC and graduate level. More than 60 per cent of parents of open category students had studied in private schools. Only 30 per cent parents of reserved category students were graduates and 80 per cent were educated in government schools and no one studied in English medium schools.

Since most of the parents of open category had their education in English it was natural that they were well-placed to transfer the skills to learn and acquire skills to become proficient in English. On the other side the reserved category students lacked this advantage. Moreover the proportion of reserved category students who had their education in English in comparison with the open category is low. Also most of the open category students had their education in private schools when compared with that of the reserved category students as the majority of these students were from government schools.

Similar findings appear in the national level study conducted by Centre for Research, Planning and Action (CERPA), New Delhi. One of the important facts which the study brought out with reference to the performance levels of students was how the teachers rated the performance of students. The opinions of teachers revealed that most of the reserved category students performed poorly when compared with the open category students and this was primarily due to their lack of understanding of the fundamentals of the subjects.

The reserved category students lacked the cultural capital which forces get them excluded from the competitive professional educational institutions. When they enter into such institutions by availing the benefits of the affirmative action policy most of the reserved category students are neither in a position to take advantage of intergenerational transfers of accumulated knowledge as the open category students. Also they are not trained in English medium and private schools which might have helped their to perform better. They try to enter such institutions with these handicaps and therefore they are doomed to be excluded from success and eventually the job market.

The affirmative action policy is not merely filling up of the quota of communities but it is a comprehensive policy so as to negate the discrimination and exclusion in education. It ensures participation of the historically marginalised groups by giving relaxations, concessions and also taking remedial measures for overcoming the cultural lag or exclusion from the field of education. Though there are some exceptions, it is not to generalise that discrimination and exclusion are rampant in all educational institutions but neither can we assume with confidence that educational institutions are free of biases, prejudices, mistreatment and discrimination. Therefore the exclusion of marginalised groups in higher and professional educational institutions is systemic due to the lack of cultural capital and non-implementation of the affirmative action policy in its true spirit.

The Affirmative Action Policy to help the SC/ST/OBC students to gain access to institutes of higher education has not succeeded on account of the lack of commitment on the part of the authorities charged with the responsibility of implementing the laid down provisions.

REFERENCES

Bourdieu, P. and Passeron, J.C., 1977, *Reproduction in Education, Society and Culture*, Sage, London.

Bourdieu, Pierre, 1973, "Cultural Capital and Social Reproduction", in Brown Richard (ed.), *Knowledge, Education and Social Change*, Tavistock Publications, London.

Davies, Ioan, 1973, "Knowledge, Education, and Power", in Brown Richard (ed.), *Knowledge, Education and Social Change*, Tavistock Publications, London.

Deshpande, S. and Yadav, Y., 2006, Redesigning Affirmative Action, *Economic and Political Weekly*, June 17, 2006.

Discussions with Reserved Category Students at University of

Mumbai and University of Pune.

Fact Sheet, 2007, *Dalits and Education*, Vikas Adhyayan Kendra, Mumbai.

Guru, Gopal, 2002, "How Egalitarian Are the Social Sciences in India?", *Economic and Political Weekly*, December 14, 2002.

Halsey, A.H., Heath, A.F. and Ridge, J.M., 1980, *Origins and Destinations: Family, Class and Education in Modern Britain*, Clarendon Press, Oxford.

Jenkins, Richard, 1992, *Pierre Bourdiue*, Routledge, London and New York.

Jenkins, Richard, 2003, *Pierre Bourdieu*, Routledge, London and New York.

Lamont, Michele and Annette, Lareau, 1988, Cultural Capital: Allusions, gaps and glissandos in recent theoretical developments, *Sociological Theory*, 6(2), 153-168.

Questionnaire Survey, 2008.

The Hindu, 24 November 2011.

Thorat Committee Report, 2007, "Caste Discrimination in AIIMS", *Economic and Political Weekly*, June 2, 2007.

Thorat, Sukhdeo, 2006, "Paying the Social Debt", *Economic and Political Weekly*, June 17, 2006.

Throat, Sukhdeo (ed.), 2008, *B.R. Ambedkar Perspectives on Social Exclusion and Inclusive Policies*, Oxford University Press, New Delhi.

Wankhede, G.G., 2008, "Accessing Higher education: Affirmative action and structured inequality-The Indian experience", *Social Change*, Vol. 38, No. 1.

Weisskopf, Thomas, 2004, "Impact of Reservation on Admissions to Higher Education in India", *Economic and Political Weekly*, September 25, 2004 .

5

Discourses of Caste in the Classroom: Reflections from Undergraduate Teaching in a Delhi University College

Smriti Singh

Introduction

Some academicians are of the view that there is the need to engage with aspects such as 'merit' and 'quality' while dealing with higher education. We could look at the issues against the backdrop of a copy of a poster (shown below) which was displayed in an elite college in Mumbai. The poster perhaps essentially had to do with the macro-issues of caste ideology and reservation policy which were implicitly being tolerated and thus in some ways propogated by that educational institution. This is a point that is undeniably significant and has rightly drawn the central ire of scholors who are against the casteist character of higher education in India. This chapter however seeks to follow a less beaten track that emerges from this poster.

A critical take, as it was probably aimed at the higher education system is embedded in a feeling of resentment arising out of perceived '*unfair*' exclusion of a student who belongs to the unreserved category. The bottom-most step of the ladder leading up to a pile of books is inscribed with the word 'Quota', referring to the reservation of seats/partial relaxation of qualifying criteria at entry level in higher education for students who belong to socially and historically disadvantaged sections

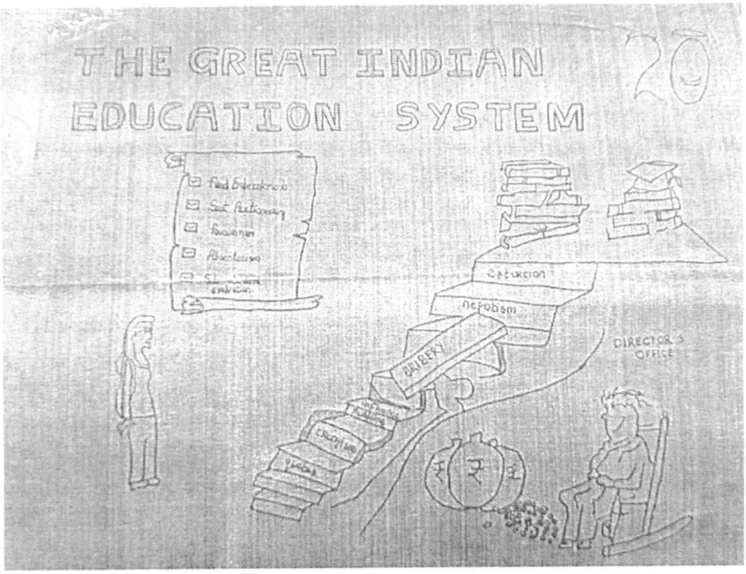

Poster at an elite college, Mumbai, 2014.

of society, as a measure towards social justice. While I agree and support the objection and critical deliberation highlighted by Prof. Wankhede, my issue with the poster here does not have to do with how authorities at the institution allowed it to be put up on display. My issue and my argument here build on what is implicit in the expressed thought and moreover with what we do about it, now that it is before us.

Expressions of casteist sentiments such as this can and must, most certainly be checked by vigilant authorities. However what the paper seeks to argue here is that checking such expressions may work to sanitise spaces of such expressions but they do nothing to address the attitudes that produce it, in the first place, that is to say, that though attitudes and their expression may coincide, they must not be mistaken as coterminous.

What is being emphasised here is that any discussion or deliberation about the 'excluded', 'marginalised' and 'discriminated against' cannot be complete without an equivalent engagement with the 'excluding', 'marginalising', and 'discriminating'. The mechanisms, processes and attitudes of discrimination associated with the latter must also be focused upon in formulation of this problem. This dimension must be focused upon as an indistinguishable part of any discussion on exclusion, that is, engaging with the privileged to highlight and make them conscious of their position of privilege and associated processes of discrimination and marginalisation.

Such a possibility emerges specifically in the context of discourses on exclusion among people. It is this realm of opinions and their expression that this paper seeks to engage with. This is likely to move the debate away from enrolments and retention, however it nonetheless engages with issues pertaining to equity and access within what Roger Slee (2010) calls 'school culture', that is, 'an agglomeration of pedagogic practices, curriculum choices, assessment regimes and the demographic and policy context of schooling'. To this category, I propose to add 'opinions and attitudes'.

This chapter builds on my experiences as a teacher for a course on contemporary issues in the Indian context for first year students in an undergraduate course in teacher education. The four year degree programme is offered by Delhi University and is taught in colleges affiliated to Delhi University. This chapter is an attempt on my part also, to make sense of a number of observations made over a course of one academic year. Hence, all arguments made here are propositional.

Modernity and Caste

Caste, as a historic regime of socio-economic relations based on ideas of ritual purity and karmic laws of justice have been one of the most resilient forms of exploitation and exclusion. Exclusion can be understood in two ways, one through issues of equity and access, and the other through what Roger Slee (2010) terms 'school cultures'. The former is a much explored theme within academic discourses surrounding caste. However, the exploration of ideas that constitute 'school culture' from the point of view of 'exclusion' within the public discourse and public sphere is rather raw. While excluding structured practices of the institutions have been captured before, the more fluid aspect of public opinion within classroom still remains an uncharted domain.

Caste within the classroom discourse provides for a very useful lens to examine an aspect of Habermas's (1989) conception of the public sphere, through building upon Frazer's (1990) critique arguing, 'Exclusion', as inherent to the character assumed by the public sphere. The chapter builds on findings from a participatory observation done in the classroom of first year students enrolled in an undergraduate course for teacher education in a college affiliated to the University of Delhi. The most commonsensical word employed in opposition to caste is 'modern' in a way that seeks to assert that caste system is obsolete and it does not fit in the urban context and its underlying principles of emergent forms of modernity.

In a rather less self-conscious manner, the usage of the word 'modern' makes for a curious case. By employment of 'modern' as a way of highlighting one's allegiance to scientific and technical rationality to govern social behaviour, one clearly also makes evident, in part the problems that this modernity causes.

At one level, the argument reveals its inability to sustain itself when one considers a dissection of the basic ontology of 'modernity' and 'modern'. Modern thought seeks to dissociate itself from traditional justifications for social and individual goals; however in doing so it chooses to base itself linearly on scientific objectivity much in the same manner as the dependence of pre-modern thought on religion. The authority of god as in religion, came to be replaced by authority of science. However, such a replacement must be understood in terms of being a discursive shift, whereby the hierarchy was reinvented using a changed meaning system. What was seen as preordained, destiny and karma came to be understood through objective criteria of scores and tests. This is equivalent to employing new rules to an old game, that is, of finding newer ways of perpetuating hierarchisation and exploitation of the historically marginalised by reinventing the ways in which exclusion reasons itself. From religious and scriptural sanction, it has become a matter of ability-inability as argued against standardised testing.

In any condition, the first and foremost reaction to any discussion on caste is a vehement negation, loud dismissal of its appeal and existence in contemporary times, especially in urban contexts or a quick distancing of oneself from it. Statements like, 'We don't believe in caste system', 'We didn't even know about our caste/we learnt about it rather recently', 'Caste system is prevalent in rural India', 'Poor are more conscious of their caste, not us.'

Essentially, the point states caste system is obsolete to urban-educated people/modern people/and that it is tied to illiteracy. What it represents is an attitude informed by the idea Satish Deshpande (2013; 32) illustrates by saying, 'Caste has already yielded all that it can and represents a ladder that can now be safely kicked away'. This attitude also, in effect sees to establish the primacy of merit over affirmative action. Deshpande further argues that, 'A language that was acquired to formulate discourses of modernity, nation, and development, all in some ways was employed and therefore acquired the language code and structure of defining set by dominant vocal caste'. And thus, ideas of education and 'modernity' and 'well educated' may only superficially mask their affiliation and allegiance to caste, making it easier to dismiss the existence of caste; however, it does nothing to the experience of caste for those who may be marginalised within that system. As Gopal Guru (2011) rightly points out while talking about the blindness of modernity and discourses of modernity to the experiences of the marginalised he suggests that in French revolution as in the Indian Constitution,

"The desire for surplus recognition presupposes a permanent gap between the lite and the subaltern cultural aspirations for recognition. This desire for surplus recognition forces the modern social elite to produce a new form of reduction, rejection and exclusion sustained by modern conditions. Modernity has an inherent tendency to exclude more in favour of a few." (Guru, 2011; 211)

Modernity, if one were to employ the Foucauldian sense to the usage of the concept it would represent a 'regime of truth'[1] in so much as to mean, "It produces conditions and sometimes even methods to classify something as truth". Universities, as modern institutions represent a curious case in this regard. So, while on the one hand emergence of Dalit politics and subaltern studies have challenged the structures of knowledge[2], on the other hand what remains unchallenged and unquestioned is the limits of universities as specialised institutions and spaces dedicated solely to intellectual endeavour and associated assumptions of primacy of mental labour over physical labour.

It is therefore safe to argue that these represent an appropriation of traditions historically associated with dominating castes and a systematic dispossession of traditions of songs, oral culture, dance, manual labour et cetera.

This process effectively segregates 'dispossession' from 'discrimination' within the ontology of caste in higher education. Such a delinking causes not only a violence on 'being' and 'becoming' of Dalit identity but must also be acknowledged to be at the base of a unanimous, almost circular engagement and emphasis on descriptions of discrimination within the narratives of sociology and social anthropology. It is a fair conclusion here that 'dispossession' along and in tandem with 'discrimination' can help evolve the caste ontologically.

Merit and Qualification

The next theme that emerges is with regard to the perceived threat to merit and qualification that affirmative action and positive discrimination represent. As a naturally flowing argument that is then posited is that any affirmative action or positive discrimination must only be given to the meritorious irrespective of their social condition, that is, the rejection of social profile as the primary basis of determination of who receives benefits of affirmative action.

The primacy of merit to social profile of an individual is definitely argued from the point of view of 'logic' and 'scientific*ity*' of objective evaluation of candidature over arguments against an inherited social profile, that one has not much say in. Social profile is inherited and thus has lesser claim over it by an individual as opposed to a more 'cultivated' 'natural talent/merit', when resources and social assets are redistributed towards the goal of social justice.

The arguments made by the students in this regard were based on positive discrimination as a contestation between sheer merit and 'privilege'. Within this context, students readily invoked their experiences of struggling to secure a seat in the elite colleges and the agony of knowing that the tagged seats were still lying vacant. Similarly they voiced their loud disapproval and discontent over students eligible for caste-based reservations seeking admission within the unreserved category thereby 'squatting' over 'general category' seat. In this regard while discussing the Mandal Commission and caste-based reservation, there was an aggressive vocalisation of the need to review the basis of reservation at entry level in universities. Vocal students argued that the only criteria for a claim to reservation must be economic vulnerability. This stance raises two set of concerns about what would constitute 'merit' and the other with respect to evolving an authentic basis of claiming 'disadvantage'.

To argue 'merit', one could draw from Prof Ivan Reid[3]'s argument. 'Merit' argued Prof Reid is a 'sum of ability and effort', the position made here renders agreement on this concept of merit and simultaneously seeks to elaborate the concept further. 'Ability' is problematic idea, in that, it leaves open the possibility of a translation of 'ability' as 'natural' ability as opposed to 'cultivated' ability. 'Cultivated' ability would also emerge from successful efforts previously made by an individual himself/herself or by generations preceding the individual. This is what ties the concept of 'ability' to history. Flowing from this argument then, it becomes clear that if individuals on the basis of their social profile were systematically excluded from making efforts in educational fields then 'merit' and 'ability' inevitably expose the nexus between caste system and its associated oppression.

This way 'ability' would also have to be dissected for its inevitable links with 'Cultural Capital[4]' by the way of 'Reconversion Strategies' that is whereby one form of capital, say economic is used to generate another form of capital, say cultural (Bourdieu, 1984). Thus, membership to social space is earned by expending or exchanging stock of economic, social or cultural capital. Further, 'ability' is also a matter of 'Habitus' that is inherited. Habitus here is to be understood as 'both the generative principle of objectively classifiable judgments and the system of classification of these practices. It is in the relationship between the two capacities which define the habitus, the capacity to produce classifiable practices and works, and the capacity to differentiate and appreciate these practices and products (taste), that the represented social world, ie, the space of life-styles, is constituted'. (Bourdieu, 1984; 170)

Another concern that is expressed in advocacy of '*merit*' is that 'merit' constructed as 'natural ability' and 'effort' combined together is crucial to safeguarding 'quality' in higher education. 'Quality' in higher education, notes Krishna Kumar (2010), has been assigned absolutely new meaning within the neoliberal discourse. Neoliberal discourse on 'quality' defines it in terms of superiority, which means picking a few from a pool of talent. It may though appear to be advocating expansion of the pool, but this expansion of the pool is not tied to social justice as much as it is tied to self-justifying system of selection. This is notwithstanding the repetitive profiles of those who are chosen. The neoliberal advocates contend that access and access alone is enough to address unequal opportunity.

The neoliberal seeks to argue its authenticity and fairness on account of 'objective' testing methods to identify talent and merit. With overpowering emphasis on outcomes, results, cross-country testing, transparency and accountability, it seeks to establish a reinvented structure to perpetuate existing hierarchies and to also simultaneously evolve newer ways in which these hierarchies project their legitimacy and authenticity, and possibly create even a new basis and framework by which they identify themselves and organise population into groups.

Krishna Kumar (2010) highlights how this approach is causing the social goal associated with education to get sidelined. He argues that education is not just a matter of human resource development towards national economic goals generally and as training for jobs, specifically. Education is also an expression of 'moral imperative of equality and justice' which must be given due value when defining 'quality' in education. Education must thus be understood as a longitudinal project towards social justice. He argues that in this sense 'quality' becomes a characteristic of an object or experience unlike the neoliberal employment of term 'quality', which solely seeks to be a means of comparison.

It would further be of interest here to suggest that the second component of 'merit', that is, 'effort' in the neoliberal incarnation invokes the karma theory as a principle and a system of justice operating with autonomous causal law. This gives the new frameworks evolved by neoliberalism, some traditional points of reference that most religions across the world subscribe to in some way or other. This must not be mistaken as an attempt to seek traditional rationale and sanction for its methods and principles by neoliberalism, but as an effort to imitate the principles of religions in the hope of gaining the same appeal as religion and science had in their heydays.

In religion, Karma theory or the principle of 'as you sow, so you reap' is embedded in the ideas of self-discipline and a keen, critical and strong surveillance of thoughts, feelings and actions (at least in principle), and a strong invocation of life after death. There are also the concepts of the interconnectedness of humans and a strong desire for escaping 'ill-fate' and the 'wrath of the supernatural'. However, in its neoliberal reincarnation, Karma or 'effort' that constitutes merit seeks to centralise the principle of the highest rewards determined by materialism and strongly situates them outside the realm of self-criticality. In this form, Karma or 'effort' seeks to delink 'merit' from structural inequalities and systematic discrimination to attach it instead to 'individual efforts'.

Authentic Basis of Claiming Disadvantage

In what follows logically from the previous section discussing debates on merit, arguments contesting what must constitute authentic basis for claiming 'social disadvantage'[5] must be students from caste Hindu families outrightly contested the 'historic underprivilege' argument on the basis of caste by arguing that their grandfathers[6] also faced economic 'disadvantage' and struggled to attain education. This was advanced as the basis for questioning the need for reservation at entry level in universities.

Historians such as Parimala Rao highlight an interesting error[7] made in this regard. She argues that although caste predisposed *Brahmins* to pursue education and knowledge, it strictly barred them from accumulation of wealth. Similarly for *Kshatriyas* the predisposition to wealth was accompanied by the singular focus on leading a luxurious life

Then, does this make it safe to argue that all castes suffered some or the other kind of disadvantage owing to their predispositions?

The answer would be negative, because of three reasons:

1. The structural experiences of modern education system favoured certain kinds of predispositions.
2. Economic capital provided initial impetus for those who were not by their origin predisposed the accumulation of wealth.
3. The oppression within the caste system towards Dalits and untouchables made for structural barriers against educational aspirations and pursuits.

It is these this structural barriers that caste Hindus seeking to retain privilege within the caste system, as it existed before the advent of modern education worked hard (both consciously and unconsciously) to uphold.

Reading the Reactions

In terms of reactions and participation within classroom discussions the two things that emerged prominently were,

1. The silence of students with Dalit identity despite provocative attacks and an aggressive questioning of their candidature, and,
2. The nature of public sphere/public domain.

The Pain of Silence: Reactions of Dalit Students

A lot has been said about how the caste Hindu students felt about caste system, affirmative action and its 'influences' on higher education in the Indian context. The paper however focuses on engagement with the privileged side of the spectrum. It is imperative to not forget that the class did not consist only of caste Hindu students and sympathisers who shared the common status of students who belonged to the unreserved category. This section may though, appear to be a digression from the core focus of the paper, and yet it is a crucial link that may offer insights into situations that are discriminatory in nature.

One of the most noteworthy points amidst the discussions on caste was the silence of the Dalit students who were as much a part of this class as the rest and bore witness to their loud and aggressive anti-Dalit stance.

The initial silence of Dalit students represented a sense of hurt, pain, possible hopelessness and the lack of feeling of belongingness. However, when the position countering the aggressive hegemonic position held by caste Hindu students was voiced, it got translated into hurt and pain into anger, and the lack of belongingness into assertion through rational argumentation. Some insights developed in this paper owe their origination to rational arguments that emerged from Dalit students in response to the hegemonic position of caste Hindu students and sympathisers.

Public Sphere/Public Discourse/ Public Domain

The last and one of the most significant points I wish to make here draws on the concluding lecture on caste system in the Indian context which I began by arguing that, *"the fact that you (caste Hindu students and sympathisers) can audaciously question the credibility of a Dalit student's candidature speaks loudly and decisively about whether caste exists or not and who does the public sphere belong to."*

The statement flows from Nancy Frazer's (1993) criticism of Habermas's[8] (1989) famous essay on public sphere. She argues that public sphere as Habermans constructs it, is sheer 'Bourgeoisie idealism' and a marginalising experience for women and other representational minorities. It assumes a politically functional individual as synonymous to men from the upper class who are free from domestic and labour obligations, relatively. The usage of the concept of public sphere in the above context draws also from Rajeev Bhargava's (2005) adaptation of Habermas's concept, wherein he states,

> By public sphere I mean a common space, in principle accessible to all, which anyone may enter with views on the common good realized wholly or partially. A maidan, a coffee house, an exhibition hall, the paan shop on the road side, the sweet shop in the locality as also the discursive and representational space available in newspapers, magazines, journals, radio, television and now the internet. (Bhargava, 2005; 14-15)

In this context, it was startling to move from a vehement dismissal of the existence of caste system to reach a point whereby we collectively acknowledged that the public sphere, the 'collective opinion' rallies the interests of a certain group, to realise one's individual position with respect to these opinions and the groups represented. Most of all, it was about realising one's position of privilege and the associated structures of discrimination produced by it.

What can be hoped for is that though the public sphere is entrenched with lopsided arguments and cosmetically enhanced appearances of existing socially-historically oppressive structures, Dalit students are increasingly seeking to reclaim the public in the public sphere. And, while I have taken leave of absece from teaching as of now, I hope that when I return, I would encounter a public sphere reflecting in classrooms that is more self-critical and conscious of itself.

REFERENCES

Bhargava, R. 2005, Introduction in Bhargava, R. and Reifeld, H. (eds.). *Civil Society, Public Sphere and Citizenship: Bialogues and Perceptions,* New Delhi: Sage.

Bourdieu, P. and Passeron, J.C., 1990, Reproduction in Education, Society and Culture. London: Sage.

Bourdieu, Pierre, 1984, *Distinction: A Social Critique of the Judgement of Taste,* trans. by Richard Nice, Harvard University Press.

Calhoun, Craig, Gerteis, Joseph, Moody, James, Pfaff, Steven and Virk, Indermohan, (eds.) 2012. *Contemporary Sociological Theory,* Blackwell, Readers in Sociology, 10.3, Oxford, UK: Wiley-Blackwell.

Deshpande, S., 2013, Caste and Castelessness, *Economic and Political Weekly*, 48(15), 32–39.

Frazer, N., 1990, Rethinking the Public Sphere: A Contribution to the Critique of Actually Existing Democracy, *Social Text*, No. 25/26, pp. 56–80.

Frazer, Nancy, 1993, Rethinking the Public Sphere: A Contribution to the Critique of Actually Existing Democracy. In Bruce Robbins (ed.), *The Phantom Public Sphere,* Minneapolis: University of Minnesota Press, pp. 1-32.

Guru, G., 2011, "Humiliation" in (ed.) Guru, G., *Humiliation: Claims and Context*, New Delhi: Oxford University Press.

Habermas, J., 1989, *The Structural Transformation of the Public Sphere: An Inquiry into a Category of Bourgeois Society.* Translated by Thomas Berger and Frederick Lawrence, Cambridge: The MIT Press.

Ketkar, S.V., 1979, *History of Caste in India,* Jaipur: Rawat Publications.

Kumar, K., 2010, Quality in Education: Competing Concepts, *Contemporary Education Dialogue,* Vol. 7, No. 1, January, 2010. pp. 7-18.

Natrajan, B., 2009, "Place and Pathology in Caste," *Economic and Political Weekly*, XLIV (51/December 19, 2009): 79–82.

Slee, R., 2010, A cheese-slicer by any other name? Shredding the sociology of inclusion. in (eds.) Apple, M.W., Ball, S.J. and Gandin, L.A., *The Routledge International Handbook of the Sociology of Education,* pp. 99-108.

ENDNOTES

1. Students (all young women) highlighted the struggle by male members and associated themselves most directly with the struggle of males in the family and justified their rage against reservation of seats at entry level in universities as being a direct product of the struggle faced by males of the family. This is interesting for it points to a clear association between patriarchy and caste.

Dr. Parimala V. Rao is the Assistant Professor, History of Education, Zakir Husain Centre for Educational Studies, Jawaharlal Nehru University, New Delhi. The points made here are based on an interaction with her to gain specific insights into the historical context of caste in education, as part of research for M Phil dissertation, submitted to the Jawaharlal Nehru University in the year 2012.

. Habermas (1989) imagines the 'public sphere' in eighteenth century England with certain characteristics that may be helpful for us to understand the university space:

- Public sphere must be understood as a communication structure rooted in the life world through the associational network of civil society.
- Public sphere must be located in institutions and associations of civil society which are loosely affiliated to the State, and definitely not an organ of the government. He includes media in this category as well.
- It is a warning system with sensors that, though unspecialised, are sensitive throughout society.
- Owing to their relationship with the State, they operate both as an instrument of governemnt as well as critical of it.

Thus, in democratic theory, public sphere must in addition, amplify the pressure of problems, that is, not only detect and identify problems but also convincingly and influentially thematise them, furnish them with possible solutions and dramatise them in such a way that they are taken up and dealt with by parliamentary complexes. (Habermas in (ed.) Calhoun et al., 2002)

6

Aiming High: Higher Education among the Kunchikorves of Dharavi

Pradeep Shinde

I. Introduction

Socio-economically, educationally and politically, the Denotified Tribes[1], are known in government parlance as *'Vimukta Jatis'* (literally free caste. The phrase refers to the so-called criminal tribes that are free from the surveillance under the Criminal Tribes Act (CTA of 1871), but remain one of the most backward tribes in India. Despite this, with a few notable exceptions (D'Souza 2001, Radhakrishna 2001, Roy Burman 2010, Simhadri 1991), there is a surprising dearth of detailed empirical studies on these tribes.[2] Kolharkar, the translator of Laxman Gaikwad's Sahitya Akademi winning autobiographical work, *Uchalya* (The Branded) observes, 'No systemic, ethnological, historical and sociological studies are available on these tribes' (Kolharkar 2005: v). It is the vernacular literature, mostly in the form of autobiography (Mane 1981, Gaikwad 2005), which has given the issues of Denotified Tribes the visibility which was denied to them. These highly acclaimed literary works tell us about the grim life that these tribes lead and the pernicious social attitude shown to them by the Indian society. When one compares the participation of Dalits and Adivasis in higher education with that of the Denotified Tribes, the latter is seen to be abysmally low. 'The literacy level among the Denotified Tribes [of Maharashtra] is only 0.06%' (http://www.

dhammaweb.net/dhamma_news/view.php?id=298), leave alone higher education. In view of this scenario that prevails among the Denotified Tribes of Maharashtra, this paper explores the participation of a Denotified Tribe, the Kunchikorves[3], in higher education in the Mumbai slum of Dharavi. Socio-economically, educationally and politically, the Kunchikorve tribe is one of the most backward Denotified Tribes of Maharashtra. Of about 2,500 Kunchikorves in Dharavi, this researcher found only 12 graduate young men and 4 graduate young women (those who have completed 10+2+3 years of education). However, none of these graduates has found employment in the Government sector in spite of their higher education, so far. All these graduates work in private sector companies in Mumbai. This paper will explore the kinds of constraints the Kunchikorves face while obtaining higher education, given the lack of cultural capital in the realm of education among them.

Education is said to 'facilitate political and human development (such as enhanced democracy, and lowered fertility and mortality rates) and provides the context for economic development' (Jeffery 2005: 19). However, the development of this nature is contingent upon equality of access to higher education. Indeed 'providing equality of access and removing systemic social exclusion have dominated policy agendas through the 1990s' (Jeffery 2005:19). Nevertheless, 'access to higher education opportunities continues to bear the stamp of multiple dimensions of inequalities—gender, caste, religion, class, locality and disability—that characterise our society' (John 2012:1). Given these constraints coupled with the social pathologies that are expressed through such social constructions as 'criminal tribes' in the past and the more recent 'a people who have no culture, language or guru', the Kunchikorve tribe had been, and continues to be, marginalised by the State as well as their upper-caste neighbours respectively. Thus exploring the participation of the Kunchikorves of Dharavi acquires significance. About thirty years ago, there was hardly any Kunchikorve who went beyond class 4, let alone higher education. But for the past 15-20 years, awareness among the Kunchikorves about education has been gradually rising. Being aware of education, however, is not enough. What is important is access. This was one of the major constraints that Kunchikorves faced, and continue to face, while accessing education let alone higher education. This slowly began to change after they found employment as sanitary workers in the Municipal Corporation of Brihan (Greater) Mumbai (popularly known as BMC) in the early seventies. This does not mean that the level of higher education among the Kunchikorves has risen substantially. However, most Kunchikorves of Dharavi eke out their living from activities in the rampantly growing informal, also known as the unorganised, sector such as broom making/selling, utensil selling for old clothes as well as sanitary contract work in the public (BMC) and private sectors (private apartments and housing colonies). Children of these families hardly go to school. Even if they do, they go to BMC-run schools where the quality of education imparted is said to be nothing but substandard[4]. Educationists attach a great deal of importance to the quality of education received at the primary and secondary levels of schooling. 'Deprivation in terms of early access to quality education is increasingly becoming the most crucial determinant of subsequent life achievement for many socially and economically marginalised groups.' (Ghosh 2006: 2430) Quality school education paves the way for higher education. If socio-economically impoverished caste/tribe groups are deprived of good school education, they tend to encounter difficulties in accessing higher or specialised education. But this deprivation is alleviated markedly with the intervention of affirmative action programmes instituted by the Central as well as The State Governments. 'There can be no doubt that a substantial share of Scheduled Caste (SC) and Scheduled Tribe (ST) students enrolment in Indian higher educational institutions is attributable to India's reservation policies' (Weisskoff 2004: 4340). And this is the mechanism which has enabled the socio-economically marginalised caste/tribe groups in India to acquire mobility (Deshpande 2013,

Galanter 1984, Parry 1999, Weisskoff 2004) because, 'quotas seek to ensure that a wider set of social groups get access to the higher education institutions that do exist, than occurs at present' (Ghosh 2006: 2429) and 'promote the equalization of life chances' (Parry 1999: 128). It is for these reasons that this paper explores the significance of reservation policy in the lives of Kunchikorves in general and higher education in particular, although accessing quotas is contingent upon one's possessing documentary evidence such as the caste certificate[5]. However, with the unequivocal implementation of neoliberal policies in terms of privatisation by the Indian State, this is all now gradually changing. With the wave of privatisation driven by neoliberal state policies (Bhowmik 2005, Kelley 2010, and Jha 2010, Kumar 2010, Patnaik 2010, and Chandrasekhar and Ghosh 2002) and its effects on BMC recruitment, the sanitation workers of the BMC in general and the Kunchikorves in particular are once again faced with the lack of a consistent source of work which may rejuvenate the language of discrimination associated with the stigma of criminality. The increasing privatisation of sanitary jobs in the form of contracts in the Sanitation Department of the BMC has led Kunchikorves to believe that there would not be new recruitments anytime soon in the future. It has been about two decades since the BMC started contracting out sanitation jobs to private contractors. Hence, the Kunchikorves are increasingly losing the hope of entering permanent employment in the BMC. Sons who thought they had a formal guarantee of future employment with the BMC after the retirement of their fathers are now having to enter the informal sector. This is what Breman (1996, 1997, 2003, Parry 2001, 2003) calls the informalisation of the formal sector. The structural transformation to which the Indian economy has been subjected has also penetrated the realm of education. 'The idea that education should be seen as a commodity that can and should be bought and sold on the market is spreading' (Jeffery 2005: 20). The idea is not only spreading, but is being seen 'as a legitimate aim' (Kumar 2011). All this has a direct bearing on the Kunchikorve tribe. For Kunchikorves the government jobs, facilitated education/higher education among them substantially, and the privatisation of these jobs may result in creating not only the uncertainty of access to economic capital, but also of acquiring higher education. The 'development' of these conditions, this paper argues, would revive the discriminatory characterisation of the Kunchikorve tribe as a *'jungli'* (primitive) people having no culture, language or guru' which, with the abrogation of the CTA and the introduction of the reservation policy, was on the verge of becoming moribund.

II. The Early Scenario

Kunchikorves migrated from the border towns of Maharashtra such as Solapur and of Karnataka such as, Bijapur, Gulbarga and Shahabad in and around 1960 and settled predominantly in Mumbai and Pune. A large number of the Kunchikorves also live in Solapur who are believed to have migrated from Karnataka. The subject of my fieldwork, between 2004, 2007 and 2011 for my doctoral programme at the Anthropology Department of the London School of Economics as also for my post doctoral fellowships at University of Kassel and the Re: Work Institute, Humboldt University, Berlin was the Kunchikorves. They migrated from Solapur during the late 1950s. Most of those who came into the city of Mumbai in the sixties and seventies survived on begging and monkey plays. The first couple of Kunchikorve families that are said to have entered the then Bombay State in 1944 presumably with a view to settle in the state did not do so. These families kept shuttling between Mumbai and their small towns and villages. The longest stay of these early migrants in Bombay is said to be in Wadala suburb near Dadar. The Kunchikorves are said to have encroached upon a small piece of land in Wadala and stayed there for about a decade and survived on daily begging. However, the families were evicted from the encroached piece of land that was earmarked for a bus depot by the state-owned company Bombay Electricity and State Transport, popularly known in Mumbai today as BEST. From there, these families entered the land mass known as Dharavi part of which was being used by the BMC as a garbage dumping ground for South Bombay. The slum, which in subsequent decades earned the somewhat denigrating epithet 'biggest slum of Asia', was nothing but a stretch of marshy land which used to be flooded during monsoon. Inhabited by the leather tanneries run by Labbai Muslim entrepreneurs of Tamilnadu and served by Dalits of the same state, as well as of Maharashtra, the slum in subsequent years became the home of migrants from almost every state of the country, except for the north-eastern states. Muslims and Dalits became the largest communities that dotted the life of Dharavi until the boom in the Indian economy in the early 1990s. Subsequently, many upper castes entered the life of Dharavi such as Marwaris and Jains who now live and run their small-scale enterprises, like jewellery, hardware and medical and provision stores, there. Many leather boutiques in Dharavi belong to Aroras and Khatris, and a couple of them to Maharashtrian Brahmins, who have established themselves in the leather manufacturing of Dharavi.

The early life spanning the period from the late sixties to the early nineties in Dharavi was often dominated by strife of various kinds. This was also a time when the right-wing Shiv Sena came into being by pursuing their xenophobic brand of politics, particularly, against South Indian migrants in Mumbai. The Tamil migrants living in Dharavi also had to bear the brunt of the xenophobia. The irony is that today the formerly Thevar migrants of Tamil Nadu are the biggest supporters of the Shiv Sena in Dharavi. The slum is also known to have been a popular hideout particularly among absconding criminals who sought refuge in the rickety structures erected by the slumlords. These powerful men, who owned hundreds of *zhopdas* (hutments), stole water and electricity for their 'tenants' in connivance with the members of the BMC bureaucracy. However, this ended with the slum clearance policy of the Congress regime in the mid-seventies. Slumlords/landsharks lost hundreds of *zhopdas* overnight. Many became paupers. One of the Kunchikorve families owned about 200 *zhopdas*, but lost all of them, except for their *zhopdas* in which they lived. The thriving bootlegging, however, was not affected by this campaign. On the contrary, it became a brisk business and provided some slum dwellers a living. Some Kunchikorves are said to have worked for the 'infamous' Varadrajan Mudaliyar aka Varda*bhai*[6] and transported Dharavi brewed illicit liquor surreptitiously to parts of South Mumbai and earned their living. These bootleggers competed with the bootleggers of the Koli village[7]. Some of these Koli bootleggers were said to be so rich that they owned plush cars and also had rich clients some of whom were leading actors of the Hindi film industry, which is known today as Bollywood. Having been turned into a cesspool by the effluents released by the small industries and housing societies that stand along its course, today the Mithi River meanders its way between the sprawling Powai Lake and the Bandra Creek. As a result of the damning pollution, the tributaries that flowed from the Mithi River were also affected severely, and so was the livelihood of the Kolis. Along with these natives of Mumbai, the slum of Dharavi thrived sheltering as it does even today, various small-scale entrepreneurs who send their products across the world.

The not-so-very-good tag the 'biggest slum of Asia' still sticks to the slum and in the consciousness of the middle-class Indian the disparaging moniker still exists. However, for the present day generation as well as for those who know about this densely populated thriving mass of human energy, Dharavi is a mini-India where thrive small-scale enterprises of various kinds. Along with representing caste and religious groups of almost all parts of the country, Dharavi houses an intricate web of small scale industries ranging from leather to hosiery to various food industries to recycling materials of different kinds. Not only have these products found their ways in Indian markets, but also to the markets of Europe, Africa and south-East Asia. Dharavi's residents therefore differ with what they call 'a perverse description of Dharavi'. Certainly, they do not discount the fact the slum is not only densely populated, but is also beset by various problems such as the deteriorating state of sanitation, and theft of water and electricity by local goons patronised by local political heavyweights. These perennial problems, as the old generation rues, put a great deal of strain on the services provided by the BMC. In the midst of this, Kunchikorves inhabit three small pockets of the slum and earn their living from various means of livelihood such as employment in the BMC's Sanitation Department, money-lending, broom making from palm leaves and selling them, utensils selling as well as contract sanitary work in the private sector of Mumbai. A few of those young men and women who have been able to access higher education come from those families that have double income earned from the BMC job and moneylending enterprise. This paper is about these men and women and the role higher education plays in transforming their socio-economic lives.

III. Ethnographic Explorations

Amol Kunchikorve, aged 44, claims to be the first lawyer from among the Kunchikorves of not only Mumbai, but also of the country. Soon after becoming a lawyer, Amol got married to his Brahmin girlfriend of four years in 2000. After staying in a joint family, which consisted of his married younger brother's family and two children, until 2002 in various parts of Dharavi, the couple moved out of the slum to a middle-class locality in Matunga and from there to one of the highly upmarket areas of Mumbai, Dadar. There, for the first four years, the couple stayed in rented houses. With his decent earnings, along with his wife's salary from an NGO job in Mumbai, and his share in the selling of a bungalow, Amol managed to buy a one-room house with an attic in Dadar for 1,000,000 (Rs 10 lakh) in 2005. The bungalow that was sold was constructed in Gulbarga town in Karnataka by his father from his earnings as a saintary worker in BMC in the early 1990s. Gulbarga was the place from where the Daravi Kunchikarves migrated to Mumbai in the late fifties. And, the hardworking lawyer is a self-made man. During his college days he helped to support his family by running a Chinese-food stall encroaching on a Dharavi pavement by paying the police *hafta* (protection money taken from food-stalls that are run on pavements in Bombay). Although his father worked as a sweeper in the BMC, his earnings were not enough to feed the family of six. But still his father encouraged the studious child and sent him to one of 'the best schools in a neighbouring suburb, where only upper middle-class children went'. Amol also did not disappoint his father. Conscious of the lack of education among poverty-ridden Kunchikorves, Amol did not give up his own education, unlike most of his Kunchikorve peers. Looking back, he says, 'I grew up in Dharavi, but never played there, I would go to play with my middle-class schoolmates in their areas.' Even after moving out of a slum, which often comes to be described by middle-class Mumbaites as filthy, to a centrally located area dotted largely by affluent sky-high residential as well as corporate towers, Amol has not broken his ties with Dharavi. That is where, along with his younger brother's as well as younger sister's families, live his father's three younger brothers and their families. Amol continues to visit them every so often. He is now concerned with his younger brother Subbu's sons' education. Amol personally ensures that his younger brother, who has a permanent job as a sweeper in the BMC, provides properly for their schooling. Subbu now works in one of the hospitals of the BMC but he still struggles to run his family due to his ill-managed money-lending network, Amol supports Subbu monetarily. Sometimes the differences over the way Subbu runs 'his money lending network' leads to arguments between the brothers but this does not affect their relationship. Subbu's 'impulsive' act of mortgaging Amol's house in the slum to a bank for 75,000 rupees without taking him into his confidence did upset Amol, for 'Amol also has his family of three to look after'. But, instead of confronting the 'irresponsible' brother, Amol paid off the mortgage. Upwardly mobile himself, Amol is as concerned about the economic mobility of the family of his younger brother Subbu as of his own. Amol's concerns are with the upbringing and schooling of his brothers' children aged 15 and 14. Standing by the Chinese-food stall, which Subbu now runs, along with his father's brother's two sons, Amol expresses his optimism for Subbu's children's future with the existing reservation facility:

> If either child of my brother passes with good grades in his 10th and 12th exams, he would be able to secure a seat in medical college through a Denotified Tribe reservation quota and would be a doctor. He would be the first doctor in our caste in the entire country, Pradeep!

While talking about his own rise from one of the densely congested parts of the slum of Dharavi, Amol attributes his success to three factors: his father's job, school and reservation benefits. With education reservation, and pursuing his aspiration of becoming a lawyer, he continued running the Chinese food-stall, which gave him the money he needed to complete his five-year law degree. His younger brother, Subbu, failed to pass 12th class and gave up school. Their father passed away soon after Amol completed his law degree; the responsibility of looking after the family fell on his shoulders. Although Subbu was involved in money-lending on a small scale, he would often meet with losses in those days. With their father's provident fund and pension money from his BMC employment, Amol got both his younger siblings married. Subbu married his classmate- cum-girlfriend and his younger sister married a BMC sweeper, a distant affine. Having helped his siblings to marry and settle down, he decided to settle down himself, and married his Brahmin girlfriend of four years, whom he had met in college. Working hard, Amol established himself in his profession and moved out of Dharavi after three years of legal practice.

Amol has a five-year-old daughter, who goes to an English medium school in Dadar. Both her parents are very particular about the kinds of things the precocious little girl should learn. One of them is the recitation of Hindu religious hymns (*shlokas*) which seems to be one of the priorities in which the mother wants the child to excel; at the top is, however, the schooling in English medium. During my interactions with the couple at their residence in Dadar, the first thing the mother would ask the child was to recite *shlokas*.

Today, Amol explains, with the government jobs of conservancy workers in the BMC's Sanitation Department, some of the Dharavi Kunchikorves, especially the moneylending class, have been able to send their children to English medium schools. Whereas those Kunchikorves who eke out their living from informal sector activities such as sanitary contract work, broom-selling, utensil selling hardly find time to even ensure that their children go to school. Talking about the general attitude of Kunchikorve parents toward their children's schooling, he says:

> Children in our locality do not go to school. Their parents slog the whole day to earn a living to survive. There is nobody to ask these children whether they go to school or not or whether they pass or fail.

But those who have acquired economic mobility because of higher education are becoming aware of education and the constructive role it plays. Although these successful individuals are moving out of Dharavi to better suburbs in the midst of middle-class families, they have not left their kinship ties behind. These individuals not only remain a source of non-material benefits (guidance and inspiration), but also become the source of material benefits of various kinds such as monetary contribution for others left behind in the slum.

Certainly this world is different from the world that exists in the Kunchikorve Nagar slum of Dharavi. The Kunchikorve girls from poor families rarely go to school and are married off as soon as they attain puberty. Even most of the young women whose fathers have BMC employment hardly go beyond Class 10 and are also married off largely to their affine. But there are also those whose fathers have double income from both the BMC job and money-lending who tend to pursue 10+2 level education. Girls from such families also have aspirations to go in for education/higher education, but face resistance from their parents and yet try to fulfil their own as well as their parents' aspirations. Vandana is one of them.

One of the very few girls from among the Kunchikorves of the Kunchikorve Nagar slum, Vandana has been able to become a commerce graduate after studying for three years post the 10+2 level. It was not easy for Vandana to complete the degree without encountering the opposition to her resolution to go in for higher education. The determined young woman was pressurised to get married to her mother's brother's son, himself a commerce graduate, by her mother herself. Vandana, supported by her father, withstood the pressure from her mother and completed her graduation. Her mother argued that Vandana could continue with her studies after getting married. But Vandana refused and stuck to her grounds saying that she would first complete her degree and then fulfil her mother's wishes. Soon after acquiring a graduate degree, a rarity among the Kunchikorve young women in Dharavi, Vandana got married to her mother's brother's son himself a commerce graduate. Along with starting her married life, Vandana started preparing for the coveted Maharashtra Public Service Commission (MPSC) exams to be able to enter the state bureaucracy. However, the family responsibilities severely constrained her efforts. Instead of continuing with her MPSC preparation, Vandana obtained a job in a private firm in a Mumbai suburb to support her family which consisted of her husband's younger brother, his wife and their two children. She had to take this decision because her husband's income from a private-company job, as well as her husband's younger brother's from sanitary contract work, were not enough for running the household which put a lot of strain on her husband. Vandana also asserted that she did not want her education to go waste. She wanted to make use of the degree fruitfully. 'What is the use of your education if you sit at home doing nothing', asserts Vandana. It was because of Vandana's income that her husband has been able to pass to his younger brother the permanent job of conservancy worker in the BMC's Sanitation Department on compassionate grounds following his father's death while in service.

The contrast is palpable: a horde of Kunchikorve women, a few of whom take their young children along to carry a small number of pans and brooms, and some carrying a burden of broom and utensils go out of Kunchikorve Nagar daily to sell their ware in Mumbai suburbs (utensil-selling women also accept old clothes along with cash), whereas Vandana just like a middle-class Indian woman goes to office to work without carrying any physical burden.

Most parents, however, do not send their daughters for higher education. After class 6 or 7, young girls are married off to their close relations such as mother's brother's son, father's sister's son or mother's brother himself after they have attained puberty. Rarely do Dharavi Kunchikorves make efforts to find alliances outside their immediate affine relations. Even if young Kunchikorve men or women are allowed to pursue higher education, they are told to get married first. Suresh's case illustrates this:

Suresh completed his three-year degree in commerce from a college in a Bandra suburb. Subsequently, he started preparing for competitive exams through the Union Public Service Commission to be a bureaucrat. However, his parents insisted that he get married first and then pursue his dream. Suresh resisted his parents' insistence for about three years but succumbed to their pressure and got married to a class 4 passed Kunchikorve young woman from a Kurla suburb. Suresh is not the first person in his family who got married after he earned his BCom. His elder brother, Naresh was the first person who had to yield to his parents' insistence.

The family having a large network of moneylending among BMC sanitary workers is one of the economically upwardly mobile families among Dharavi Kunchikorves. With the income earned from Suresh's father's BMC job of sanitary worker and his mother's savings from the vocation of a temple priestess, the family invested in the enterprise of moneylending through the process of *bhishi*[8] and gradually established itself as one of the fast rising moneylending families. The family which survived on daily alms collected by Suresh's mother to overcome the marital discord with a husband who became addicted to alcohol and philandering some twenty-five years ago, attributes its economic rise to the BMC job and sons' higher education. Although unschooled, Suresh's mother had faith in education and made sure that her sons would acquire higher education.

Although Suresh continues to pursue his aspiration to become an IAS officer, he also involves himself in expanding his family's moneylending enterprise that their parents established. Both Suresh and his brother Naresh are two of the very few Kunchikorve graduates who are trying to secure the path of social, along with economic security. They attribute their success in the economic arena to the reservation policy which they availed of for acquiring higher education in the form of the graduate degrees that they earned. Indeed, the family's ascent in economic mobility is meteoric, but its attitude towards their sons as well as their daughter (who was married off at the age of 17 to her mother's brother's son) is still governed by the old notion that unmarried sons/daughters tend be spoilt if not married off early. Almost all Kunchikorves believe in this maxim.

As far as their sons' higher education is concerned, Kunchikorve parents tend to give way to their sons' aspiration for higher education. The same cannot be said about the attitude towards their daughters. Of course Vandana is an exception to the rule, but most of the Kunchikorve girls who go to school tend to drop out after class 7 or 8 and are married off. They are first told to get married and then think of continuing education. This is also contingent upon the wish of her husband or in-laws who oppose their daughters-in-law acquiring education/higher education. Kunchikorve parents often expressed this possibility that their daughters in-law would send her to school or college because the Kunchikorves exchange daughters between themselves. So the mother of a daughter gets her daughter married into the same family from which she has come. So the mother vouches that her brother would continue her daughter's education once she is married to him or to his son. Except for Vandana, I did not find a Kunchikorve young woman who has pursued higher education after getting married.

IV. Denotified Tribes and Reservation Policy

In recognition of the malign effects of the CTA, both in depriving the Denotified Tribes of constitutional rights and on account of the social stigma and socio-economic deprivation they had suffered as 'criminal tribes', the Criminal Tribes Act Enquiry Committee of India recommended shortly after independence that they should be recognised as beneficiaries of reservations policy and other benefits as a separate category on par with other castes (Rathod 2000: 1). Yet this was ignored. Still today, at the Central Government or Constitutional level, there exists no 'Schedule' of Denotified Tribes and hence no Constitutional reservations or other benefits are available for them as such.

The social category generally known as the Denotified and Nomadic Tribes of India covers a population of approximately six crore [60 million]. Some of them are included in the list of Scheduled Castes, some others in the Schedule of Tribes, and quite a few in the category Other Backward Classes. But there are many of these tribes, which do not find place in any of the above. (Devy 2006: 21)

The Kunchikorve appear as 'Makadwale or Kochi Korva' on the state-wise Central List of Other Backward Classes (OBCs).[9] However, the Constitution also gives the individual states considerable power not only to constitute their own lists but also to determine state-level reservations and otherwise facilitate the advancement of any socially and educationally backward class members. In 1949, the Antrolikar Committee was appointed by the State of Bombay to study the effects of the repeal of the CTA 1924 (D'Souza 2001: 67–68). While recommending a particularly harsh version of the Habitual offenders' Act (HOA), it did also address the issue of rehabilitation of the Denotified communities (Dandekar 2009: 4) and special education (D'Souza 2001: 67–68). Although its recommendations were not taken up by the Bombay Presidency, one could speculate that it might have been influential in forming the reservation policy of the State of Maharashtra (which was created in 1960).

The newly formed State of Maharashtra issued The Government Resolution in Education and Social Welfare Department No CBC-1361/M on 21 November 1961.[10] This established the right of *Vimukta Jatis* (Denotified Tribes) and nomadic tribes to employment and education reservations in the public sector (totalling 4% for both groups taken together). The resolution also contained a list of 13 recognised *Vimukta Jatis* (one more was added in 1977). The Kunchikorves appear as one of the 'synonyms' of Kaikadi:[11] Kaikadi sub-castes are the following: Dhontale, Korva, Makadwale or Kunchikorva, Pamlor and Krovi. Today the Denotified Tribes have a 3%, reservation quota for employment and education as well as in departmental promotions. In 2004 a new Act came into force in Maharashtra entitled 'The Maharashtra State Public Services (Reservation for Scheduled Castes, Scheduled Tribes, Denotified Tribes *(Vimukata Jatis)* and Other Backward Classes) Act 2001 (Jogdand: 2004: 3344, emphasis added), specifying that the Denotified Tribes of Maharashtra have a 3% reservation quota in education as well as in employment and 3% in departmental promotions. However, it is not clear when the 1961 Government Resolution was put on a statutory footing or when the precise 3% reservation quota was granted specifically to Denotified Tribes by the State of Maharashtra.

V. Debating the Reservation Policy of India

Although hailed as an empowering mechanism for the socio-economically disadvantaged, the policy has not been without its critics. Scholars from disciplines ranging from anthropology, political science and sociology to history have taken various stances in viewing and debating reservations in India. Keeping these debates in mind, this paper will analyse the Kunchikorve experience of the policy.

Béteille is one of the staunchest critics of the reservation policy of India. His scepticism reflects his concerns for modernising institutions such as universities, hospitals, laboratories, banks and bureaucracy whose values, if subject to the implementation of reservation quota, would be compromised. He argues, 'Today the disagreement is not so much about the value of these modern institutions as about the criteria by which access to positions of respect and responsibility in them should be regulated' (Béteille 1991: 591). Specifically, he argues that the problem is:

> ...the compatibility between the requirements of institutional well-being and the claims made by or on behalf of disadvantaged groups in the name of distributive justice. How far can such claims be accommodated without damage to the interior lives of these institutions? I believe that it is disingenuous to pretend that every institution can accommodate without any strain all the claims that are made on it in the name of distributive justice. (ibid.: 591)

Béteille specifically criticises the way that reservation policy perpetuates caste, the very system whose ill effects it seeks to redress. He asks, "On what ground can individuals now claim distributive shares for themselves in the name of their caste after having repudiated their moral obligations to it?":

In the traditional order, the village priest or the village barber or the village scavenger had a moral right to claim a share of the social product in the name of caste because each of them was bound by the moral authority of the caste of which he was a member. That moral authority has been, for good or evil, shattered for ever. (ibid.: 592)

'Equality of opportunity' will mean very little if at every turn the individual is shadowed by the caste or the community into which he was born' (Béteille 1983: 130). Critical of caste as the basis for addressing the social inequality it created, he is equally critical of the idea of individual rights and entitlements. He therefore suggests that 'quotas for disadvantaged groups are best viewed as matters not on grounds of rights and justice but on those of policy and utility' (1991a: 593). It is on those grounds that he argues that ultimately the costs to institutional well-being, and to the poor, of relying on 'ascriptive criteria' (ibid: 596), as in reservation policies, would be too severe. Both in perpetuating the caste system, which is antithetical to the subculture of modern institutions and in overriding (modern) principles of merit-based equal opportunity, the reservation system will not produce overall utility, according to Béteille (drawing on Parry's summary of Béteille (Parry 1999: 3–4)).

Based on his ethnographic work on the Satnami caste, ex-untouchable caste-members in the Bhilai Steel Plant (BSP) town, Central India, Parry agrees with Béteille on the appropriate ground for assessing the value of reservations but comes to the opposite factual conclusion. Arguing for reservations from a utilitarian policy-oriented perspective, he provides a '*defence* of reservations ... not in terms of rights, but in terms of policy and utility' (Parry 1999: 130, emphasis added). The policy of reservation, Parry contends, has meant that 'apart from direct benefits from BSP employment, there was also a proliferation of indirect benefits—both material and immaterial—that was spread more widely' (ibid.: 162). The economic mobility thus earned has enabled them to multiply their earnings, making properties and investing in lucrative self-employment, leading the young upwardly mobile Satnami youth to acquire higher education. Reservations, Parry shows, have not only brought about economic benefits to the Satnamis' lives but also decreased caste discrimination substantially outside the workplace. 'Without reservations in public sector employment, the tenacity of the prejudices against them would be significantly stronger' (ibid.: 162).

Parry also takes issue with Béteille's assessment of the negative impact of job reservations on the well-being of institutions, in this instance the steel plant. He examines various instances where reservation-related or 'ascription'-based practices led to not following the formal rules associated with 'modern' institutions—and found no significant impairment of efficiency. He draws the overall conclusion that:

> in this particular instance the 'bottom line' may be less clearly in deficit than Béteille's pessimism might lead us to suppose. More specifically, I want to suggest that there is little evidence that reservation does impair the productive purpose of the steel plant, or seriously undermine its institutional culture; that in

> this context there are other more serious threats to the principle of equality of opportunity, and that here the direct and indirect benefits of job reservation are in fact quite widely diffused. (ibid: 131)

Galanter's observations on the changes brought about by job reservation policy, broadly complements Parry's account: 'The reservation of jobs has given to a sizeable portion of the beneficiary groups earnings as well as the security, information, patronage and prestige that go with government employment' (1984: 189). However, Galanter does not think that education reservations have been successful, because, he suggests, it has been a costly exercise[12] (1986: 78).

Parry's and Galanter's observations are important in understanding the Kunchikorve experience of the reservation policy. Following, Parry (1999) and Galanter (1984, 1999) and Deshpande (2013) who also adopts the policy approach and Béteille (1983, 1991), this paper has explored the utility of the policy of reservation among not only for the Kunchikorves who are employed in sanitation work for the BMC, but also those who are not.

While thirty years ago Kunchikorves may not have been aware of the importance of education reservations, a few of their children, those who managed to acquire specialized education, are increasingly becoming aware of the role that the reservation policy plays in advancing one's educational profile, leading to socio-economic upward mobility. The mobility attained by the Kunchikorves in the realms of economy and education, this paper shows, is characterised by the redistributive effect. These young men have not become complacent with their own economic and educational mobility. They are as much concerned about providing education to their own children as to their siblings. Higher education, facilitated by reservation, not only brings about changes in one's material conditions (buying movable as well as immovable assets), but also in non-material conditions (providing children good school education in English medium schools and so on). The impact of higher education also modernises one's mindset. These educated men often talk assertively against moneyed moneylending men that these men are not doing any constructive work for the community. They are also critical of certain traditional structures such as the *jat panchayat* (caste assembly) that the Kunchikorves organise to resolve their internal matters such as divorce and property issues among themselves. They believe that the men who preside over such hearings do not remain impartial and also tend to succumb to the influence of families involved in a dispute. To avoid this, the educated Kunchikorves feel, members of the Kunchikorve tribe should approach modern law enforcement institutions such as courts and police for resolving their issues and not the 'obsolete *panchayat*'. The old generation, however apparently happy for the young educated Kunchikorves, tend to be dismissive of their suggestions. 'Panchayat is our tradition', argues sixty-five year old Ganganna. The *panchayat* members believe that these young men should respect their elders. The tension between the old generation and the new generation is palpable. It suggests that the members of the young generation who have acquired socio-economic mobility from the reservation policy have not become complacent with their lives. These members express their concerns for those who have been left behind in the slums. These educated men often visit their kith and kin in the slums to know about their well-being and also invite them occasionally to their houses in the middle-class localities where they have moved in. In other words, whatever little benefits these educated Kunchikorves have achieved are shared by them with their relatives in the slum. Indeed, these middle-class members tend to feel at times encumbered with the expectations of their less privileged kin and affine members. But the brighter side is that they still make attempts to fulfil those expectations.

This scenario shows that the Kunchikorves who obtained higher education and the material and non-material benefits accrued thereof share them with their less privileged kin/affine members. The disposition shown by these upwardly mobile Kunchikorves suggests that the criticism made against reservation policy that it spawns elitism (Patel 2014: 195, Sachidanand 1977) holds no water.

The Kunchikorve case shows similarities with what Mendelsohn and Vicziany observe for the untouchables, 'the creation of a more privileged group among untouchables could well be of benefit to the general untouchable population'(1998: 255, quoted in Weisskoff, Parry 1999, Deshpande 2013). Along with this, the ethnographic evidence from Dharavi slum presented here shows that the creamy layer/dominant class structure argument lacks credible evidence to back itself up with empirical evidence and hence may best be termed as mere sophistry. Weisskoff observes, 'The paucity of hard evidence on the post-university careers of reservation policy beneficiaries points to the great need for more research on this topic' (Weisskoff: 2004: 4348). Also, reservations benefits, in the form of a sanitary worker in the BMC and the departmental promotion of *mukkadam* therein, availed by the Kunchikorve sanitary worker and with whose help s/he provided their children higher education shows that they did not adversely affect the well-being of the BMC (contra Beteille 1991: 591). In fact, I would go so far as to say that it is the protective discrimination policy that has enabled children of Kunchikorve sanitary workers to pursue far cleaner jobs than the dehumanising ones that their elders have been doing since the early seventies. This transformation has certainly reduced the tenacity of the casteist jibes hurled at them by their upper-caste neighbours (Parry 1999, Deshpande 2013, Weisskoff 2004) and to some extent enabled the beneficiaries to 'build capacities' (contra Patel 2014: 200) to join the mainstream Indian society. Patel (2014) further argues that reserving seats for higher education has done very little for Scheduled Caste students, the real solution lies in providing 'good school education' (Patel 2014: 1995), an illusory objective that can only be achieved through an affirmative action programme. Indeed, good school education is necessary. But the manner in which it is being touted by some Indian sociologists shows that good school education is a panacea that bears the potential to annihilate the caste discrimination against SC and ST and to ensure the well-being of modern institutions in Indian society. However, this elixir seems to be misplaced given the nature and quality of school education that exist in the country. The standard of teaching imparted in schools run by municipalities as well as the state (government)in urban and rural India respectively is widely criticised and termed as substandard by scholars and educationists (Jeffery 2005, Page 2005, Parry 1999, and Subrahmanian 2005). The second variety is as non-state/ unaided schools, which offer mostly English medium education. These schools are run by private managements or trusts. Most standard-conscious middle-class Indian parents prefer these non-state schools to the ones that are run by municipalities and district councils because they believe that the former maintain a high standard in their teaching and impart quality education, which is believed to be more expensive, than the latter. Another category of schools is called elite schools. Although a few elite schools were started by British administrators in colonial times, a lot of them mushroomed after the liberalisation of the Indian economy. Apart from charging a whopping one-time donation which is believed to run into several lakhs, these schools charge huge amounts of money as admission fee as well as other charges that run into several lakhs every year. A cursory look at the fee structure provided by these schools tells us that these schools are beyond the reach of ordinary Indians; leave alone, socio-economically marginalised SC, ST and Denotified Tribes (DNT) students who live largely in sprawling urban slums and in rural areas of the country. In view of this institutionalised discrimination against these sections of Indian society, it is difficult to be sanguine about 'good school education' which sociologists, like Patel (2014), advocate. One of the more nuanced arguments for making reservations more effective comes from Deshpande (2013). She argues that, 'Affirmative action programmes neither lowers productivity nor promotes casteism' (contra Beteille) (Deshpande 2013: 185). To make affirmative action programmes more comprehensive and successful, she suggests 'providing entry into jobs or into education institutions is not sufficient. There have to be supplementary measures that need to be mandatorily incorporated: remedial teaching, counselling and other measures to lower the incidence of drop-outs, skill enhancing programmes and so forth, which will ensure the benefits of entry into prestigious jobs and educational programmes are fully utilized' (Deshpande: 2013:83). Given the rampant privatisation of education that has been taking place in India since the early 1990s under the neoliberal influence (Kumar 2011, Tilak 2013), for socio-economically deprived Denotified Tribes like Kunchikorves, the hope of accessing quality school education may never materialise, unless the welfare/development state's intervention ensures the children of these tribes access quality schooling. Until this optimism is actualised, the available evidence (Deshpande 2013, Parry 1999, Weisskoff 2004, Galanter 1984) on India's reservation policy shows that the much-talked-about policy has indeed enabled members, albeit a very few of the Kunchikorve tribe to transform their lives by gaining mobility in the realms of social economy and education. However, this largely depends on an unambiguous caste categorisation which the Kunchikorves lack.

VI. Ambiguous Categorisation

So far we have discussed the impact of reservation in higher education among some Kunchikorve men and women. These examples show that members of the Kunchikorve tribe, due to the stigma of being treated as a 'criminal people' face exclusion while accessing education/higher education which is very much contingent upon the affirmative action programme known as reservation. However, reservation cannot be had if the member of a socially discriminated caste/tribe group possesses no caste certificate, which further facilitates access to higher education a great deal. Although such a member socially belongs to a marginalised caste/tribe group, bureaucratically speaking, s/he bears an ambiguous caste identity in the records of the state. This is exemplified by the following case.

In 2000, Satish's father, with his brothers' help, managed to make him permanent in the Sanitation Department of the BMC. Before moving out of Dharavi, Satish lived in a joint family that included Satish's wife, their three children, his BMC sweeper mother, his father's second wife (his mother's younger sister), his broom making/selling step-brother and his wife and their child, and his six young siblings in a cramped two-storey dwelling. As part of his family obligations, he got his two younger brothers married to distant affines before he moved out of Dharavi to what he calls 'posh Municipal Quarters' in Malad suburb in Mumbai.

One of Satish's two sons passed standard 10th exam with a second division in 2012. Expectedly a jubilant Satish expressing happiness distributed sweets to his neighbours. 'As a next course of action', he said, 'I would admit my son in the science stream in order to make him a doctor or engineer'. He therefore started making inquiries. I happened to be one of his first points of contact. He asked me how his son could get admission in one of the best colleges in Mumbai like Ruia or Ruparel. 'If not these then Somaiya or Jhunjhunwalla college in Ghatkopar will also do', said Satish self-approvingly, without realising that with a second division his son would find it very difficult to get admission in one of these colleges in the science stream. A friend did apprise him of the tough competition his son would have to face to get a place in the science stream. Moreover, since the admission to 10+2 courses is now centralised, unlike a decade ago when colleges would admit students according to the percentage with which a student would pass the class 10th exam[13]. This dampened the spirits of a concerned father who was not able to continue with his schooling because he had to support his large family. It was all thanks to the reservation policy which enabled him to obtain the permanent job of sweeper in BMC. Satish sensed that his son would not be able to secure admission in a well-known college through the centralised admission system. I then suggested to him that instead of getting disappointed he should use the reservation quota meant for Denotified Tribes of 3%, his son could find a seat in a science college in a Mumbai suburb. Satish outrightly rejected the suggestion. I was surprised at his dismissive approach to the available option which could have helped his son secure admission.

Since Satish possessed a caste certificate for himself which his son could have used to procure one for him to be able to avail of a seat in the science stream through reservation. On the basis of the same caste certificate, Satish had claimed a permanent job in the BMC's Sanitation Department. But Satish was not inclined to use reservation for his son with the help of that certificate. 'Why not?'The question stymied me. I asked Satish. Hesitatingly, Satish answered, 'My caste certificate is not from Mumbai. It is from Solapur'. Although Satish was born and brought up in Dharavi, he procured his caste certificate from Solapur. It was because Satish's father, who was from Mumbai and retired from the BMC as a sweeper, he did not possess the caste certificate for himself. So Satish had to procure one for himself from Solapur by using his kin connections (his father's elder brother's daughter lives in Solapur). This was the reason for his reluctance to use the caste certificate obtained from a city than the one in which he was born to access reservation benefits for his son. My conversation with him happened in 2012 when his son passed class 10th exams. In the meanwhile, Satish got his caste certificate verified by the Caste Certificate Verification Committee of the Government of Maharashtra without facing any questions on the caste certificate. Now his son is set to enter the realm of higher education which very few of his caste members have been able to do. Although the young man is not very happy with the percentage of marks (48%) he has secured in his class XII science exams, he believes he will be able to pursue higher education further because of the caste certificate he possesses.

Because of poverty and illiteracy, the first generation of the Kunchikorves, who lived in Bombay city before it became part of Maharashtra, could not obtain domicile certificates showing that they had lived in Bombay before 1 May 1960. 'It was simply not possible for our people to have domicile certificates on the basis of which we could have obtained caste certificates today. 'They were illiterate and moved from one place to another to earn a living to survive', says Arun Kunchikorve, a 40 year-old sanitary worker of the BMC. Arun's generation was born and brought up in Bombay; they are undoubtedly Maharashtra domiciles. Their elders, who migrated from villages of formerly Bombay and Karnataka States to Bombay city before Maharashtra State came into being, never acquired domicile certificates on or before 1 May 1960. The possession of domicile certificate would have established the fact that they have been Maharashtra residents enabling their later generations to apply for caste certificates to the office of Mumbai District Collectorate. The effect of this deficiency is that Kunchikorves are treated by the State as 'outsiders'. They cannot, as a result, avail of state benefits such as reserved jobs in the state government and reserved seats for higher education, enjoyed by the native disadvantaged castes/tribes of that State[14]. Since the first generation of Kunchikorves failed to acquire the certificates of domicile and caste, the same is continuing with the second generation. However, the present generation in Dharavi today does not blame their elders for having possessed no domicile or caste certificates, which would have allowed them to prove that they are as Maharashtrian as sons of the soil themselves. Rather, these second-generation members blame the poverty and illiteracy-ridden nomadic existence that their elders led. Until they obtained BMC employment, they did not know which certificate entailed which privileges. For this generation of Kunchikorves, the aspiration to obtain education started taking root after they gained economic mobility through BMC jobs. But today the non-availability of domicile certificate, as well as the father's caste certificate, is still a hurdle for most Kunchikorves in Dharavi. However, this paper shows that these Kunchikorves have not reconciled themselves to this deficiency; instead, they use their kin/affine connections, close as well as distant, in Mumbai and Solapur to procure caste certificates. Such connections tend to be influenced by customary obligation, which facilitates the issue of a caste certificate. It is mainly the Dharavi Kunchikorves who migrated from Karnataka, rather than those from Solapur, who do not possess domicile certificates; they are able to get help from the Solapur

Kunchikorves, through affine obligations, in obtaining caste certificates. If not for the Kunchikorves of Solapur, a large number of the 'Kunchikorve migrants' from Karnataka would not have succeeded in obtaining BMC employment. Kin and affines come to each other's aid because kinship bonds bear deeply rooted obligations that Kunchikorves have carried out from one generation to another. Such practices prepare them to accommodate concerns of their kin/affine members. However, those who claim to have procured 'authentic caste certificates', do not seem bothered about their authenticity. Unless or until the manufactured caste certificate is required to be validated by the Caste Certificate Validation Committee of the State of Maharashtra (CCVC), it remains unquestioned. Yet the deficiency that makes these Kunchikorves go to Solapur for redressal resurfaces when claiming another reservation benefit, that is departmental promotion, with the 'manufactured' caste certificate (Shinde 2011). Unlike the older generation about forty years ago, today many young Kunchikorves have realised the importance of these certificates and utilise their kin/affine connections across two cities of the State of Maharashtra to 'manufacture' caste certificates in order to obtain reservation benefits (Shinde 2011). Without these benefits, Kunchikorves would find it difficult to access higher education. Most Kunchikorves tend to discontinue education after passing their class tenth and work as contract workers for the BMC's Sanitation Department with a private contractor. They detest sanitary work in private establishments in Mumbai and its suburbs. The reason that these young men give for their inability is that they feel discouraged about not possessing caste certificates which could help them to get the Government scholarships while pursuing higher education.

Some Kunchikorves are highly conscious of the fact that, had it not been for reservation, it would have been difficult for Kunchikorves to achieve whatever little they have achieved today. Therefore, the Kunchikorves of the Dharavi slum demand that Government of Maharashtra revise the stringent 1960 criterion soon. Without the revision of such arbitrary bureaucratic conditions, Government claims to address the Kunchikorves' socio-economic deprivation are nothing but sophistry. Dharavi Kunchikorves also object to the fact that the category of Denotified Tribes as a whole has only a 3% reservation quota, unlike the SCs and STs who enjoy 14% and 8% reservations respectively; in turn there are several Denotified Tribes competing among themselves for the very small quota.

After the country gained independence, the 'Criminal Tribes' were decriminalised by the Indian State in 1952 by declaring that these tribes would not be subjected to the same treatment as was meted out to them under the British colonial rule. They were to be treated as free citizens of the country. However, even today, the Denotified Tribes have not been completely out of the gaze of the State. The consequence of this categorisation is such that they would never be free from the gaze of state. Denotified Tribes in order to avail reservation benefits must prove by furnishing documentary evidence such as domicile certificate and the caste certificate. This means that the Kunchikorves who have lived in the State of Maharashtra since it came into being in May, 1960, believe that they socially belong to the Kunchikorve tribe. But due to poverty caused by social stigma, they do not possess documentary evidence in the form a caste certificate. Hence, looking at it from the State's prism they do not belong to any category sans a caste certificate. So they cannot avail of reservation benefits thus depriving themselves of the facility of accessing higher education. In other words, their categorisation is ambiguous.[15] Even those Kunchikorves who have caste certificates have now started encountering difficulties in accessing job reservations in the BMC's Sanitation Department, because the jobs have been privatised.

VII. Withering the Welfare/Development State[16]

The colonial form of the state categorised erstwhile nomadic tribes as 'criminal tribes' in 1871, paradoxically the same form, which has also been theorised as a derivative (Chatterjee 1986), of the colonial state that Indians inherited from the outgoing colonial regime which denotified the 'criminal tribes' of the stigmatising identity in 1952. However, the state while recognising the denotification also made it mandatory that the claim of denotified tribe members to avail of its policies for their empowerment/welfare would not be recognised unless they provide the caste certificate to substantiate their social/oral claim. The caste certificate can be had only if s/he possesses a domicile certificate which authenticates the claim that the Kunchikorve has stayed in the State since or before 1 May 1960. Those who fulfil the required conditions have claimed reservation benefits on the basis of which they have been able to acquire socio-economic and, to a very limited extent, educational mobility. But those who do not possess these certificates attribute the shortcoming to the life of poverty, illiteracy and unemployment from which their previous generations suffered in Mumbai. Facing caste jibes, most Kunchikorves, however, have remained outside the purview of the welfare/development state's policies and continue to suffer from poverty, illiteracy and unemployment, for they do not possess domicile certificates and the caste certificates. Thus this problem has continued to trouble the subsequent generations, except those who could 'manufacture' a caste certificate by using their kin/affine connections across two cities of Maharashtra, namely Mumbai and Solapur. The State of Maharashtra, although committed to empower Kunchikorves, refuses to accept any other solution to the categorisation problem for Kunchikorves than the caste certificate for allowing them to have access to reservation benefits. Such an approach of Maharashtra State highlights the disjuncture between policy (socioeconomic empowerment of the weaker sections) and practice (not recognising the oral claim of those Kunchikorves who do not possess caste certificates or failing to address this issue by evolving some other mechanism) (see Subrahmanian 2005 in the context of school education of SC and ST children in Madhya Pradesh). However, given the privatisation of the government/formal sector, influenced by the doctrine of neoliberalism, by the State of Maharashtra, the existence of protective discrimination policies is now running the risk of becoming obsolete. The neoliberal agenda stresses the role of private corporations in controlling the economic affairs of a sovereign nation by furthering the interest of private capital and by the process of decentralisation of State institutions (Kelley 2010, Kumar 2010, Patnaik 2010, and Bhowmik 2005). Conceived of individual conglomerates, these corporations believe that State control is inimical to improve the efficiency and standards of its institutions. Similarly, the Indian State in the name of improving the standard of education pursued in government-run institutions has allowed private corporations to enter the realm of education considerably. 'The idea that educational institutions can be run along market principles has gained both currency and a sense of normalcy (Kumar 2011: 38). 'This has changed the nature, character, and strength of the State which has had a strong influence on quite a few dimensions of higher education—access, quality, equity, funding, governance, and so on' (Tilak 2013: 42).

In view of this 'development', it could be argued that because of the rampant privatisation of the welfare/ development state, Kunchikorves are having to face new challenges as far as their participation in higher education and government employment is concerned. Since the BMC, as part of its privatization drive in its Department of Sanitation, where Kunchikorves found permanent employment and gained economic mobility for the last four decades, has started contracting out its jobs. Due to this policy, the chances of Kunchikorves finding permanent employment under reservation policy there are being adversely affected. Whatever little Kunchikorves have achieved from BMC employment is likely to be overridden by the increasing privatisation of it. With the monetary capital earned from the BMC job, Kunchikorves could send their children to school. As a result, a few of these children without any cultural capital in the field of education have succeeded in acquiring higher education today. What I am trying to point out here is the enabling role the welfare/ development state has played in the lives of such a historically discriminated against people as the Kunchikorve. With the increasing adoption of the neoliberal policies Kunchikorves without substantially doing away with the primordial identities based on caste, gender and religion, the Indian state would find empowering the discriminated against Denotified Tribes difficult. In this climate of neoliberalism, Kunchikorves, as well as their future generations, without the intervention of an affirmative action policy such as reservations will find accessing education/higher education and government employment difficult in the future. It is the consistent source of income from the permanent employment in the BMC which enabled some Kunchikorves to achieve economic mobility which has further helped them to realise their aspiration for higher education. If both are privatised completely, there is a fear among the Kunchikorves that the social pathologies that have stalked them for many decades may resurface to haunt them.

VIII. Conclusion

For the Kunchikorve tribe, the path to education/higher education has been, historically, strewn with various forms of discrimination imposed on them through such constructions as 'a people having instincts to commit crimes' by the British Colonial State since 1871. Such a categorization not only divested Kunchikorves of the potential of becoming social beings, but also of economic beings. Once dispossessed of socio-economic capital, Kunchikorves were also alienated from accessing education, let alone higher education. It is with the help of the government employment (*sarakri naukari*) in the BMC's Department of Sanitation, Kunchikorves of Dharavi have been able to provide their children higher education, argues this paper. Exploring the connection between government employment and higher education acquires significance, for the Kunchikorve tribe with its categorisation as 'a criminal tribe' under the CTA of 1871, which was formally abrogated in 1952 by the Indian State. However, [Denotified] Tribes have now been reclassified under, 'the Habitual Offenders Act, 1958 in various states' (Heredia 2007: 12). In other words, the consequences of the stigma still reverberate, which dispossessed Kunchikorves of access to education and employment through the casteist jibes of their neighbours as well as law enforcement agencies that look at these tribe members suspiciously. Nevertheless, with the help of the government jobs which enabled some of the first generation Kunchikorves to avail of reservation benefits they started sending their children, mostly boys, to school. With this hard-earned mobility the second-generation Kunchikorves have been able to obtain higher education and jobs in private companies (unlike their elders who survived on begging as well as informal sector activities and many of them still do), and lead middle-class lives. However, those who drop out due to poverty after class seven or eight eke out their living from sanitary contract work as *safai kamgar* for BMC works. These contract workers believe that the experience gained from contract work with private contract workers would help them consolidate their chances to secure permanent employment in the BMC in the future. However, their expectations, given the rampant privatisation of sanitary jobs in the BMC, may be difficult to fulfil in the future. The rapid shrinking of BMC jobs, a direct consequence of liberalisation of the Indian economy, is shrinking the chances of Kunchikorves finding permanent work in the BMC and elsewhere for their succeeding generations. This is not only jeopardising Kunchikorves' chances of securing a certain source of income, but is also affecting their aspirations adversely. Moreover, kinship demands especially on girls, as this paper shows, deprive them severely not only of education but also of higher education. If given access to higher education, the Kunchikorve young woman negotiates her marginalisation successfully and contributes substantially for the well-being not only of her family but also that of her affines. However, this assertion, it could be argued, is contingent upon the intervention of the 'welfare/development state', which is unfortunately succumbing to the prescriptions of neoliberal policies. This 'development' does not seem to augur well for the socio-economically marginalised communities, like the Kunchikorves, in India.

REFERENCES

Bates, C. 1995. Race, Caste and Tribe in Central India: The Early Origins of Indian Anthropometry. *Edinburgh Papers South Asian Studies* Number 3.

Béteille, A. 1983. *The Idea of Natural Equality and Other Essays*. Delhi: Oxford University Press.

Béteille, A. 1991. Distributive Justice and Institutional Well-being, *Economic and Political Weekly*, 26(11/12) annual number, pp. 591–600.

Bhowmik, S. 2005. Globalization, Governance and Labour in Kameshwar Chaudhary (ed), *Globalization, Governance Reforms and Development in India*. New Delhi: Sage.

Breman, J. 1996. *Footloose Labour: Working in India's Informal Economy*. Cambridge: Cambridge University Press.

Breman, J. 1997. *Wage Hunters and Gatherers: Search for Work in the Urban and Rural Economy of South Gujarat*. Delhi: Oxford University Press.

Breman, J. 2003. *The Labouring Poor in India: Patterns of Exploitation, Subordination, and Exclusion*. Delhi: Oxford University Press.

Chandrasekhar, C.P. and Jayati Ghosh. 2002. *The Market That Failed*. New Delhi: Leftword books.

Chatterjee, P. 1986. *Nationalist Thought and the Colonial World: A Derivative Discourse*. London: Zed Books.

D'Souza, D. 2001. *Branded by Law: Looking at India's Denotified Tribes*. New Delhi: Penguin.

Dandekar, A. 2009. Disenfranchised by History: The Tribes and Their Narratives, Mukt–SAAD. Available at: www. indianfolklore. org/journals/index. php/Mukt/article 4/ MUKT – SAAD/November 09.

Deshpande, A. 2013. *Affirmative Action in India*. Delhi: Oxford University Press.

Devy, G.N. 2006. *A Nomad Called Thief*. New Delhi: Orient Longman.

Gaikwad, Laxman, 2005. *Uchalya (The Branded)*. New Delhi: Sahitya Akademi.

Galanter, M. 1984. *Competing Equalities: Law and the Backward Classes in India*. Delhi: Oxford University Press.

Galanter, M. 1986. The 'Compensatory Discrimination': Theme in the Indian Commitment to Human Rights. *India International Centre Quarterly*, 13(3–4), December.

Galanter, M. 1999. Pursuing Equality: An Assessment of India's Policy of Compensatory Discrimination for Disadvantaged Groups, in S. Kaviraj (ed.), *Politics in India*. Delhi: Oxford University Press, pp. 187–99.

Ghosh, J. 2006. Case for Caste-based Quotas in Higher Education, *Economic and Political Weekly*, June 17, Vol. 41, Issue No. 24.

Heredia, R. 2007. Denotified and Nomadic Tribes: The Challenge of Free and Equal Citizenship. Occasional paper series, Department of Sociology, University of Pune.

Jeffery, P. 2005. Introduction: Hearts, Minds and Pockets in Chopra Radhika and Patricia Jeffery (eds), *Educational Regimes in Contemporary India*. New Delhi: Sage.

Jha, P. 2010a. Employment in the Time of Liberalization in Kelley, M. and Deepika D'Souza (eds), in collaboration with Helmut Reifeld, *The World Bank in India: Undermining Sovereignty, Distorting Development, Independent People's Tribunals on the World Bank in India*. Hyderabad: Orient Blackswan.

Jha, P. 2010b. Globalization and Labour in India: Emerging Challenges and Responses in Bieler, A. et al. *Labour and Challenges in Globalization: What Prospects for Transnational Solidarity*? University of KwaZulu-Natal Press.

Jodhka, S. 2010. 'In the Name of Globalization: Meritocracy, Productivity, and the Hidden Language of Caste', in Sukhadeo Thorat and Katherine S. Newman (eds), *Blocked by Caste: Economic Discrimination in Modern India*, New Delhi: Oxford University Press.

Jogdand, P.G. 2004. Reservation in Private Sector: Legislation in Maharashtra'. *Economic and Political Weekly*, 39(30), 24–30 July, pp. 3344–346.

John, M. 2012. *Equality in Higher Education: Indentifying Critical Gender Concerns* (*Policy Brief*), UN Women, New Delhi.

Kelley, M. 2010. Introduction in World Bank out of India, in *The World Bank in India: Undermining Sovereignty, Distorting Development, Independent People's Tribunals on the World Bank in India*. Hyderabad: Orient Blackswan.

Kolharkar, P.A. 2005. Translator's Note in Gaikwad, L. 2005 (1998).

Uchalya (The Branded). Trans. from the Marathi by P.A. Kolharkar New Delhi: Sahitya Akademi.

Kumar, A. 2010. The Economic Aspects of World Bank Activities in India, in Kelley, M and Deepika D'Souza (eds), Ibid.

Kumar, K. 2011. Teaching and the Neo-liberal State. *Economic and Political Weekly*, Vol. XLVI, No. 21, May 21.

Limbale, Sharankumar. 2004. *Towards an Aesthetic of Dalit Literature*. New Delhi: Orient Longman.

Mane, L. 1981. *Upara: An Outsider*. New Delhi: Sahitya Akademi.

Mendelsohn, O. and M. Vicziany. 1998. *The Untouchables: Subordination, Poverty and the State in Modern India*. Cambridge: Cambridge University Press.

Page, E. 2005. Negotiation and Compromise: Gender and Government Elementary Education in Radhika Chopra and Patricia Jeffery (eds), in collaboration with Helmut Reifield, *Educational Regimes in Contemporary India*. New Delhi: Sage.

Parry, J. 1999. Two Cheers for Reservations, in R. Guha and J. Parry (eds.), *Institutions and Inequalities: Essays in Honour of Andre Béteille*. Delhi: Oxford University Press.

Parry, J. 2001. Ankalu's Errant Wife: Sex, Marriage and Industry in Contemporary Chhattisgarh. *Modern Asian Studies*, 35(2), pp. 783–820.

Parry, J. 2003. Nehru's Dream and the Village Waiting Room: Long Distance Labour Migrants to a Central Indian Steel Town. *Contributions to Indian Sociology*, 37(1/2).

Parry, J. 2005. Changing Childhoods in Industrial Chhattisgarh, in R. Chopra and P. Jeffery (eds.), *Educational Regimes in Contemporary India*. New Delhi: Sage.

Patel, T. 2014: Stigma Goes Backstage: Reservation in Jobs and Education, in Paramjit S. Judge (ed), *Towards Sociology of Dalits*, Vol. I. Readings in Indian Sociology, Series editor Ishwar Modi. New Delhi: Sage.

Patnaik, P. 2010. The Changing Role of the World Bank in India in Kelley, M and Deepika D'Souza (eds), Ibid.

Radhakrishna, M. 2001. *Dishonoured by History: Criminal Tribes and British Colonial Policy*. Hyderabad: Orient Longman.

Rathod, M. 2000. Denotified and Nomadic Tribes in Maharashtra, The Denotified and Nomadic Tribes Rights Action Group

Newsletter, April–June and July-September, 2000, transcribed November 2000. Available at: http://sickle. bwh. harvard. edu/india_tribes. html.

Roy Burman J.J. 2010. *Ethnography of a Denotified Tribe: The Laman Banjara*. New Delhi: Mittal.

Sachidanand 1977. *The Harijan Elite*. Faridabad: Thompson Press.

Shinde, P.K. 2011. Kunchikorve Worlds of Work, unpublished PhD thesis, London School of Economics and Political Science, London.

Shinde, P. 2016. The Political Technologies of Caste: Manufacturing A Caste Certificate in a Mumbai Slum, *South Asia: Journal of South Asian Studies,* Volume, 39, Issue-1.

Simhadri Y.C. 1991. *Denotified Tribes, A Sociological Analysis*. New Delhi: Classical Publishing House.

Subrahmanian, R. 2005. Education Exclusion and the Developmental State in Radhika Chopra and Patricia Jeffery (eds), in collaboration with Helmut Reifeld, Ibid.

Tilak JBG, 2013. Higher Education in the BRIC Member-Countries: Comparative Patterns and Policies. *Economic and Political Weekly,* April 6, 2013, Vol. XLVIII, No. 14.

Weisskopf, T. 2004. Impact of Reservation on Admissions to Higher Education in India. *Economic and Political Weekly,* September 25, 2004. Vol. 39, Issue No. 39.

Internet websites

http://indiankanoon. org/doc/108364/

http://www. firstfoundation. in/socio_casteslist_Maha. htm

http://www. dhammaweb. net/dhamma_news/view.php?id= 298 (accessed on 23/04/2014)

NOTES

1. The category of Denotified Tribes, also known as ex-'criminal tribes', comprises petty traders, pastoralists, and itinerant and nomadic tribes that were categorised under the Criminal Tribes Act (CTA) 1871 as 'criminal tribes' by the colonial state of British India. The CTA authorised the government to declare any 'tribe, gang or class' to be a criminal tribe on the basis that they were 'addicted to the systematic commission of non-bailable offences' (Radhakrishna 2001: 45). (The process by which a tribe

was officially designated as a criminal tribe was called 'notification'. Hence tribes declared 'criminal tribes' were also referred to as 'Notified Tribes'.) 'The criminalization of certain tribes, for example, provided a means of controlling turbulent populations in the more inaccessible or 'lawless' parts of the subcontinent' (Bates 1995:10). Once a tribe was notified as a criminal tribe, its individual members were registered and subject to a wide range of controls, involving, on the one hand, police powers of monitoring and surveillance, search, arrest and detention and, on the other hand, forcible removal from particular areas and resettlement elsewhere. 'Restrictions on movement meant that adult male members of such groups could be forced to report weekly to the local police' and police had powers to search and arrest without warrant any member of the tribe found outside the prescribed area without a pass (Gaikwad 2008). In the name of the welfare of children, the authorities were empowered to separate the children of a 'criminal tribe' from their parents (Radhakrishna 2001, D'Souza 1999). After India gained independence from British, the young republic repealed the CTA in 1949 and denotified the tribes in 1952, re-categorising the 'notified criminal tribes' as Denotified Tribes or *Vimukta* (free) *Jatis*. However, members of these tribes remained *vimukta* only until 1959 when, under the Habitual Offenders Act (HOA), the State again brought members of ex-criminal tribes under surveillance. 'The HOAs preserved most of the provisions of the former CT Act, except the premise implicit in it that an entire community could be 'born' criminals' (Devy 2006: 22). At one point in his Sahitya Akademi award winning book, *Upara* (Outsider), Laxman Mane, a Kaikadi, the tribe of which the Kunchikorves are believed to be a subtribe, expresses his frustration at the position of nomadic tribes as compared to ex-'untouchables': 'A Mahar has at least his profession of removing dead animals' skins. He does have a roof above his head though it may not be in a good condition. But I... 'Mother Earth has no place for me; my hands never reach the sky'. A man who resides at places where people come to defecate, is he not an untouchable? If he is not, then who is he? And he who moves from place to place to earn his livelihood, what is he?' (Mane 1982: 141).

2. Because of this paucity of empirical studies, most of the empirical evidence that I invoke to support my argument in the context of higher education as well as reservation vis-à-vis the Kunchikorve tribe comes from the studies that discuss SC and ST students' participation in higher education. Moreover, there are also similarities between these marginalised groups as far as experiencing discriminations of various kinds is concerned. Like SCs, Denotified Tribes, along with being treated as untouchables in many parts of India (Gaikwad 2005, Mane 1982), continue to be treated as 'criminals' and, a result, assaulted (D'Souza 2001, Dandekar 2009). 'The DNTs are the most depressed sections of society and all of them are regarded as Dalits' (Limbale, 2004: 137).
3. Because one of their occupations has until recently been that of organising monkey plays/dance to earn a living, the Kunchikorves are also called *Makadwalla*. However, many socio-economically upwardly mobile Kunchikorves feel offended by this nomenclature. Also, they are at times derisively referred to as 'monkeys' (*makad*) by their neighbours.
4. This Dharavi school, attended by the majority of those children whose parents work in the unorganised sector and where the prospects of later success in life are dismal, is a counterpart to the government school in the Bhilai Steel Plant township that Parry talks about (2005: 292).
5. This document shows that the bearer of it belongs to the caste/tribe groups that were, and continue to be subjected, to social discrimination and hence are entitled to claim welfare measures through reservations. Otherwise, however stigmatised one may be, s/he without the coveted caste certificate would not be able to access reservation benefits at all.
6. In the popular imagination of Dharaviites, 'Varda*bhai*' remains as a Robin Hood type character fighting against the rich for the poor. This character, essayed by the legendary Indian actor Kamal Haasan, also became the main protagonist of the Mani Ratnam directed biopic, '*Nayagan*' ('The Leader'). The movie was selected by India as its official entry for the Academy Awards of 1987, but could not win an award. In 2005, the movie

was shortlisted by the Time Magazine as one of the best 100 movies of all time.

7. The Koli village, which predates Dharavi, remains in the popular imagination as a place famous for its delicious crabs, caught from the adjoining creek, which today like its neighbour the Mithi River, wears the look of a large sewer that flows sluggishly.
8. A *bhishi* is formed by a collective of twenty members, which may be led by one of them, who is called the agent. If it is a 100,000- rupee-*bhishi*, each member puts in 5,000 rupees monthly, amounting to a total of 100,000 rupees, which is auctioned every month as organised by the agent. This cycle goes on for 19 months until each member is able to 'buy 100,000 rupees'. Whatever amount the monthly auction is bought for by the member whose bid outdoes the others is equally distributed among the nineteen members. The very first *bhishi*, as a rule goes to the agent without auctioning the amount in recognition of his efforts in organising the *bhishi*. Along with this benefit, however, come risks. It is the agent's responsibility to collect the monthly money from his *bhishi* group without fail and organise its auctioning every month for 20 months. The auction takes place mostly at the agent's house in the first week of every month, with the payment of an additional amount of 500 rupees, known as a government price. The amount to be auctioned in a *bhishi* varies from group to group (*bhishi* to *bhishi*). That most preferred among the permanently employed BMC sanitation workers/moneylenders is a 100,000-rupee *bhishi*, whereas those who work under private contractors and for private buildings prefer a 20,000 rupee one (Shinde 2011).
9. In the Central List (i.e. Central Government) of OBCs, under Maharashtra is listed as Entry Number 177: 'Kaikadi [in Bombay, Thana, Kolaba, Ratnagiri, Nashik, Dhule, Jalgaon, Pune, Ahmednagar, Satara, Sangli, Kolhapur, Sholapur, Aurangabad, Nanded districts and Rajura Tehsil of Chandrapur District] and the following are recognised 'throughout the State: Dhontle; Korva; Makadwale or Kochi Korva; Pamlor, Korvi.' See below for why Kunchikorve are

also known as Makadwale (http://www. firstfoundation. in/ socio_casteslist_Maha. htm).

10. See, for example *Kum. Tanuja D/O MaganlalRajpal* vs *State Of Maharashtra* on 3 November, 1988: 1; (1988) 90 BOMLR 541, 1989 MhLJ 99 (http://indiankanoon. org/doc/108364/). This resolution is cited in numerous cases concerning the validity of caste certificates.
11. Maharashtra Goverment Letter No. CBC-10/2006/P. No. 94/ MVC-5 of Dept of Social Justice, Cultural Affairs & Special Assistance, 25 May 2006 (http://www. firstfoundation. in/ socio_casteslist_ Maha. htm).
12. This may be located as a problem of implementation rather than a fundamental flaw of reservation policy as such. Thus, Mendelsohn and Vicziany argue that: The [reservation] scheme has been far from impeccably administered: non-performance has sprung from a habitual lack of bureaucratic performance in India, reinforced in this instance by the traditional discrimination practised against Untouchables. (1998: 134; see also Ghosh 2006).
13. This autonomy soon came to be manipulated by colleges themselves leading the State to introduce a centralised system for admitting students to 10+2 courses.
14. Those Denotified Tribe members who do not possess, or have been unable to obtain, the caste certificate cannot claim reservation benefits only on the basis of an oral claim. Such members then come to be categorised by the State as belonging to the open category to which belong the upper-castes. However, if these members prove that they have lived in Maharashtra for the last fifteen yearswith documentary evidence such as a caste certificate acquired from their 'native' state from where they migrated to Maharashtra, along with the ration card and domicile certificate obtained from Maharashtra, can be put into the Other Backward Classes (OBC) category.
15. Most Kunchikorves from Dharavi claim to have belonged to the Kunchikorve tribe, a Denotified Tribe of Maharashtra. However, they do not possess any documentary evidence to support their claim. They attribute this lack of evidence to the

poverty and illiteracy from which their earlier generations that entered the Bombay State in 1950s suffered. As a result, the first generation settlers could not collect documentary evidence to prove that they have been domiciles of the state of Maharashtra since 1 May 1960, the day the State came into being, and hence are a Denotified Tribe of that State. Interestingly, most of those Kunchikorves who have found employment in the BMC on the basis of 3% reservation meant for the Denotified Tribes of Maharashtra used their kin/affine connections in a western Maharashtra city, Solapur to procure caste certificates.

16. Theoretically speaking, the welfare state is different from that of the development state. The politics of the former is against the market and of the latter, unlike the neoliberal state, does not completely discard the market nor does it give a free hand. Under the rubric of the welfare state in India came into existence the reservation policy for the empowerment of SCs and STs in the 1950s. Since then the policy continues to exist today even in the regime of the development state, and hence I am using these two terms together. The subtitle also intends to convey the increasing adoption of neoliberal policies such as privatisation, liberalisation by the development state in India to the extent that the Indian State is being termed as a neoliberal state embracing private capital (Bhowmik 2005, Kelly 2010, Jha 2010, Kumar 2010, Patnaik 2010, and Chandrasekhar and Ghosh 2002).

7

Higher Education, Conflict Resolution and Peace Building in Rural Areas of Jammu and Kashmir State

Renu Nanda

The highest education is that which does not merely give us information but makes our life in harmony with all existence.

–Rabindranath Tagore

Violent conflicts are on the rise all over the human race. Worldwide, an estimated 25 million people are displaced by conflicts and the number is ever-increasing. Conflicts not only lead to deaths, destruction of property, displacements, trauma, poverty etc but also leave a tremendous negative impact on the societies and demolish them. In a multi-racial, multi-religious, multi-cultural country like India there is always a challenge on ethnic, communal or cultural issues creating conflicts. The contradiction between the privileged and deprived sections of the people, educated and illiterate people, people of higher castes and lower castes within the same religion, social discrimination between men and women, and even th trends of political defeat of small sections of the population are the major sources of origin of conflicts. Conflicts are threats to the peace and security of all nations around the world and thus cause human suffering. These need to be avoided and the societies have to look for ways to overcome the situations through peace and create peaceful societies where people would work together to resolve conflicts, develop morally, treat each other with justice, satisfy basic needs, and respect each other.

Resolution of conflict without resorting to violence is an indispensable condition for establishing peace in the society. Peace is an attitude towards life which strengthens social cohesion and makes life worth living. In the ongoing discussions on conflict resolution and peace-building in conflict zones, it has been found that promotion of higher education has opened new vistas of opportunity for youth to have better employment and income pursuits thereby improving their quality of life. With the extension of awareness at the global level, the education sector especially the higher education system has been expanding throughout the world to meet the ever-increasing need of trained manpower for improving the economic conditions in the world. In fact, higher education has been a potent force in shaping the civil society and also the vehicle for rapid economic growth and generation of employment opportunities for millions of young people. In societies that have experienced violent conflict, higher education has a diverse and imperative responsibility in the longer-term, in the post-conflict period to help succeeding generations to avoid violent conflicts and potentially contribute towards future peace building. Higher education is the input to enhance India's competitiveness in the worldwide economy. Therefore, ensuring access to quality education for all, in particular for the poor and rural population, is central to the economic and social development.

The rapid expansion of the education system has brought out several significant issues related to the standards of its quality and equal availability of higher education facilities to all the categories of people of the society. More than 70 per cent of India's population live in rural areas. Educating people in rural areas is essential for substantial development and rural economic competitiveness of our country and challenging at the same time as issues of equity, quality and access remain areas of concern. Usually in India, higher education institutions are mostly located in cities, main towns etc where it is not possible for the rural youth to stay away from their families as they may be the only breadwinners of their families. Apart from this, the poor communication as well as transportation system of the rural areas also hinders equal access to higher education. The most important problem in the higher education system in India as well as in Jammu and Kashmir is the lack of quality of the institutions in rural areas. In the words of India's Prime Minister Manmohan Singh, 'Too many of our higher education institutions are simply not up to the mark. Too many of them have simply not kept abreast with changes that have taken place in the world around us.... ., still producing graduates in subjects that job market no longer requires.... Not one Indian university today figures in top 200 universities of the world.'

As a result, a considerable number of our youth have become victims of ideological and monetary allurements on account of lack of income and employment opportunities. They are not able to fully understand the disastrous consequences of conflict and violence. The pattern of education and its delivery mechanism, changes in higher education, in India have traditionally been slow, in terms of its pattern and delivery, mainly because of the elitist nature and the ivory tower existence of its institutions. Therefore, the present paper will be of assistance to know the existing state of higher education system in Jammu and Kashmir region and understand the need for creating an effective institutional delivery mechanism in rural areas of Jammu and Kashmir State. It will help us impart education to the young population as well as suggest suitable recommendations for establishing an effective educational delivery model in rural areas that maintains a climate of peace and tranquility in J&K State. In this chapter the research is based on secondary data. The data is taken from different research reports, journals, websites, research papers and *Economic Survey, 2013-14 (J&K)*. The research is based on the study of Gross Enrolment Ratio (GER) of higher education in urban and rural areas of J&K State.

Jammu and Kashmir, Northern-most state of India, shares its borders with Himachal Pradesh and Punjab, and the neighbouring countries of Pakistan, China as well as Afghanistan. The State consists of three regions: Jammu, the Kashmir Valley and Ladakh. Even though the State of Jammu and Kashmir has ethnic, linguistic, religious and cultural diversity, yet it is a perfect example of unity in diversity. It is also one of the most violence-infested states in India which has been witnessing a protracted conflict for over a quarter century now. This implies that young people up to the age of 24-25 years have never seen a peaceful Valley. Their interaction with people in and outside the Valley is laden with mistrust, suspicion and terror. There is deep-rooted fear, anxiety and mistrust due to sustained exposure to violence. Conflict in J&K is affecting the children's innocent minds. The youth have higher suicidal tendencies and they have lost interest in social, domestic and educational activities. Young students have been used for grenade throwing in the past. Many young Kashmiri boys used for stone pelting in 2010 during Kashmir summer unrest were between the ages of 13-19 years. Psychic disorders, drug abuse and personality changes are rampant and children naturally absorb the spirit of violence in the atmosphere. Thus, there is a dire need to stop the armed conflict in this region besides restructuring the society by equipping the youth in the valley with creative techniques and tools so that they are able to break free from the cycle of violence. The hope for a more peaceful future in the Valley lies in strengthening the lost faith in its dynamic and thinking civil society. Thus, education is needed for J&K children that can actualise their potentialities in helping them learn how to make peace with themselves and with others, to live in harmony and unity with self, humankind and with nature. Mostly, the reason for the terror campaign in our State is poverty, religious factors and the lack of education. The youth who join the terror groups are those who do not have education and employment and other basic things to survive; so if we have to eradicate the problem we should first educate and provide employment to the people of rural areas.

Over the past few years though the State Government has been trying to revive the education situation in Jammu and Kashmir and has been motivating more and more people to stay on in the State for higher studies. The Government runs many Centre and State-supported schemes, especially for the rural/backward/underprivileged sections of the society, so that they are not deprived of education. It includes providing free education up to college level, mobile institutions for the nomadic population, scholarships, free books and uniforms to deserving students. Yet the State is educationally relatively backward. Against the national literacy rate of 74.0 per cent, the State has a literacy figure of 68.74 per cent; literacy among males is 78.26 per cent and that of females is 58.01 per cent (2011 census). In the national educational scenario, J&K is subsumed as educationally backward with reference to the established indices namely, literacy rate, teacher-pupil ratio, drop-out rate and the absorption pattern of the educated persons.

Higher Education in Jammu and Kashmir State

The standard of higher education is an essential factor in promoting economic development and it indicates the levels of general and specific knowledge, achievement and learning. Beyond this, it is the natural incubator and safeguard of citizenship and democratic values. It results in material and intellectual well-being of human beings and is the basis for foresightedness that triggers change, resolves conflict and develops peace. However, in Jammu and Kashmir, social structures as well as economic limitations have influenced the pace of higher educational development since last two decades. The major issues plaguing the higher education sector are the burgeoning dearth of human resources, physical infrastructure, permanent and well-trained faculty and absence of updated syllabi as per the global standards. In J&K, the Department of Higher Education is charged with the responsibility to monitor and regulate the dissemination of higher education above 10+2 level in the State by extending education facilities by opening of the colleges and universities. The access to higher education is measured in terms of Gross Enrolment ratio. The Gross Enrolment ratio for the State of J&K was 10.36 per cent in 2007-08 which increased to 18.2% (provisional) in 2011-12 which is higher than the national GER of 15 per cent. The enrolment accordingly increased from 77,000 in 2004-05 to 1,35,264 in 2012-13.

The overall enrollment in the higher education sector including universities, private institutions and agricultural/ medical institutions has increased approximately to 2,77,000 in the 11th Five Year Plan. The enrolment in higher education for the academic year 2013-14 is 1,79,398, which includes Govt Degree Colleges 1,36,163, B Ed Collges 26,080 and Universities (Kashmir University, Jammu University, Baba Gulam Shah Badshah University and Islamic University of Science & Technology, Pulwama).

Table No. 1 showing number of Universities in J&K along with the year of establishment:-

Name of The University	*Year of Establishment*
University of Kashmir	1949
University of Jammu	1969
SKUAST Kashmir	1982
SKUAST Jammu	1999
SMVD University Jammu	2004
Baba Ghulam Shah Badshah University	2005
Islamic University of Science & Technology	2005
Central University of Kashmir	2009
Central University of Jammu	Fully established in 2011

The Government of India, MHRD has set a GER target of 22 per cent at the national level to be achieved by 2020. The State is also aiming at achieving this GER target of 22 per cent by the end of 2020. However, it requires a matching expansion in the capacity of educational institutions vis-a-vis the strategy centred on enhancing the intake capacity of educational institutions. For every two lakh population in the age group of 18-23 an additional university is required to be established and for every one lakh population in the age group of 18-23, 10 colleges are required to be established. Based on these projections there is still scope for establishment of more universities and colleges in the State. To reduce the disparities based on gender, caste and region and to provide equal opportunities of higher education to the age group of 18-23 is a major challenge to be overcome. The GER in urban areas is higher compared to rural and backward areas and the same is the case with male/female disparities in the enrolment rate. The GOI has identified 374 districts as educationally backward out of which 11 districts are in the J&K State. All these districts are being covered with one college each with 50 per cent state contribution. To bridge the gap between the male and female enrolment, the endeavour will be to provide one women's college in all the districts which are at present without a women's college.

If we look at the higher education system of our J&K State, deficiencies and shortcomings are obvious at every stage and everywhere. Our State without having a concrete policy and planning has tried to go in for mushroom growth of institutions in the form of colleges and universities. Currently the State has already initiated a process to improve the educational scenario and has made several efforts to establish higher learning institutions at several locations to cover the rural bases, even though it involves huge budgetary expenses. The number of state-run colleges since 2005 increased manifold and over 50 new colleges got established in less than a decade's time; thus bringing the total number of government-run colleges in the State around 95. At present there are 47 government colleges in Kashmir region, 45 in Jammu and 3 in Ladakh. However, almost all colleges lack permanent teaching faculty and every year the State is hiring thousands of Ph D, NET, SET and M Phil qualified candidates on contract basis to meet the academic requirements. Taking the example of Jammu region the status of government-run colleges is as under: the Government Women's College Parade established in 1953 has 98 permanent and 25 contractual appointees; Government Degree College Kathua set up in 1961, has 54 permanent and 39 contractual staff; Government Degree College Reasi established in 2003, has 6 permanent and 18 contractual faculty members; Government Degree College RS Pura set up during 2005, has 19 permanent and 12 contractual lecturers; Government Degree College Bani set up in 2008, has 1 permanent and 7 contractual staff, and Government Degree College Mahanpur established in 2011, has only 4 contractual faculty members. In the Kashmir region, however, the situation is worse as the colleges are understaffed and are run by 80 per cent contractual faculty members. The Government Women's College Baramulla set up during 1986 has 17 permanent and 60 contractual lecturers; Government Degree College for Boys set up in 1963 has 26 permanent and 51 contractual staff; Government Degree College Kupwara established in 1988 has 7 permanent and 29 contractual lecturers, Government Degree College Pattan established in 2005 has 22 contractual and 6 permanent lecturers and Government Women's College Srinagar set up in 1950 has 50 permanent and 50 contractual teaching faculty members.

Though, in our State, the higher education is reaching every nook and corner the fact is that establishing more and more colleges will not serve the purpose. The move in fact, is welcome but it should have been accompanied by the rapid enhancement of human resources and physical infrastructure. These newly established colleges present a dismal scenario as most of them have been opened in rented structures or clubbed with the existing higher secondary schools. The State needs to gear up its machinery to improve the physical infrastructure as well as the human resources (both teaching and non-teaching) required for smooth functioning of these colleges. Thus before opening more new colleges there is the need to improve the conditions of existing ones; otherwise the colleges will merely serve the purpose of just enrolling the students and conducting examinations rather than disseminating knowledge. The establishing of colleges and universities has taken place more on the basis of political rather than on societal/ideological considerations. Yet it is a salutary step because the J&K State has been in the drought of institutions of higher learning which could be accommodative and productive in nature. The J&K State has not been able to compete in educational ventures with the other states of the country and the notion to compare its educational standards with the world standards would not be in order.

Effective Institutional Delivery Mechanism

The magnitude is exemplified by the 'Education for All' movement, a global commitment to provide quality basic education for all children, youth and adults, which links directly with the UN Millennium Development Goals. Sustainable development of quality primary education is dependent on complementary development in the secondary and tertiary education sectors. With economies relying more and more on the generation and application of knowledge, productivity is increasingly dependent on the development and spread of technological innovations. The dilemma of inadequate higher education capacity, dwindling government support, low enrolments, have resulted in limited and unequal access to higher education. There is the need for large scale interventions to improve the higher education sector as it is directly related to the employment sector; the stress should be on vocational education leading to better placements in the job market. The need of the hour is to learn the latest technologies available and government institutes need to be equipped with the latest infrastructure so that students are better informed in rural areas.

The State of Jammu and Kashmir has shown high economic growth but has not been able to meet the aspirations of the youth who are looking for opportunities for education and employment. Frequent disturbances have created an atmosphere of uncertainty, impacting employment creation which has alienated the youth. The State has to make up for the lost time and lost opportunities for its youth by increasing the number of institutions of higher education in J&K. In addition, the student intake in the existing institutions must be stepped up significantly by enhancing the faculty capability and positions. While this would be an appropriate medium-term intervention, an immediate short term-solution would be to encourage the J&K youth to take advantage of the educational institutions of higher education in the rest of the country. The recent youth turmoil in Kashmir, though political, was also in a sense indicative of alienation and possibly disappointment at the lack of opportunities in the State. On the one hand, the long years of militancy and violence have taken toll of the educational institutions in the State, especially in the Valley. There has been damage to the physical infrastructure and the disturbances have also eroded the intellectual capital. On the other hand, the youth have had to live with disruptions in education, which have impacted their ability to compete. The relatively better off, were able to send their children abroad or to reputed institutions within the country but others with limited means did not have this option. Currently the State has already initiated a process to improve the educational scenario and has made several efforts to establish higher learning institutions near every doorstep to cover the rural bases, even though it involves huge budgetary expenses.

Educational Interventions

In India, at present there are 60 Distance Learning Institutions (DLIs), including 9 Open Universities. Indira Gandhi National Open University (IGNOU) has emerged as one of the India's pioneering and biggest open university and the second biggest in the world after Central Radio and Television University, China, Established in 1985. The aim was to provide cost-effective, quality education to large sections of population including those living in remote and far-flung areas. It was also intended to provide ample opportunities to those, who for one reason or the other, could not seek or improve their educational standards. These educational interventions are essentially based on the supply of instructional material for home study but have to be supported by personal contact programmes (PCP), library facilities, study centres, audio-visual aids, and students' responses.

The evolution of technologies over the past decade, in particular the utilisation of such telecommunications technologies as satellites, has increased know-how to effectively deliver distance education and integrate ICTs into educational systems. Many countries have achieved success in combining pedagogical and organisational goals to create innovative educational solutions using modern information and communication technologies. The early experiences and a large number of the present distance training initiatives have focused on increasing access to and enhancing the kind and quality of instruction through the delivery of education materials at a distance. These include both distance-education based on postal exchange of educational correspondence between teachers and remote learners, and the use of radio and television to broadcast non-interactive education programmes.

Today, distance education consists of a richer set of practices. These include education activities with geographical or time drift between teachers and learners with possibilities for self-paced education, instructor and tutor-facilitated education and instructor-led education. Open learning is yet another concept that introduces additional flexibility in the learning process and in curricula certification. The goal is to facilitate access to education for learners facing constraints when it comes to admission and required prerequisites, pace of learning, and to alternate ways to earn certification and qualification. Open learning can include both distance training and distance education. Open learning is well adapted to life-long learning and professional development outside the traditional academic environment. The State of J&K being hilly has wider scope for open and distance education. Keeping in view the low literacy on the one hand and the challenges of reaching lakhs of unreached people spread throughout the State, adoption of open learning and its effective delivery through the distance mode seems to be inevitable choice on the other.

Since 1986, IGNOU has also been imparting education in the State. As such, it is an opportune time to introspect the delivery system adopted by IGNOU in J&K to assess its success matrix of educational programmes, in terms of their effectiveness and impact as also to evaluate its delivery system. Has the objective of educating all sections of the society, living even in the remotest corners and backward regions been accomplished as to nullify the imbalances in the development of education in the State? There has been an increase in enrolment and academic programmes and courses, being offered by IGNOU have multiplied in J&K State. However, the nature of facilities and support system required to sustain such academic endeavours have to match up such an expansion. Access to education is not only about access to technology but also access to content, services, and expertise, through different forms ranging from off-line databases (such as directories, training materials, guidelines) to distant publishers, databases, web sites, and other open distance learning resources that can or cannot be reached in real time.

The new educational and technological channels (like ICT, EDUSAT, e-learning, internet, telecommunications) require of educational planners and providers the operation of a variety of specialised sub-systems interacting with each other and managed in a very comprehensive way. The development, delivery and management of e-learning has emerged as a complex process that includes different stages and requires a large variety of actors and modalities of work, producing deliverables, products and services. The educational delivery system is in some ways similar to an industrial process: there are learners, teachers and trainers, instructions and multimedia designers, information and ICT professionals, managers, and decision makers, and all these must work smoothly together. Live video instruction is the most popular and fastest growing delivery mode in the developed world and this technology is starting to be used in India also—there is insufficient data to confirm whether this technology is yet available in the rural areas of our State. Through open learning, therefore, India as well as our State is able to relieve some of the ever-increasing pressure that is building up on higher education. Technology-enhanced learning has the potential to achieve good results and partly solve the problem of teachers' training as well as students' learning.

Issues and Challenges

1. Peaceful behaviour does not occur in a vacuum. It is nested within the context of the family and other primary social groups like the clan, peer groups and

through arts, songs, drama, proverbs and storytelling. In J&K state, the family plays pivotal roles in the transmission and inculcation of societal acceptable values and norms. Currently, the forces of globalisation have negatively influenced the family, making it to lose its grip on its individual members and its potency to prepare people for peaceful living. The socialising power of the family in helping its members to cultivate the needed values which higher education will later build upon has rather been frustrated by modernisation articulated by the forces of globalisation. The expectation that these missing values will easily be built into people by the system was dashed, because of the challenges confronting it which are equally created by globalisation.

2. Curriculum dictates what should be taught, when and how it should be taught. Apart from the fact that the curricula of most tertiary institutions are obsolete and are in dire need of reform, they do not contain peace programmes. They are lacking in all facets to meet up with the developmental trends in the areas of peace, security, conflict resolution and non-violent education. Where such programmes are provided, they are inadequate and may not reflect the needs and aspirations of State societies. This is because they are basically drawn from foreign experiences which may not find the right environment at home for its application.
3. Staff in higher education institutions in J&K, whether teaching or non-teaching have poor orientations concerning the theoretical and practical underpinning of issues relating to peace. The financial implication of training people abroad often stands as a barrier in developing staff in this area. Homegrown institutions offering courses in peace studies are limited in supply, and the majority of their staff are not formally trained

in the area. Hence, their performance abilities will be adversely affected in terms of empowerment, productivity and scholarship.

4. Material resources such as textbooks, films, tapes, monographs etc on peace are scarce in higher educational institutions of J&K State. The available materials are rather difficult to come by and where they are found, they are highly expensive to acquire, putting institutions offering the courses in a tight corner to actually to acquire them. Shortages of materials on peace and staff problems are the main challenges preventing these institutions from empowering youths effectively in the area of peace in J&K.
5. There are limited available research materials in the area of peace in the State. The majority of the materials available are of foreign origin and cannot be comprehensively used to reflect local peculiarities. Acute shortage of staff, material resources, and funds are the main impediments to the realisation of scholarly research works on peace studies, and are consequently producing negative effects on youth empowerment for peace.
6. The nature of knowledge that globalisation is radiating is questionable. While in some quarters, the gains of globalisation are impressive, in J&K, globalisation is making people to form unclear pictures of reality. It has brought with it confusing and stressful environment for most people. This resulted in preventing people, especially the younger generation, from forming clear values about peace and non-violent behaviours. Higher institutions of learning are not free from the adverse consequences of globalisation in the State. Their coping strategies in reacting to the speedy occurrences of events are rather slow, manifesting in a highly demanding environment, with little capacity for such types of

institutions to cope and respond adequately. Hence, students are ill-prepared to face the challenges of life.

7. In rural areas of J&K State, the school dropout rate is more than urban areas. Even during college-life also because of the family burden, poor infrastructural facilities, lack of monetary support, apathy towards education etc we can see a high percentage of dropouts among rural students.
8. Poverty is one of the main issues and indicates a condition in which a person fails to maintain a living standard adequate for a comfortable lifestyle. Mere growth of economy cannot bring social justice and balanced development unless it is coupled with poverty alleviation and employment generating opportunities for deprived and marginalised sections of the society. The survey conducted by the State during 2007-08 put the BPL population at 21.63 per cent. A host of poverty alleviation programmes are in operation in the State mostly with Central assistance.
9. On the one hand, Gross Enrolment Ratio (GER) stands low for the overall population, while on the other there are large variations among the various categories of population based on urban or rural habitation and rich and poor. Due to regional disparities in economic development and uneven distribution of institutions of higher education, higher education is not equally available to the different sections of the society.
10. The Gross Enrolment Ratio (GER) measures, the access level by taking the ratio of persons in all age groups enrolled in various programmes to total population in the age group of 18 to 23 in rural areas. The access to higher education for all eligible students in the State is a major issue before the policy makers.

Recommendations

1. There is an urgent need to create awareness amongst rural youth about the different programmes being

offered by the higher education system so that they can learn while earning and develop their income sources in a more effective way.

2. For an effective delivery mechanism, study material should be learner-based. Persons with experience should be selected.
3. Infrastructural facilities of higher learning institutions (like open/distance education, IGNOU) for effective delivery mechanisms are less in comparison to the formal system of learning. They will have to make use of the infrastructural and other facilities of the existing schools/colleges. Therefore, it is very essential to maintain proper co-ordination/liaison with them.
4. As an alternative to face-to-face teaching, such types of delivery models have not gained full acceptance. A way round the constraint is found where equal status is awarded to the degrees given in traditional teaching systems.
5. Interactive communication has new watchwords like: teleconferencing, radio-paging, satellite communication and group telephone tutorials. A beginning should be made even partially to facilitate higher education programmes through the distance mode in the country based on the new system of delivery.
6. Due care must be taken for developing skills for enhancing teaching-learning transactions, creating a conducive academic environment, putting technology-enabled learning into practice wherever possible, generation of employment and alleviation of poverty in rural areas to bring about the desired socio-economic development of Jammu and Kashmir.
7. Electronic media packages and the support system should prominently supplement the printed study materials. Access to the facilities and services pertaining to media packages must be ensured at

different study centres, across the country as early as possible. Mere supply of media and other electronic support systems by institutional delivery model to different regional study centres does not have any such meaning that the students, either use them or have easy access to them.

8. Proper planning and coordination with the postal authorities is needed for the dispatch of course materials. Study material should be prepared in a given time frame and dispatched properly.
9. Success of these delivery models to a great extent depends on the regular receipt of studiously prepared lessons and honestly done assignments by the learners. Efforts should be made so that learners take interest to complete their task and in doing research on current issues prevalent in the State instead of merely copying the material.
10. The utilisation of funds for developing these models effectively in the State should be increased. To build a high quality education system, adequate funding must be made available by the Central and State Governments to improve quality, and at the same time, make higher education affordable to all specially to the families in the rural areas where income level of the people is low and access problems are higher.

In the socio-economic development of a nation, human capital has a very crucial role. It has been found that the higher education system is essential for national, social and economic development of the country. There is the need of value-based higher education system which empowers the youth for self-sustainability by inculcating employment skills and reducing poverty. No doubt, higher education is reaching every doorstep. It is good to see the rural areas being covered. The two higher education institutes providing an effective institutional delivery mechanism for the rural youth to promote higher education, which in turn enhance their income as well as the sources for employment in Jammu and Kashmir, would have to make more efforts to integrate these mechanisms into their core development processes and policies. This would surely contribute to the overall development of the human resources in the State of J&K. A delivery model whereby educational interventions could enhance income and employment possibilities among the educated sections who are located on the international border or in rural areas of the State. Empowered educated youth through an effective delivery mechanism work as representatives of peace alongside those responsible for terrorism and violence. If apt location-specific institutional interventions are made operational, they could facilitate the building of a climate of peace and harmony including in the conflict affected areas in the State.

Eventually, we need to loom and espouse advanced flow of higher education for our rapid economic growth paradigm coupled with rising income levels which shall usher in a metamorphosis in the educational scenario of our State. 'Hope springs eternal in the human breast' says Shakespeare. The hope of a better education system coming to prevail in our State shall remain rooted in our hearts.

REFERENCES

Adi, S.M., 2007. 'Higher Education in Rural Areas', *University News*, 12 (March 19-25), pp. 16-17.

Agarwal, P. 2006, 'Higher Education in India: The Need for Change', Working Paper No. 180, Indian Council for Research on International Economic Relation (ICRIER), India.

Agarwal, P. 2007, 'Higher Education in India: Growth, Concerns and Change Agenda, *Higher Education Quarterly*, 6 (12), pp. 197-207.

Bliss, S. 2010. Peace Building and Conflict Resolution: A Global Education Learning Emphases. Retrieved from: http://www. globaleducation. edna. edu. au/globaled/go/pid/554

Bora, Abhijit. 2012, 'Higher Education Consolidation of Existing Facilities', *academe,* Vol. XV, No. 1, January, Academic Staff College, Himachal Pradesh University.

Brett, R. 2003. 'Why Do Adolescents Volunteer for Armed Forces or Armed Groups?', Paper presented at the Spanish Red Cross Conference, Valencia, Spain, November 5-7.

Government of Jammu & Kashmir, *Economic Survey, J&K, 2013-14.*

Lewis. G. Ralph and Smith, H. Dougals. 1998. *Total Quality in Higher Education*, Deep & Deep Publications, New Delhi.

Schaffer, T.C. (2005). Kashmir the Economics of Peace Building, a report of the CSIS South Asia Group with the Kashmir Study Group Newspaper, *Kashmir Greater*, 28/09/2012.

Siddique, M.A. 2010, 'Rural-Urban Disparity in Higher Education', *University News*, Vol. 48, No. 28.

WEBSITES

http://www. dailykashmirimages. com/news-a-bleak-future-for-higher-education-52014. aspx#sthash. ssrE8AS1. dpuf

8

Access to Higher Education: Issues and Challenges of Students with Disability

Vaishali Kolhe

Background

First of all, it is tough for students with disability to reach at the stage of higher education. Access to higher education is a laborious task for such students due to three main factors; one is 'diversity among students with disability' and second is 'social construction of disability' the way meaning of disability is perceived by the university stakeholders in shaping policies and services for them. Third is 'lack of awareness' among university stakeholders that leads to unwillingness and resistance to change for inclusion of disabled students. This resistance is observed from entry level to every stage of higher education. This non-accepting attitude due to lack of awareness, results in facing painstaking challenges by disabled students at every step-in fulfilment of their academic goals. This impacts their overall development as individual in terms of personhood, identity construction and citizenship.

How prepared are our universities and higher educational institutions to provide access to higher education for students with disability by the ways of equal opportunities and requisite services? What are the attitudes of higher educational bodies and professionals towards such students? In the Indian context, the traditional and stereotypical mindset of society does not accept disability as a 'natural human phenomenon' but views it as 'different with stigma' which discredits the potential of students with disability. Such societal outlook may reinforce attitudes of higher education authorities and institutions in providing limited services for them.

The issues of students with disabilities in higher education are diverse and multifaceted. The current status of students with disability in higher education exhibits high level of vulnerability. This vulnerability cuts across intersectionality within the structures of body, mind, class, caste, gender and sexualities. This shows the pattern of invisibility and powerlessness faced by them leading to multilevel disadvantage and academic exclusion. The total graduate population of persons with disability is 12,46,857. The male population is 8,39,702 and the female population is 4,07,155 (Census of India, 2011). The graduate male-female population ratio is 3:1. ***One third of the total graduates with disability comprises female graduates. They face a triple disadvantage*** as in addition to disability, they are vulnerable to abuse and face lack of financial support that lead to female graduates dropping out of academia. Lack of specific knowledge, skills and experience perhaps lead to the unpreparedness of university stakeholders to deal with issues faced by disabled students. The attitudes of teachers, staff and administration are, especially, some of the main reasons for the disabled students' academic exclusion. Another reason is the lack of a database of disabled students at the university level. Lack of financial support is common reason for female graduates to drop out from universities. This lack of financial and academic support with namesake services is the key issue of concern. This requires efforts from universities to have dialogue with teachers and disabled students and identify individual needs of such students and accordingly plan the classroom teaching pedagogy. Classroom level inclusion is a basic unit to bring about access to higher education and inclusion of students with disability in their ecology. It is about how the teacher is able to design the teaching plan, lecture, teaching learning material and student learning exercises keeping in mind the type of communication mode that will best aid students with disability.

This requires conscious efforts to transform the pedagogical modalities as required for better acquisition of knowledge and skills by the disabled students. This kind of change requires fundamental policy reforms using the experiences of such student. It may be called a bottom-up approach to provide free and compulsory education to them to enjoy their life with dignity. An institutionalised enabling of such services at university level is key in this age. The first step towards this is the identification of their needs at the curricular level. Based on this needs assessment the basic services such as provision of books, class notes, library facilities can be initiated followed by long term services of curricular changes, accessibility, software, ICT technology aids, etc., can be initiated. Inclusion at higher education is understood by observing the marginalised learners' needs and intentionally identifying a space for their inclusion by giving equal access and opportunity to learn by planning from developing curriculum to pedagogy formulation. The idea is 'to be included universally with equal access' to education as their human rights. This further requires a creation of academic centers such as a centre for disability studies at each university to collate insiders' voices to develop a rights-based framework and inclusive services for disabled students.

A multimodal/multisensory human interactive design and information communication technology (ICT) is required to bridge the gaps in teaching and learning for the students with disability for promoting equal access in inclusive education. The starting point is developing and enabling 'equal accessibility policy at university level from the admission to getting the degree'. This begins from responding to their diverse needs from the choosing a subject of choice, responding to admission needs and access to classrooms, class notes, books and academic resources, library, campus navigations, practical, hostels, food, playing games, examinations, class assignments, research and orientation to academic environment, etc.

Understanding individual needs of the students with disability in planning and designing curriculum at classroom level is a prerequisite for facilitating inclusive/the better facilitation of education at higher levels. The philosophy of inclusion is towards 'Occupiability of all learners in classroom curriculum domain of teaching and providing learning with equal access'. Occupiability is a description of affordance offered by the teaching environment for pause and movement for durable occupation towards enhancing student-teacher engagement/person-place engagement i.e. students, university stakeholders, teachers, peers and staff engagement. This may be understood by ways in which the durable occupation of teaching environment is facilitated or hampered by architectural design action (Himanshu Burte, 2008). What factors hamper or facilitate occupation of teaching the student with disability in the concerned learning environment is understood by implemented by architectural design action. Universal Design which brings the larger philosophy of equitable space to all is useful here. 'Universal design is the design and composition of different products and environments to be usable by all people, to the greatest extent possible, without the need for adaption or specialized design' (Aslaksen, 2007). The development of five principles of Universal Design India follows a sequential process of co-creation to address the diverse needs of users across ability, age, socio-economic strata and culture (Mullick, 2011; Khare, 2011, Raheja 2011) 1. Equitable/Saman, 2. Usable/Sahaj, 3. Cultural/Sanskritik, 4. Economy/ Sasta, 5. Aesthetics/Sundar.

The philosophy of inclusive design, often called "Universal Design" or "Design for All." It is a way of thinking that can be applied in any form of design or activity, infrastructure, urban and rural habitat, curriculum, transport, housing, food, program or service involving interface of people with disability with structures of physical, social environment.

Inclusive education is possible by implementing and institutionalizing universal design at higher education. This also includes flexible adaptations in classroom, curriculum & teachers teaching modality matching to their impairment, disability and diverse learners' needs without compromising all learners' outcomes. This may be achieved using principles of universal design and multisensory/ multimodal approach with flexibility. This process enables equal access and social inclusion of students with disability reinforcing user centric engagement of all diverse learners. This multimodal engagement provides the foundation for inclusive academic environment to the learners who are students with disability. This process of student centric engagements with understanding individual's learning needs formulates the building blocks of inclusive process. Also, weaving voices of students with disability and diversity and facilitating bottom up approach to develop rights based framework using "Nothing about us without us" as stated in the United Nations Convention for Rights for Persons with Disability (UNCRPD) framework ratified by India to change its policies for inclusion of persons with disability. It can further be studied by user centric design to occupy all types of learners and providing equal opportunity to students with or without disability in higher education. The question is how our university /higher education policy is prepared today to enable students with disabilities and diversity towards equal opportunities and equal accessibility to higher education. Currently the persons with disability are categorized in 21 categories as per "Rights of Persons with Disability Act 2016. Hence inclusion at the university level will have to work towards including 21 categories of students with disability in higher education with inclusivity in classroom design, curriculum planning and design and exams. The answer lies in the UNCRPD statement "Nothing about us without all of us" by developing a framework by inclusion of voices of students with disability, their capabilities, strengths and their individual needs of various subjects. This can be done through the identification of problems and barriers at structural, architectural, physical and academic level faced by disabled students in accessing higher education.

The earlier Persons with Disability (PWD) Act 1995 had just seven disabilities listed. Today, there are 21 categories that apply. Those with 40% disability in any of these categories is recognized by the Government as a disabled person and is eligible to get all the services and provisions given by the

Government of India. This includes a 4% reservation that is being introduced in a new Bill. This reservation is applicable to the educational institutions as well. This move should help disabled students secure admissions and hope for a better adjustments and adaptations in engaging in any activity of enjoyment of rights equally with others.

Introduction

An attempt has been made to examine the 'issues and challenges of students with disability in higher education' at Tata Institute of Social Sciences (TISS), Mumbai through qualitative study and thematic inquiry. TISS has various services for disabled students like unique library for visually impaired students established in 2009 and the Centre for Disability Studies and Action established in 2006. Due to these services a conscious effort has been made to understand the issues and concerns in the disability sector and higher education issues of disabled students. The study is based on observations of struggles faced by students with disability and responding to their needs and concerns at individual capacity. The chapter aims to highlight academic adaption of students at the university level. These challenges are mainly accessibility issues faced at following levels. 1. Architectural Barriers that deny access to university buildings, roads, classrooms, library, hostels, canteen, furniture, washrooms and other amenities. 2. Academic barriers include access to academic resources like books, class notes, and articles in accessible format, and problems in accessing subject specific curriculum and technical aspects, barriers faced in classroom teaching and learning, preparing notes in accessible format and website accessibility becomes an issue of concern. Extracting notes in general and specific subjects, getting books from library research software are not accessible for doing independent data analysis, accessibility at the entrance exam, access to classroom, inaccessible notice boards, getting scribes in exams is problem along with payment to scribes/writers 3. Institutional and administrative barriers is the lacuna in governance mechanisms and rules in the university system that perceives disability as less important and tends to exclude disabled people while issuing circulars, exam notices, eye cards, etc. Academic information in the form of notices notice boards, circulars and university news do not reach disabled students in time. 4. Social and attitudinal barriers are due to a lack of awareness of disability among university staff, faculty, peers among university stakeholders, getting accessible hostel/ accommodation. This indicates an urgent need to create an institutionalised mechanism/'equal access policy' at university level and digital accessibility services. This mechanism may involve feedback of student with disability and develop a framework with philosophy of 'universal design' for facilitating inclusion. This entire system aims to dialogue with university stakeholders like teachers, peers and administration to meet academic needs of students with disability. Also there is need to redesign the higher education policy with principle of "Creation of rights-accessible enabling environment" with voices of student with disability and initiating inclusive process with the UNCRPD statement, i.e. 'Nothing about us without all of us'.

The findings suggest four major recommendations; first conducting regular Access Audit/Disability Inclusion Audit to reduce architectural barriers and modify the university buildings and infrastructure with disabled friendly standards of barrier free environment of the Government of India. Second is developing data of students with disability at university level to implement 4% reservation and government schemes i.e. scholarships and book bank schemes. Third is creating institutional mechanism of equal opportunity unit/equal accessibility unit conducting needs assessment and responsible for addressing disability issues and resolving individualised educational and academic needs of student with disability. Third developing university resource centres and centre for disability studies and equal accessibility units, sign language units for developing guidelines and call for action. Fourth is creating a accessibility committee of persons with disability to monitor the accessibility issues at curricular level and implement it with feedback of students with disability. This may help the university to develop disabled friendly university guidelines and call for action with need based services for students with disabilities.

TISS initiative: Access Rights Mission: The TISS initiative for inclusion is a field action project of the Centre for Disability Studies and Action seeks to create an innovative, needs base approach towards education framework that aims to take initiative towards greater inclusion using affirmative action and reasonable accommodation.

I. Conceptual Aspects

Disability Definitions & Inclusion

According to the current definitions in the context of Indian laws, "persons with disabilities" would mean to include anyone who suffers a minimum 40% disability and it must be certified by a medical authority specified by the government. This medical model of disability shifts the onus of responsibility and pressure to persons with disabilities to continually strive for rehabilitation, treatments & medical interventions. The concept of 'disability' must be redefined both socially and legally to accommodate its broader aspects with a view to making every area of the lives of such disabled persons inclusive and accessible. By widening the purview of the definition of disability, state and non-state actors alike will be able to reach out to the most vulnerable sections of society and amplify their efforts in making sure that persons with disabilities claim the benefits and provisions afforded to them under various International and National laws.

Therefore, not only is this definition of 'persons with disabilities' limiting because of its medical assessment based definition, it also excludes other persons who suffer less than 40% disabilities from receiving benefits related to accessibility for persons with disabilities; these are disabilities nevertheless and still act as a barrier to the individual's effective enjoyment of his/her inherent right to live life with dignity in accordance with the provisions of the Indian constitution. Though newer definitions of disability have expanded the view of what qualifies as a disability, the benchmark of 40% disabilities is both regressive and restrictive.

> The Bill of Rights for Persons with Disability 2016 constitutes three separate categories of persons with disabilities:
> Section 2(q) "persons with disabilities" which is defined as per the UNCRPD as any persons with long term physical, mental, intellectual or sensory impairment, which may hinder his full and effective participation in society equally with others.
> Section 2(p) "persons with benchmark disabilities" which means a person with not less than 40% of a specified disability, which includes around 19 separate disabilities including the seven already mentioned in the PWD Act, and
> Section 2(r), which defines a "person with high support needs" as a person with a benchmark disability who needs high support.

The following concepts related to higher education and university education are defined under Rights for Person with Disability Bill 2016 are mentioned below, which requires appropriate implementation at university level to create a disabled friendly university/higher education institutions.

> Section 2(t) 'reasonable accommodation' means necessary and appropriate modification and adjustments, without imposing a disproportionate or undue burden in a particular case, to ensure to persons with disabilities the enjoyment or exercise of rights equally with others.
> Section 2(c) 'barrier' means any factor including communicational, cultural, economic, environmental, institutional, political, social or structural factors which hampers the full and effective participation of persons with disabilities in society
> Section 2(z) 'universal design' means the design of products, environments, programmes and services to be usable by all people to the greatest extent possible, without the need for adaptation or specialised design and shall apply to assistive devices including advanced technologies for particular group

of persons with disabilities.
Section 2(f) 'communication' includes means and formats of communication, languages, display of text, Braille, tactile communication, signs, large print, accessible multimedia, written, audio, plain-language, human-reader, augmentative and alternative modes and accessible information and communication technology.

Section 38 Under Duties and Responsibilities of the Appropriate Government

Section 38(d): provide orientation and sensitisation at the school, college, University and professional training level on the human condition of disability and the rights of persons with disabilities;
Section 38(f): ensure that the rights of persons with disabilities are included in the curriculum in Universities and colleges.
Section 15: The appropriate Government and the local authorities shall endeavour that all educational institutions funded by them provide inclusive education to the children with disabilities and towards that end
Section 15(i): admit persons with disability without discrimination and provide education and opportunities for sports and recreation activities equally with others;
Section 15(ii): make building, campus and various facilities accessible;
Section 15(iii): provide reasonable accommodation according to the individual's requirements;
Section 15(iv): provide necessary support individualised or otherwise in environments that maximise academic and social development consistent with the goal of full inclusion;
Section 15 (v): ensure that the education to persons who are blind or deaf or both is imparted in the most appropriate languages and modes and means of communication;
Section 46(2): Human Resource Development: All universities shall promote teaching and research in disability studies including establishment of study centres for such studies.
The Lok Sabha passed RWPD 2016 replacing the existing PWD Act 1995 enacted 21 years ago.

The salient features of the Rights of Persons with Disabilities Act 2016 are:

1. Disability has been defined based on an evolving and dynamic concept.
2. The types of disabilities have been increased from existing 7 to 21 and the Central Government will have the power to add more types of disabilities.
3. The 21 disabilities are given below:- Blindness, Low-vision, Leprosy Cured persons, Hearing Impairment (deaf and hard of hearing), Loco motor Disability, Dwarfism, Intellectual Disability, Mental Illness, Autism Spectrum Disorder, Cerebral Palsy, Muscular Dystrophy, Chronic Neurological conditions, Specific Learning Disabilities, Multiple Sclerosis, Speech and Language disability, Thalassemia, Hemophilia, Sickle Cell disease, Multiple Disabilities including deaf-blindness, Acid Attack victim, Parkinson's disease. Hence University may have to work with 21 categories of students with disability as per the RPWD Act 2016.

II. Theory and Disability

Disability and Normality

Auguste Comte, a French philosopher who founded the discipline of sociology and the doctrine of positivism introduced the concept of 'normality' which implied a state of order and balance; so when he viewed disability with this idea of order and balance, he recognized the pathology of disability to be an 'excess' or 'deficiency'. (in their book 'Damned for their difference'. The cultural construction of deaf people as disabled' authors Jan Branson & Don Miller are of the opinion that the ideology is one of normality). The medical model originated because it was founded on the principle of normality. It aims 'to restore the disabled person to normality,' (Oliver, 1990) 'By contrast, the social model of disability locates the experience of disability in the social environment, aims to dismantle the social and physical barriers in participation and inclusion of PWD.' (Kayess & French, 2008) The social model of disability is the embodiment of UNCRPD's slogan which calls for the dynamic participation of persons with disabilities in bringing about changes in disability rights and the laws.

The social model of disability has unified persons with disabilities in their common struggle for disability rights while also acting as a powerful device of liberation that by means of purposeful collective action can transform society. (Disability KaR-Enabling disabled people to reduce poverty; Briefing Note: The social model of disability, human rights and development by Bill Albert September 2004).

The UNCRPD's concept of a 'person with disabilities' suggests fluidity and accommodation, which is crucial to understanding and developing guidelines in the context of an evolving jurisprudence on disability rights with emphasis on inclusion and accessibility. It has been instrumental in bringing about a paradigm shift in the way the world views issues of disability and in empowering persons with disabilities to grow beyond perceived limitations imposed by the society at large. Disability from birth is known an 'congenital' disability as a result of insult to the brain before or during the birth of the child during his/her prenatal(before birth), perinatal(during birth) and postnatal(after birth) period of life. Based on injury, infection, genetic causes may result in any type or degree of impairment/disability e.g. visual impairment, hearing impairment, locomotor impairment, multiple disability, autism and intellectual disability.

III. Disability Concept

Disability is a result of interaction of a person with his/her environment. A facilitating environment will enable the person to access any structure or design with ease and without much efforts. On the other hand The Inhibiting environment will create restrictions or barriers to the equal opportunities and equal access to the resources. Barriers can be classified as structural/ architectural, institutional, academic, social and attitudinal.

1. Structural barrier is physical/structural design creating a barrier. Staircases are a barrier to a wheelchair user.

2. Institutional barrier is preventive restrictions related to the rule, governance, administrative barriers increasing the restrictions for the individual.
3. Academic barrier Barriers in reading books, writing notes, accessing library, accessing circulars, exam question papers, assignments as they are not in accessible format.
4. Attitudinal Barrier is rooted in cultural stereotypes and personal biases and exhibits in behaviour of the persons during social interaction as well as interface.

Medical Model of Disability

The loss of an organ is called as impairment. Disability is 'inability to perform' due to the loss of an organ in the body. In this way disability has a biological construct. Medical model dominates with social model of disability and emphasises the core value of treating the body to be able body.

Social Model of Disability

The Social Model of Disability highlights the societal stereotypical belief system and karma theory. Hence disability is socially constructed due to the socio-political context of a society. It is rooted in rigid stereotypical values, myths and biases which results in prejudiced attitudes and stigmatised behaviour with PWD. Stigma further discredits the potential of the persons and subjects to othering process and social exclusion.

Classification of Disability

A. International Classification of Impairment, Disability, Handicapped (WHO/1980)

It prefers medical model of disability to make them able body by expert treatment.

Impairment is any visible structural/anatomical loss of physical or sense organs in an individual. The loss of a little finger is impairment.

Disability is usually a consequence of impairment, is the functional inability of an individual to perform any activity in the manner or within the range considered 'normal' for any human being; Disability interferes in the performance of daily activities by an individual. Due to loss of little finger, someone is unable/disable to write.

Handicapped involves social disadvantages due to disability and impairment and an affected person is known as a handicapped individual. Someone is unable to marry and face social disadvantage due to loss of little finger.

B. International Classification of Impairment, Activity, Participation (ICF 2002)

This refers to Social Model of Disability and destigmatised disability. The term 'disability' is substituted by 'activity' and 'handicapped' is substituted by 'participation'. Participation is divided into two factors Contextual/Personal factors and Environment Factors. a. Environmental factors affecting participation: physical, social, attitudinal, academic and institutional barriers and identifying intervention to provide equal access to all resources.

b. Personal Factors affecting participation: Personal factors affecting participation. ICF puts the notions of 'health' and 'disability' in a new light. It acknowledges that every human being can experience a decrement in health and thereby experience some disability. It fosters 'mainstreams' the experience of disability and recognises it as a universal human experience. By shifting the focus from cause to impact it places all health conditions on an equal footing allowing them to be compared using a common metric – the ruler of health and disability. (ICF 2002).

C. United Nations Convention for Rights of Persons with Disability (UNCRPD 2007) was ratified by India and augmenting its legislation with rights based approach.

Accessibility as Human Right context

Accessibility is the human right as as per UNCRPD which specifically recognises Accessibility (under Articles 9 and 21) that access to information, communications and services, including the internet, is a human right. This applicable to rights of student with disability in higher education under Article 9.

IV. UNCRPD Context

India is one of the first countries which has signed and ratified the United Nations Convention on Rights of Persons with Disabilities (UNCRPD) 2007 to change its national legal system for inclusion of people with disability. Therefore, the Government of India is having an obligation under International Law to give effect to the Convention on rights of Persons with Disabilities within its Indian legal system by implementing the principle of 'Nothing about us without us' in its Constitution. If you observe the Constitution of India, originally, the identity of persons with disability is viewed as powerless and invisible in its status. This prohibits the citizens with disability to participate equally in society and hampers their dignity to live.

Since past two years there has been a paradigm shift observed in the representation of persons with disability in framing bodies to implement UNCRPD due to international pressure regarding implementation inclusion principle of 'Nothing about us without us' on the Indian government. The philosophy of inclusion is promoted by the above statement by including the voices of persons with disability in framing the policies using bottom up approach. Finally, the RPWD 2016 was passed with 21 categories of diverse disabilities and redefining disability as a evolving and dynamic concept on 14th December 2016.

Inclusion in Context of Higher Education

Inclusion has academic and social benefits for all students, whether with or without disabilities, such as increased communication and social interaction opportunities, age-appropriate models of behaviour skills, more active participation in the school community, individualised education goals, as well as access to the rich core curriculum (Grenot-Scheyer et al, 1996). Teachers' attitudes have been found to influence the process and the outcome of inclusion to a great extent (Avramidis et al, 2000). Attitudinal prejudice in mainstream schools hindered the development of formal relationships and successful inclusion in classroom. This becomes a barrier to learning and thus for future success (Shah, 2007). Inclusion values diversity not assimilation (Balland 1997). Cultural and social values dominating the minds of policymakers and society at large and have caused barriers to inclusion (Alur, 1998).

Status of Students with Disability in Higher Education

Status of students with disability in higher education is matter of concern due to their invisible status and academic exclusion. The total graduate population of persons with disability is 12,46,857. The male population is 8,39,702 and female population is 4,07,155. One third of total population comprises of female graduates with disability. The male: female ratio of graduates with disability is 3:1. This exhibits need for serious engagement into issues of students with disability.

Universities have to think about providing facilities to 21 categories of students with disability in higher education to facilitate inclusion. One of possibility to provide government schemes to 21 categories of students with disability is by providing unique identity cards UDID to them. This will help to create maintain a data base of SWD and allow to get all schemes eligible for them.

V. Requirements:

Paradigm shift

Laws related to special education or children with special needs (CWSN) exemplify the notion of 'disability' being a natural phenomenon that sees students with disability not as objects that are broken and need fixing, but as individuals who are essentially unique and function differently from others. A disability can not and must never be allowed to 'define a person's potential, humanity or character.'(Snow, 2013). 'Inaccessible environments create disability by creating barriers to participation and inclusion'. (WHO, 2011).

Inclusion Context

Inclusion is a philosophy that has it roots in social justice, and the de-institutionalisation and civil rights movements of the sixties. Inclusion is a philosophy and as such does not directly inform pedagogy or curriculum. There is a need for a theoretical foundation for special education that addresses this dilemma of the application of policy to practice (De Valenzuela, Connery & Musanti, 2000, p. 113). The term 'inclusion' within education evokes great interest, debate and discourse all over the world (Alur, 2001). Essentially it cannot be overlooked that India has the highest absolute number of out of school children (UNESCO Institute for Statistics 2005) and it is one of the country's most unlikely to meet aims which is 'education for all' goals by 2015 (UNESCO, 2005). Inclusive education is championed as a means to remove barriers, improve outcomes and remove discrimination (Lindsay, 2003).

Higher Education Context

The Indian higher education system is presently facing several challenges. The challenge of global competitiveness has been added to other demanding tasks such as access, equity, relevance, quality, privatisation and internationalisation in the face of a resource crunch. (Ved Prakash, 2007).

A well developed and equitable system of higher education that promotes quality learning as a consequence of both teaching and research is central for success in the emerging knowledge economy. It is widely acknowledged that education contributes significantly to economic development. It is, imperative for developing countries, to give due importance to both the quantitative and qualitative expansion of higher education (Ved Prakash, 2007). Skill development play a very important role in empowering today's youth and one needs to understand significance of inclusion of students with disability in higher education.

VI. Inclusion as a Change Process

Classroom level inclusion is a basic unit for brining out

transformation within mindsets of learners and inclusion of student with disability. Its about initiating process of changing teaching learning pedagogy as per individuals needs of students and especially students with disability and changing the entire curriculum and teacher's teaching modalities required to acquire the knowledge of student with disability however this amplifies learning of peers. Inclusion is a matter of universal access, Interactive communication technology, accessible infrastructure, classroom communication and provision of equal opportunities to the student with disability in higher education context.

Inclusion in higher education means redesigning the teaching pedagogy with enhanced flexibility and adaptability to facilitate student centric learning. This requires opening curriculum boundaries to meet the individual needs of students with disability without compromising all learners needs. The inclusion process is developing new ways of identifying students needs and evolving into a curricular-building process with principle of Universal Design. Principle of Universal design enables access to all the academic resources in higher education by breaking barriers. e.g. architectural, attitudinal, academic and social barriers. Inclusion is a process and can be implemented at following levels.

1. Universal Access is the first dimension for bringing Inclusion of student with disability in the higher education context by enabling equal access to all to higher education resources. Enabling inclusion of students with disability by provision of the accessible infrastructure, Institutional resources, academic resources/teaching learning material with accessibility to all. This enabling environment with equitable distribution of resources facilitates equal learning opportunities by formulating new academic goals to meet the learning needs of students with disability.

2. Interactive Communication Technology is a second dimension towards bringing inclusion of student with disability. The reforms in Information and Computer Technology (ICT) has played a significant role in providing access to students with disability across their life span and especially in higher education. The Jaws software, NVDA software, Voice synthesizer, ICT, mobile technologies, Communication APPs like Jellow, Social networking technologies has played a key role in enhancing the learning's of students with disabilities in higher education.

3. Mode of Communication is the third dimension for brining inclusion of student with disability in the higher education context. The mode of human communication has two parts, one is receptive communication and the other is expressive communication. If student with disability has Deafness uses sign language, The mode of communication is sign language-nonverbal communication with limited vocabulary. Hence, teaching shall be aided by a sign language interpreter for completing receptive communication for interpreting meanings. If the learner is deaf and blind and her mode of receptive and expressive communication is Braille, then it's difficult for teachers to use verbal mode of communication which is affected. Hence, the teacher may have to learn Braille to communicate and provide all class notes to her in Braille. Hence, the teaching pedagogy shall be done keeping in mind learners' mode of communication.

4. Schemes, Policies Towards Inclusive Pedagogy and Curriculum is a fourth dimension to bring inclusion process for student with disability. The Rights of Persons with Disabilities Draft Bill of 2014 was restructured to implement the UNCRPD framework to facilitate the rights based framework through inclusion in the higher education policy and teacher education scheme.

UGC guidelines of Persons with Disability XII Plan constitutes three major facilities for students with disability

a. Teacher Preparation in Special Education (TEPSE) The Teacher Preparation in Special Education (TEPSE) scheme is meant for assisting Departments of Education to launch special education teacher preparation programmes to prepare special teachers to teach in both special and inclusive settings. The scheme provides financial assistance to offer B.Ed. and M.Ed.

b. Higher Education for Persons with Special Needs (HEPSN): creating awareness about the capabilities of differently-abled persons, constructing facilities aimed at improving accessibility, purchase of equipment to enrich learning, etc. Establishment of Enabling Units in order to develop awareness, providing necessary guidance and counselling.

B.1 Equal Opportunity/Enabling Unit: 1. Facilitate admission of differently-abled persons in various courses; 2. Provide guidance and counselling; 3. Create awareness; 4. Assist differently-abled graduates to gain employment in the public as well as private sectors. A budgetary provision of Rs. 40,000 per unit per year will be made by the UGC .

B.2 Accessible Environment: The institutions create special facilities such as ramps, rails and special toilets. One-time grant of up to Rs.10 lakhs per university is provided. Access audits by experts; develop architectural/ construction plans as per guidelines on accessibility prescribed by Chief Commissioner of Disabilities, Government of India (website: www.ccdisabilities.nic.in).

B.3 Providing Special Equipment to augment educational services for differently-abled persons: Availability of accessible learning devices such as computers with screen reading software, low- vision aids, scanners, mobility devices. The UGC will provide an ad hoc one-time grant of up to Rs. 8 lakhs per university during the Twelfth Plan period.

C. Visually-Challenged Teachers: The current budget for schemes providing Reader's Allowance and funds for purchase of Braille books, recorded materials, etc. is very low and is focused on special education approach instead of inclusive education. Hence, guidelines and 'calls for action' document shall be prepared for higher education level by using UNCRPD, Education for all, EFA and UGC and RUSA to transform policy for empowerment of students with disability through creating space for Inclusion of PWD.

5. Inclusive Infrastructure and Academic Resources in Accessible Format: Under SIPDA schemes from ministry and social justice and empowerment provides 50 lakhs per building to make it accessible to universities and 20 lakhs for website accessibility.

6. Inclusive Classrooms and Library: Inclusive classrooms where teachers are using multisensory /multicommunication approach to include all vulnerabilities and student centric needs. of students with disabilities. Also, equip to provide the class notes in accessible format as per needs of student's disability. Also, make change in exam and assessment styles in order to suit the capability of students with disability. Library shall have the all the academic resources books in accessible format and facility of readers and writers for exams and study purpose. Also, it should have software and ICT for better accessibility for students with all disabilities.

VII. Problem Areas

Observations and Findings: Issues and Challenges of Students with Disabilities:

Architectural Barriers:

- Absence of Any sensory Cue for PWD (Diverse sensory impairments).
- University Buildings are inaccessible due to steep stairs and lack of tactile pavements
- The overall contrast value of signage by improving better colour scheme for low vision.
- Alternative route plan/Navigation route plan to access to the entrance of campus needs to be identified and created for ease in movement by diverse disability stake holders.
- Unstructured route for mobility impairments and wheelchair users.
- Low maintenance and uncombined pavements.
- Absence of tactile and sensory blocks on the pathways.
- Absence of adequate curb/kerbs cuts near the entrance zone

Academic Barriers:

- Website inaccessibility creates barrier in everyday learning.
- Reading material books are not in soft copy and accessible format.
- Scanning of books is essential to read the book and that is difficult. Academic material is not accessible; library facilities are not adequate to access the books.
- Non-availability of Braille printer.
- Accessible furniture, accessible class notes.

Classroom and learning issues

- At Classroom Level: cannot take notes simultaneously, PPT is not accessible/voice recording. Problems in recollecting the previous lecture. Lectures are not in accessible format.
- Library: Availability of software for academic purpose, Jaws software for visually impaired. Software called dragon converts voice into text and very useful for students with visual and hearing impaired and dyslexia. Book finder facility required in the library for helping to identify books, journals, scanning and editing relevant books on an urgent basis. Readers and writers' facility is required to read and convert material into audio format and transcriptions. Scanning facility is a must with editing facility.
- Study Issues: Compendium for each subject is must for students with disabilities in accessible form; without compendium, it is very difficult to access all the fundamental knowledge required by the student to conceptualize, there is problem of chapter fragmentation, when a chapter is scanned student try and scan the book in order to conceptualize which is time consuming hence compendium is preferred by the students with hearing, autism and learning disability.

- Orientation at various levels: Career guidance job cell, field work supervisor, fieldwork partners, and classmate's level. General students level, research level, student's union level, etc.
- Volunteer facility with writers and readers' facility to be institutionalised.
- Guidelines for students with disability to facilitate classes/exam fieldwork/net/library/jobs.
- Skill development: Skill oriented course with enough material available to them and facilitation in usage of the skill as effectively as other students
- Exam and assignment: Accessibility in writing the exam with scribe / writer is essential.
- Scribe guidelines should be made as per the feedback of students.

Accessibility Issues

1. Website & Moodle Accessibility: Information and academic material level from admission to completion.
2. Architectural Accessibility: Access to University Buildings and infrastructure.
3. Academic curriculum is not accessible, therefore accessible format is required.
4. Classroom accessibility in learning: Teachers teaching pedagogy and lectures are not accessible.
5. Exam Accessibility and Provisions: Scribe provision is inadequate and question papers are not in accessible format.
6. Library and reading materials are not accessible to SWD. Library resources are in the forms of books and e-journals, e-database. The books are not available in soft copies and architectural barriers are faced by SWD. Orthopedic and students using wheel chairs have not gone to library in entire three years of graduation as it is located at the top floor with no lift facility.

VIII. Recommendations

A. Recommendations and four categories of accessibility barriers in Higher Education & TISS Initiative TISS-Initiative

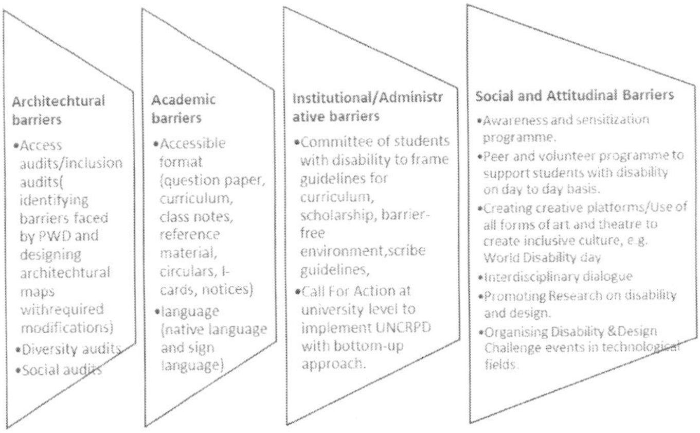

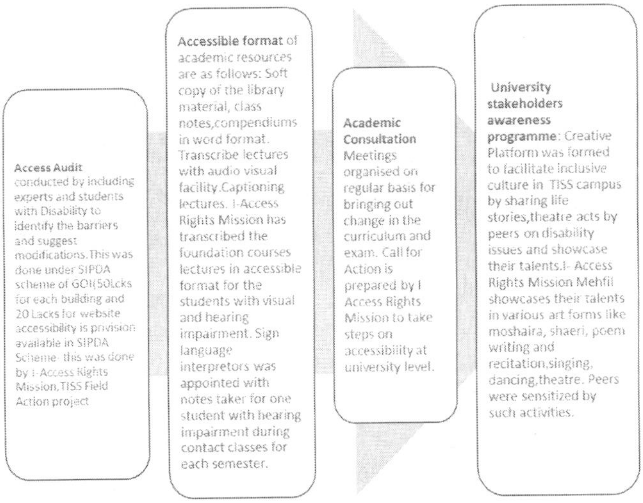

B. Six A's of Enabling Inclusion

1. Awareness, 2. Accessibility 3. Assistive devices 4. Academic Resources and Services 5. Attitude 6. Academic Teaching Pedagogies

1. Awareness

1. Awareness and Sensitization programs for all stakeholders at university level which involves teachers, peers, administration staff, security guards and peons.
2. Creating a data base of students with disability with social stratification and gender categorization.
3. Counselling and Orientation at entry level on disability facilities during 1st semester till adjustment.
4. Awareness programmes using all art forms such as film festivals, art festivals to promote inclusive culture in the university campus.

2. Accessibility

1. Website Accessibility and academic circulars as per WCAG, 2.0 guidelines. All university websites shall be accessible for PWD
2. Barrier free environment with modification at classroom and campus by Access Audit and Inclusion audit in identification of architectural barriers inside and outside university buildings, auditoriums, play grounds, classrooms, pathways, roads with voices of students with disability to develop accessibility guidelines.
3. Access to Transport in campus: travel within campus and out of campus for fieldwork, research/academic work and data collection.
4. Developing Accessibility committee of students with disability with head of department/principle for developing Disability Action Plan with students and faculty with disability towards disabled-friendly university.
5. Classroom Accessibility with Basic mobility and navigation services: Students with blindness, Neurological disability, multiple disability and wheel chair users requires escorts every day to reach to

classroom due to inaccessible environment. e.g. Escort service and peers volunteer can help them to reach to classroom daily.

6. Washrooms, Dining Hall and Canteen, Accessible Washrooms with fitment of ramps, mirror, grab bars. Texture contrast, colour contrast, Escort service to reach at Dining hall, Peer assistance for inclusive sitting arrangement.
7. Accessible Hostel: accessible lodging with accessible toilets and bathrooms.
8. Field work/Internship peer support facility, accessibility route and transport facility.
9. Access to Scribe and scribe guidelines can be developed and list of scribes can be kept ready at the university level for emergency, Workshops for developing scribes will be useful for university level.

3. Assistive Technology and Assistive devices

1. Need based Software, apps, Screen readers, talking Calculator.
2. Aids and appliances for learning purposes and software and apps can assist in teaching process too.
3. Library may have additional library for visually impaired with all assistive devices and ICT software and can also apply for ADIP schemes to gets appliances from GOI.
4. Language and Mode of Communication

a. Student with Blindness: Braille & tactile embossed notes, reading material is required.
b. Low Vision: Colour contrast and Texture Contrast is required with clear instructions for understanding, font changes required, Blind Students: visual auditory and tactile mode of communication.
c. Learning Disability: Integrated & multi-sensory stimulation is required for quality learning, films, PPT, audiovisual logic are modes of communication.
d. Student with Deafness: PPT, visual & sign language

mode of communication is to be used since they understand through pictorial logic

e. Cross Disability Issues: A students with blindness with student with deafness and hence accessible assistive devices and software with ICT are required.

f. Research and Data Collection accessibility: Software SPSS for quantitative data analysis is not accessible for student with blindness which discourages them to take quantitative research; Hence research scribes shall be allotted for research and data analysis

g. Exams/Entrance Exam and Online tests in accessible format with extra 20 minutes per hour. For scribe arrangement scribe guidelines shall be followed. Scribe shall be arranged by colleges and scribe list shall be put up on university notice board and website. Remuneration for scribes shall be given by university.

4. Academic Resources and Services

1. Academic resource (books, journals, class notes) in accessible format.
2. Exams with proper scribe arrangement.
3. Accessible Exam Hall and accessible furniture.
4. Accessible question paper and options with understanding of specific needs. Exams/ Entrance Exam and Online tests in accessible format with extra 20 minutes per hour. Scribe arrangement Scribe guidelines shall be followed. Scribe shall be arranged by colleges and scribe list shall be put up on university notice board and website, Remuneration for scribes shall be given by university.
5. Academic Resources and Need based Curriculum: books, curriculum and assessment patterns for addressing the needs of students with disability are required.
6. The schemes for students with disability in higher education are as follows:

1. HEPSN scheme
2. TEPSE scheme
3. Equal Opportunity Cell
4. Scholarship as per government of India
5. Rajiv Gandhi fellowships and overseas fellowships.

5. *Attitude*

1. Preparing Films, Programs on Students with Disability and Creative Art based Sensitization program for Teachers, Staff and Peers for being sensitive to the needs of students with disability and treating them with dignity.
2. Access-ability events, Celebration of World Disability Day every year and acknowledging staff and students with disability of college.
3. Disability Etiquettes: 1. Treating with Dignity, 2. Communicate naturally, 3. No Stare please, 4. Sharing openly, 5. Dialogue to discover, 6. Infinite capability 7. Positive attitude

6. *Academic Teaching Pedagogies*

1. Need based Pedagogies with inclusion of PWD and in accessible format.
   a. Students with Learning Disability benefits from Audio visual form of learning. Films and creative art based assignments aid in their learning.
   b. Students with Deafness or Speech and Hearing Disability requires visual text/soft copy of all lectures in advance. Sign language interpreter is must for students with deafness in everyday contact classes. Compendiums of each subjects with descriptive simple language and pictorial diagram's is required. Question paper in simple language with diagrams is helpful. For conceptual understanding, Visual aids films, pictorial lectures in diagram logic is useful. Teacher has to take efforts to create pictorial/visual diagrams of

abstract concepts.

   c. Students with Low Vision: PPT, Increased space on board, bigger font e-notes and e-books is required.
   d. Persons with Blindness require Audio recorded lectures, Embossed diagrams, Auditory and Tactile aids, transcribed notes, use of screen reading software, Apps, ICT devices
2. Interventions: Individualised Tutorial required to maximize learning as per their learning modality and communication pattern(verbal, nonverbal or sign language). Specific interventions during exams as question paper in accessible format/simple language so that students with deafness can comprehend adequately.
3. Access to Exam, assignment and Class Presentation: Teaching, learning and exam paper in accessible format and easy to understand with adequate options.
4. Teaching learning material(TLM)
   a. Students with Hearing impairment/deafness may requires sign language interpreters, PPT with captions and visual stimuli.
   b. Students with Low Vision required reading material in colour contrast (yellow and black), visuals PPT with bigger font 20 size and Arial type.
   c. Students with blindness require TLM in Braille or audio recorded lectures with transcriptions.
   d. Learning Disability: Audio Visual, Film, sensory moving pedagogy.
   e. Students with Mental Illness: Experiential Art, theatre based learning is better.

Exam Specific Recommendations for Students with Disability in Higher Education

Examination Coordination

A. University/College with Equal Opportunity Cell at

college/university level

B. Exam department at college/university level

C. Specific subject Teachers having students with disability at college level

Coordination of above three authorities of higher education to take responsibility of exams services to the Students with disability of the 21 categories as per Bill RPWD 2016. List of student with disability shall be prepared by exam department in advance and answer book shall have symbol of disability for identifying and providing needful services.

1. Provisions and Services for Student with Disability:

1. Distance: The nearest center from residence for the examination shall be provided for the person with disability.
2. Extra Time: shall be given 20 minutes extra for every 1 hour.
3. Technical Need: Question paper in bigger font size (20 font size, Arial font) shall be made available, colour contrast, sufficient light to view at paper for low vision students.
4. Scribe or writer's service.
5. Accessible and computerized examination.
6. Large print.
7. Audio Recordings Questions: Oral answers can be audio recorded mobile or tape recorder and sent by email to examiner.
8. Assistive Devices: Students shall be allowed to use magnifying glass and sketch pen, in the examination.
9. Technology & Software: Zoom software, NVDA, JAWS, talking calculator, Screen magnification software.
10. Exam Notification by Mobile SMS shall be sent to students for seating arrangement.
11. Scribe: It is the responsibility of the university/college to provide a scribe for the student with disability and

the parents should help them in searching for one, if they are aware of any scribe.

12. Diagrams: If the student is unable to draw diagrams properly a substitute question can also be provided.
13. Accessible Aids/Material for Practical Exams: Practical examination for science and technology, psychology, Commerce subjects: provision of accessible material is required, this may be aided by recorded verbal exams/Video exams.
14. Technical: Students with blindness shall use Trailer Frame during the examination.
15. Calculators: Students shall be allowed to use calculators during the examination for complex calculations of accounts, commerce, etc.
16. Technical: Students shall be allowed to use Abacus and Geometrical appliances during examination according to their needs.
17. Software: Students shall be provided a screen reading software–NVDA, JAWs in computer according to student's requirement. Students will have to take permission from the University Examination Board. (College will take responsibility for communication).
18. Option of Audio Recorded Exams: Students shall be provided with audio recorded questions and answers may be recorded.
19. Option of Braille Exam: Option for writing exam in Braille.
20. Braille Exam: If there is Braille exam and marks should not be deducted for mistakes in writing.
21. Alternative Questions: Instead of diagrams, images and maps student shall be given alternative questions.
22. Options in Compulsory Subjects: For those students who are not able to complete compulsory subjects e.g. Maths/Statistics due to their impairment, the exemption to such subject shall be provided.
23. Notice Board: All the instruction shall be put up clearly

on a notice board regarding examination.

24. Accessible Format: Mathematical subject and Computer Science, Economics, Science & Psychology subject questions shall be made in accessible format (visual logical diagrams) and comprehensive.
25. Sign Language: Sign language interpreter shall be provided during exams as per requirement.
26. Scribe: It is the responsibility of the college to arrange appropriate scribe and the parents should help them in searching for one, College should prepare scribe list.
27. Accessible Examination Hall: Separate exam hall or shall be accessible with accessible furniture.
28. Associated Disability: Student with associated / multiple disabilities shall be permitted to take a scribe to type or to write or to write some part of paper. This scribe should be selected carefully and S/he shall be able to understand & comprehend these students language.
29. Serious Medical Emergency: In case of Medical Episode or long term hospitalization the year shall not get wasted but alternative exam arrangements would be made.

IX. Need for Inclusive Dialogue

Inclusive Dialogue:

There is a requirement of a dialogue in all academic disciplines on the issue of disability and enabling an inclusive education among all students and promoting equal access for students with disability in higher education. The dialogue among key stakeholder i.e. teacher, staff, student and peers should be held to experience the interface with disability. This is a journey towards creating a space for understanding and accepting disability with its unique similarity and initiating process of coming together towards social cohesion and inclusion. This dialogue aims towards developing an academically flexible and multisensory learning environment for equal participation of student with disability at classroom level for creating inclusive environment. This process of change among various disciplines stakeholders may enhance interdisciplinary and transdisciplinary academic development reinforcing inclusive culture in higher education.

Inclusion Code: The inclusion code is 'lived experiences in embodiment/within body' of person with disability. This lived experience can be qualitatively and quantitatively categorized to develop a university level framework in higher education.

Conclusion

There is a need to implement an integrated support system and guideline based on various provisions of International & National level protocols like the UNCRPD, the PWD Act 1995, the National Trust Act 1999, The Marrakesh VIP Treaty, The Biwako Millennium Framework (BMF), the Rights of Persons with Disabilities Act 2016 and the University Grants Commission (UGC) guidelines. There is a need to develop a framework that lays emphasis on accessibility and includes various stakeholders such as peers, teachers, university administration, ICTs, structural changes, and social attitudes which would help create an inclusive and accessible learning experience for students with disabilities. Training and research must be provided for stakeholders on accessibility issues facing persons with disabilities. Understanding individual needs and concerns of student with disability is prerequisite for facilitating inclusion. Article 24, 2(e) UNCRPD recommends individualized support measures for maximizing academic & social development with the goal of full inclusion. Students with disabilities must be recipients of an inclusive education system right from primary to higher education level with the view of developing their talents, creativity and skills while affirming their sense of confidence, dignity and self-esteem. While also sensitizing stakeholders in the field of higher education towards the needs of students with disabilities and ensure continued commitment towards conducting Inclusion Audits (audit by insiders: including students with disability of the campus are involved in mapping physical and social barriers for developing guidelines to create disabled friendly environment at university level) and Access Audits (audit done by diverse persons with disability and experts to identify barriers in architecture and institution).

The next step would be to ensure that admission procedures and educational material required by such students with disabilities are made in accessible formats and multimodal methods of teaching & learning are employed in general educational settings along with other students. The same process must be followed at the time of examinations, research, field trips and dissertations.

Taking steps at university level for students with disabilities on accessibility and inclusion based issues is possible by conducting through needs assessment which means identifying individual needs of the students with disabilities under general/ everyday issues and subject specific issues. This can be quantitatively and qualitatively categorized to find out possibility of bridging gaps in teaching and learning till they obtain their degrees. Guidelines needs to be developed for teachers and peers regarding Students with disabilities and work towards designing class notes, lectures and curricular taking into account 21 categories of students with disability and initiate basic idea of universal design required to ease the curriculum for their better adaptability, accessibility and initiating inclusion.

Students with disability are profound resource to the country to bring out policy level changes towards inclusion of disability issues in higher education. Continuing this dialogue and facilitate it in all academic disciplines & enabling an inclusive education among all students with and without disability.

Also the dialogue among key stakeholder i.e. teacher, staff, student and peers to experience the interface with disability that aims at developing an academically flexible and multisensory learning environment promoting equal participation of student with disability at academic level. This process will bring an insight building change in all stakeholders of various disciplines may enhance interdisciplinary and transdisciplinary development towards including disability studies and newer disciplines. The consultation with examination authorities and academic stakeholders largely teachers, library and administrative staff will be helpful in developing needs based framework to enable students with disability to learn better. There is a need to start Centre for disability studies in every university and dialogue on disability issues and develop evidence based knowldege and curriculum as subject of importance and initiate bottom up approach at university level using UNCRPD statement nothing about us without all of us for progressive development of students with disability. This aims to promote equal access to higher education among students with disability and valuing their experiences as inclusion code to follow for bridging the gaps in bring about inclusive higher education.

REFERENCES

Albert, B. 2004, The Social Model of Disability, *Human Rights,* Sage Publications.

Alur, M. and Timmons, V. 2009, *Inclusive Education Across Cultures, Crossing Boundaries and Sharing Ideas,* Sage Publications.

Asslaksen, F. 1997, *Universal Design: Planning and Design for All.* Gladnet Collection.

Avramidis, E., Bayliss, P., and Burden, R. 2000, A Survey into Mainstream Teachers' Attitudes Towards the Inclusion of Children with Special Educational Needs in the Ordinary School in One Local Education Authority, *Educational Psychology,* 20(2), 191-121.

Beckett, A.E. 2008, "Challenging Disabling Attitudes, Building an Inclusive Society": Considering the Role of Education in Encouraging Non-disabled Children to Develop Positive Attitudes Towards Disabled People, *British Journal of Sociology of Education,* 30 (3), 317-329.

Burte, H. 2008, *Space for Engagement: The Indian Art Place and a*

Habitational Approach to Architecture. Calcutta: Seagull Books.

De-Valenzuela JS, Connery MC and Musanti SI, 2000, The Theoretical Foundations of Professional Development in Special Education. *Remedial Spec. Educ.* 21(2):111-120.

Grenot-Scheyer, M., Staub, D., Peck, C.A. & Schwartz, I.S. 1998, Reciprocity and Friendships: Listening to the Voices of Children and Youth With and Without Disabilities. In L.H. Meyer, H.S. Park, M Grenot-Scheyer, I.S. Schwartz & B. Harry (eds.), Making Friends: The Influences of Culture and Development, (pp. 149-167), Baltimore, MD: Paul H. Brookes.

Gupta, Asha, 2005, "Judicialization of Education: The Fee Cut Controversy in India." *International Higher Education* 38, Winter.

Kayess, R., and French, P. 2008, Out of Darkness into Light? Introducing the Convention on the Rights of Persons with Disabilities. *Oxford Journals*, 1-34.

Khare, R., Abir, M., and Gaurav, R. 2011, *Universal Design India Principles@ 2011, A Collaborative Process to Design Principles.* (Rep.).

Kolhe Vaishali, 2009, Inclusive Education : A Developmental Policy Addressing Social Exclusion, *Critical Enquiry Journal*, April – June, Vol., Issue-II.

Oliver, M. 1990, *The Politics of Disablement,* MacMillan, London.

Prakash, V. 2011, Concerns About Autonomy and Academic Freedom in Higher Education Institutions. *Economic and Political Weekly* (16), April.

Prakash, V. 2007, Trends in Growth and Financing of Higher Education in India. *Economic and Political Weekly* 42(31).

Rose R. and Cole, C. 2002, Special and Mainstream School Collaboration for the Promotion of Inclusion, *Journal of Research in Special Educational Needs,* 2(2): 1-17.

Sharma, M. 2012, Revisiting the Dialogue of Inclusive Education: The Indian Course, *Mainstream,* Vol. L, No. 19.

Singal, N. 2007, Inclusive Education in India: International Concept, National Interpretation, *International Journal of Disability, Development and Education.*

Triliva, S., Anagnostopoulou, T., Hatzinikolao, S., Chimienti, G., and Mastorakou, A. 2009, Sensitization of Students to Issues Relating to Disability, *European Journal of Counselling Psychology.*

UGC, 2012, *University Grants Commission Guidelines for Persons with Disabilities Scheme in Universities.* New Delhi, India.

UNCRPD, 2008, *Convention on the Rights of Persons with Disabilities.*

UNESCO. 2014, *Concept note & Programme: ICT & Disability: Pursuing Inclusive Development through Technology,* New Delhi: UNESCO.

UNESCO, 2014, *Concept Note: From Exclusion to Empowerment-Role of ICTs for Persons with Disabilities,* New Delhi: UNESCO.

UNESCO, 2015, *Position Paper on Education Post* -2015, UNESCO.

UNESCO, 2015, *UNESCO Education.* Retrieved July 7, 2015, from UNESCO.ORG: http://www.unesco.org/new/en/education/themes/strengthening-educationsystems/inclusive-education/people-with-disabilities/.

UNESCO-IITE, 2006, *ICTs in Education for People with Special Needs.* Moscow: UNESCO Institute for Information Technologies in Education (IITE).

USOF, 2011, *Concept Paper-Access to ICTs and ICT Enabled Services for Persons with Disabilities in Rural India,* New Delhi: Ministry of Communications & IT, Department of Telecommunications, USOF.

Ved Prakash, 2007, Trends in Growth and Financing of Higher Education in India, *Economic and Political Weekly,* August.

Watkins, A., Tokareva, N., and Turner, M., 2011, ICTs in Education for People with Disabilities, *Review of Innovative Practice.* Moscow: UNESCO, European Agency for Development in Special Needs Education.

WHO, W.B. 2011, *World Report on Disability,* Geneva: WHO.

9

Counter-Hegemonic Assertions of Marginalised Students in University Campuses in India*

Gaurav J. Pathania

Setting the Debate

In the past two decades, student compositions of Indian universities have undergone rapid transformations with the increasing number of students from socially marginalised sections[1]. As more and more students from the lower strata of society access higher education and confront a campus culture that does not reflect theirs, they begin to challenge the dominant ideological activism (both the Left and the Right) that has long existed in campuses. Historically, marginalised students have faced discrimination but have recently raised their voices to challenge various realms of the campus culture which represent the 'dominant' culture for them. These contestations appear in several forms; at the social level, eg opposing all Hindu festivals; at the pedagogical/institutional level, eg highlighting various types of caste discrimination in academic evaluation, and in the process of implementing reservation policy and in representation. The basis of these resistances lies in cultural-

* This is an extended version of the original article published in a SOAS Journal *South Asia Research,* titled "Food Politics and Counter–Hegemonic Assertion in Indian University Campuses", (2016) Vol. 36(2), pp. 261-277.

historic logics. This activism has started new debates about democratic processes in campuses. Hence, the last decade provides substantial evidence to analyse this resistance in university campuses. This chapter presents qualitative data collected from 2009 to 2014 from five major institutions of higher education namely, Jawaharlal Nehru University (JNU), Osmania University (OU), University of Hyderabad (UoH), the English Foreign Language University (EFLU) at Hyderabad and Tata Institute of Social Sciences (TISS). In recent years, these campuses were in the limelight for their student activism.

Higher Education and Marginalisation/Exclusion in India

Constitutionally, India is a secular country. More than 80 per cent population in the country is Hindu and rest are Muslim, Christian, Sikh, Jain, Buddhist etc. Therefore, Indian society in general has a dominant Hindu society. However, the impact of this dominance is visible in every socio-economic sphere of life. Because of the caste system, a large majority of India remained uneducated for centuries and now because of positive discrimination in the Constitution, they have become part of the education system. There exists a cultural gap (between the upper and lower castes) when they enter into the education system as the majority of children learn in their 'social environment' (home and neighbourhood) and what they receive in our classrooms. It affects the process of how a student grasps the knowledge imparted in the classroom. John Ogbu, talking about the American school system argues that black American schoolchildren are handicapped because the home does not provide them with the cultural patterns necessary for the types of learning characteristics of the school and the larger society (Wilson 2003: 453). Further he states that except for black children, all other immigrant students quickly adapt to the 'euro-centric' educational system (ibid 88). Taking a clue from Ogbu, one can easily observe the Indian school system where Dalit students learn things which they do not experience in their home environment. Explaining the culture-of-poverty argument in the case of India, inequality in access to education[2], as Thorat (2004: 47) pointed out, is a core feature of the caste system. To him, the problem Dalits encounter relates to the curriculum and courses in the higher educational institutes. We also do not make use of writers who have developed a body of knowledge based on the local realities; therefore, individuals such as Ambedkar, Phule and others do not have a place in our educational system. While explaining the same situation, he raised a point on Dalits' behalf that 'Scheduled castes face problems in the curriculum and courses... as they are unable to relate themselves to what they study. The courses do not reflect the life experiences of the society in which they live'. Rather, they are exposed only to the dominant ideological traditions of specific disciplines rather than evolving Indian realities. According to Gramsci, education is not a matter of handing out 'encyclopaedic knowledge' but of developing and disciplining the awareness which the learner already possesses[3] (Forgacs 2014: 54).

Even within schools, the emphasis upon the stratification of knowledge may promote interests in certain subjects or groupings at the expense of others. By the time marginalised/ Dalit students enter into the university system, they unconsciously absorb information which has no practical relevance in their life. In other words, our (the Indian) university system does not offer any critical tool to understand our own social behaviour. Thus, there has been a tendency, according to Bernstein, to view the structuring of knowledge in schools in isolation from other symbolic arrangements of society (1975: 169). Moreover, as the Indian education system is highly stratified or layered, the absence of transparency in higher education and the nexus of networks of exclusion operate formally and informally on campuses to reproduce caste inequalities in the metropolitan university (Rege 2010: 89). Rege further argues that universities and other centres of higher learning have become the cockpits for caste, regional and linguistic conflict and intrigue (ibid 90). Therefore, universities can be understood as sites of struggle, of 'both domination and contestation'.

The cultural hegemony has over the years precipitated several major counter-cultural movements among Dalits. There have been various movements to counter the dominant culture, ie 'Hindutava' in the nineteenth and twentieth centuries. Jyoti Rao Phule and later B R Ambedkar have been two important figures who offered a counter-Hindutava force. In South India, Periyar, Narayana Guru and many others continued their resistance against socio-religious practices of Hinduism in an anti-Dravidian movement. To counter Hindutva would, according to Thirumaavalavan, be (towards) an annihilation of caste. Thirumaavalavan (2004: 6) argues that Hindutva and casteism entered into our arts and culture assumed different forms. These movements are significant attempts to bring Ambedkar's ideas to the forefront. The subsequent inclusion of Ambedkar in the university syllabus gave birth to a countervailing struggle to transcend Hinduism. It is in this context that the paper locates the evolution of an intellectual Dalit tradition in Indian university campuses.

How University Becomes a Space for the Hegemonic Culture

The 'dominant' campus culture is usually the culture of socially powerful groups (that need not be the culture of the majority of people). This dominant culture receives support and legitimacy from social institutions that constitute the major belief system (Andersen and Taylor 2013: 35). This culture is the standard by which the other cultures are judged and thus, projected as the 'popular culture'. This projection leads to the 'marginalisation' of other cultures. The process of marginalisation occurs at the institutional level. Thus, in the process of transmitting knowledge in any institution, whether it is family, religion or education, society is governed by the 'popular culture'. In this way, a cultural hegemony is maintained. In his theory of 'cultural hegemony', Gramsci is concerned with the question of force. Hegemony, he believes, is a more sensitive and therefore more critical term than 'domination', which fails to acknowledge the active role of subordinate people in the operation of power. Gramsci made a few points to explain hegemony: first, hegemonic ideology is formed as a constellation of interests of ruling classes; second, it accommodates specificities of historical and cultural living of subaltern classes; third, hegemony cannot be established at once—it must be established gradually through struggles of different kinds; fourth, hegemonic ideology is hegemonic only when it depends on common sense. Hegemony solicits the active consent of subaltern classes and thus maintains the domination of ruling classes. Thus, hegemony maintains the domination over subaltern classes with the aid of their active consent. That is why Gramsci calls hegemony as domination with consent[4]. Hegemony is not to be confused with domination or with consent manufacturing consciousness.

Gramsci posits that every relationship of 'hegemony' is necessarily an educational relationship (Gramsci, 1971: 350); he argues that 'everybody is already cultured but in a primordial and undisciplined' manner. Therefore, for Gramsci, hegemony is always contested; it is only ever a temporary resolution of a continual conflict[5]. As a result, counter-hegemony[6] begins with a resolution of common sense in contradiction. The construction of counter-hegemony involves two steps: one, determination of the truth-content from these transvalued universals by a symptomatic reading, ie, there is a coming back from the displaced universal to its original point; two, movement towards a higher moment of the universal. In other words, false consciousness cannot hide the truth; it reveals the truth. Semmes (1992: 1) defines cultural hegemony as the systematic negation of one culture by another for the purpose of manipulation and control (also at 1992: 47).

Counter-hegemony is a qualitative extension of the signs of the displaced hegemonic power that reveals the true position of the elite, from which follows counter-hegemony as a leap (Chaudhuri 1998: 19). Gramsci highlights that the fundamental impetus behind cultural hegemony is the historical phenomenon of Hindu culture based on structural hierarchy that rationalises the supremacy of caste Hindus and exploitation of lower castes. Hegemony simultaneously constitutes a critical consciousness[7], doesn't it?

Sociology of Food

Food is an important element in maintaining the caste hegemony in India. Food is part of our socio-cultural life (Bourdieu, 1986). Similarly, eating is a familiar act because it is universal, but it is also a formal act because there are social expectations around consumption that vary by culture and context. According to Levi Strauss (2008), food can be considered a symbolic text. Levi Strauss articulates the more specific, linguistically based, semiotic processes for using food as text for sending other types of messages. These messages might be about personal, cultural and social identity. Levi Strauss suggests that food—the making of it, the presentation of it, sharing of it, and even disposal of it, in contexts where food is not expected—carries significant social meaning that can be denuded or denigrated when forced or taken up in official ways.

The dominant culture, ie 'Hindu culture', as mentioned earlier, has captured the public sphere of Indian society. In Hinduism, food has been linked with the concept of purity and pollution and the way it has been consumed. Thus, it has a caste character to it. 'purity'/'pollution' is one of the key characteristics that maintains the caste system. According to Hindu religious text, any 'beef' product should not be consumed publically[8]as the cow is considered the holiest animal on earth. Thus, Hindus refer to it as *gau mata* (mother cow) and holy cow. Similarly, Hindu texts have defined particular types of food for every caste. Even types of cooked and raw food have been specified caste-wise.

The priest castes, Brahmins form the top of the caste hierarchy. Brahmin castes have a completely different food culture than the lower castes. According to ancient Hindu texts, lower castes were supposed to survive on the left-over food from the upper castes or they were given rotten meat. The style of cooking and the consumption of raw food is also decided. Hence, it is not just a matter of 'beef and pork' consumption; in fact, everything which is consumed publically is controlled by the dominant culture. In other words, lower castes were not allowed to consume any healthy or fresh food. If they violated this practice they would be often face violent punishment by upper castes.

On 2 April 1936, a report appeared in the newspapers that an untouchable of Chakwara village, who had returned from a pilgrimage, had arranged to give a dinner to his fellow untouchables of the village as an act of religious piety. The host desired to treat the guests to a sumptuous meal and the items served included *ghee* (butter). But while the assembly of untouchables was engaged in partaking of the food, the Hindus in the hundreds, rushed to the scene armed with lathis, despoiled the food and attacked the untouchables who left the food they were served with and ran for their lives. Quoting this event, Dr Ambedkar argues:

> The Hindus of Chakwara village thought otherwise and in righteous indignation avenged themselves for the wrong done to them by the untouchables, who insulted them by treating ghee as an item of their food which they ought to have known could not be theirs, consistently with the dignity of the Hindus. This means that an untouchable must not use ghee even if he can afford to buy it, since it is an act of arrogance towards Hindus. (Ambedkar 2000: 7) [9]

Since the beginning, the aim of the Dalit movement in India has been focused on the demand for equal access to public spaces. Ambedkar, the leader of untouchables started a temple entry movement as a symbolic struggle to ensure universal access to public spaces. According to Omvedt (2004: 21) 'Dalits, since at least the nineteenth century, have fought for education, for wastelands for cultivation, for temple entry and above all, for access to public spaces and the use of roads and public transport'. Similary, the Mahad Satyagraha for water rights for Dalits in 1927, under the leadership of Anantrao Chitre and Dr Ambedkar, marked the new beginning of Dalit battles against the caste Hindu society and its non-egalitarian culture.

This hegemony over food does not diminish even in the time of globalisation which offers countless choices to India, the world's largest democracy. However, globalisation in India, according to a sociologist and social activist G. Aloysius, claims that Indian has not seen globalisation yet: 'You go to any McDonald store in India; you cannot get a hamburger. Because the dominant culture ie Hindu culture of this country has controlled our dietary habits.'[10] 'Aloysius' concern is valid if we talk about the basic principle of right and choice of food in a democratic country. What globalisation does is that it offers us all the choices across geography. But how (or why) does a popular global brand such as McDonald's change its policy (menu) according to the existing hegemonic culture? Interestingly, McDonald's, known globally for its hamburgers, has opened vegetarian stores in Jammu and Amritsar- religious pilgrimages of Hindus and Sikhs. 'Hindutva forces want to welcome economic globalization but do not want to have anything to do with the process of cultural globalization' explains Illaiah (2007: 138). He raises a critical question that 'Hindutava organisations do not ask why the buffalo, that gives us most of our milk, is not sacred'. Thus, finally the question finds its answer in the purity-pollution debates. Dalit student activism in Indian campuses raises a number of questions around this dominant/hegemonic culture which decides the food menu of every university hostel. This is also a critical question for the existence of 'critical education' which Giroux and others suggest in their writings.

Hegemony and Food Politics on Campus

The majority of campuses in India offer a vegetarian menu, especially in North India. Non-vegetarian is limited to chicken and mutton dishes. As a matter of fact, the majority of the population from North-East India (consisting of seven states) and South Indian states consume pork and beef as part of their diet. Similarly, the majority of South Indian Dalit students prefer beef over other types of meat.[11] Students from these states are scattered all over India in various universities. Yet in the hostel they do not have access to the kind of food which they eat at home. Ignoring food diversity, an exclusive preference of a particular variety of food, identified with a specific culture, especially on the occasion of the cultural festival of a university, is a marker of hegemony of a specific culture over the plural cultural terrain of the campus. In 1997, when the hostel mess secretary of EFLU decided to serve beef in the hostel, this move was welcomed by a significant group of students (including Bengalis, Malayalis, Muslims, Christians and a handful of Dalit students). With their non-traditional activism, Dalit students' methods of criticising the national iconic figure provoked the upper castes. At times, this activism resulted in campus fights whereby police cases were registered against the students. Serious debates around 'culture', 'food habits' and 'purity-impurity' erupted in campuses as well as social media.

As a step towards equality in representation, the Dalit Students Union at HCU in 2006 demanded that it should be allowed to set up a beef stall in the annual food festival celebrated by the university known as *Sukoon*. It was argued that beef constitutes an important part of the food habits of Dalits and is thus part and parcel of Dalit culture. Besides, such food culture is equally shared by Muslims and a few others from caste Hindu cultural backgrounds. The university administration, the executive body of the university, was 'irritated', to quote one of the Dalit Students Union delegates, by this request. It instantly denied permission for the stall on the grounds that 'consumption of beef... (in the campus) creates caste and communal tensions' (Gundimeda 2009: 131).

In 2010, in JNU, a new group called *The New Materialist* (TNM) was formed by Dalits, Tribal, Backwards and left-leaning students. The group is based on the ideologies of Marx, Periyar and Ambedkar. With its aim to fight against caste, it brought up a demand to include beef and pork in the food served in the canteens at JNU. According to the members of TNM, the university campus, dominated by the left-aligned organisations and ideology is Brahminical in nature. This group organised various talks and debates on food culture[12]. Another joint forum 'Committee for the Democratic Right to Choice of Food' was formed where TNM played a major role. In 2012 they issues a pamphlet regarding organising a beef festival on 17 September

2012 in the campus in the occasion of Saheed Bhagat Singh's Birth Anniversary. This was opposed by the ABVP and many right wing organisations in Delhi.[13] Finally, to control the situation, the university administration rusticated one student who was leading the agitation. Pamphlets pasted on campus by the local police warned of the illegality of consuming beef in Delhi; thus the programme was cancelled.

An event of open beef cooking was organised by students of EFLU in 2012. The pamphlet[14]regarding this event states, 'Democracy in EFLU by the Brahmins, of the Brahmins and for the Brahmins'. According to them, the 'tabooisation of non-vegetarianism, and beef eating in particular, is part of a process of cultural and food fascism promulgated by the Brahmanical castes, who only want their vegetarian diet as the idealised diet'. This event was disrupted by students opposing it who resorted to stone pelting and vandalisation of the food prepared. According to the activists, 'as long as the university spaces were dominated by the upper caste, their culture was hegemonic in all aspects of university life, including the kind of food that was served in hostels.' Most of these activists argue that 'beef is the cheapest and most nutritious food available for Dalits'. A large number of students frequent Kalyani Biryani hotels, located in the pockets of Hyderabad and Secunderabad and they buy beef to cook in their rooms.

However, the case of Osmania University in Hyderabad was unprecedented. In 2012 a 'beef festival' organised by Dalit and leftist student groups in the campus[15] was quite an unprecedented affair. This was perhaps the first time that Osmania students raised their voice in favour of beef eating. Beef was cooked together by the students in front of the Dr. B R Ambedkar New Research Scholars' Hostel (known as NRS). What was striking was that most political formations did not know how to react to this 'festival'. ABVP tried to oppose but their effort was in vain. Outside of the networks of Dalit activism there do not seem to be many takers for what these groups call a movement against 'Food Fascism' (*EPW* 2012: 8).

This is the first time in the history of modern India that a political challenge was thrown, apparently with some success, to the Hindutava politics around the cow. News reports suggest that Osmania University's beef festival has become something that has set a precedent and plans are now afoot in various parts of the country to organise such beef and/or meat festivals to highlight 'non brahmanical' food traditions (*EPW* 2012: 8).

Dalit and other student unions criticised the university administration: how does beef consumption create caste and communal tensions? Beef is consumed outside the university campus as well, and does not appear to create such tensions between the consumers and non-consumers of beef. The administration's rejection of a beef stall was taken as a rejection of Dalit culture by the Dalit Students Union, which organised a number of protests against the decision and led an untiring campaign among the students. Its determined efforts divided students into two diametrically opposed groups, one supporting the installation of the stall and the other opposing it. 'Beef after fish, is the most consumed meat in India. Beef and pork are the integral dietary components of more than 40 per cent of India's population, particularly of India's marginalised communities[16].' Why is the public trying to maintain 'vegetarian hegemony[17]'?

A similar story was repeated (played out) in 2014 at the Tata Institute of Social Sciences (TISS) where students demanded the inclusion of beef and pork in the hostel food menu. It even became an important issue in the students' union elections. They claimed that beef and pork are staple foods of Dalits and tribes, especially of the North Eastern tribal communities in campus. According to Dalit and tribal students, the 'intention is not to create a divide but to make a campus more inclusive wherein everybody's cultural dimensions, including their food habits, will be respected and understood in the larger context of the country's diversity and civility'.[18] Eventually the beef debate turned into a 'cow-buffalo' debate. In these meetings Professor Kancha Illaiah was invited to speak. In his words, the buffalo is portrayed in Hindu iconography as the bearer of the God of Death, and as the demon killed by the Goddess Durga as the behest of Rama (Illaiah xxxi 2007). Buffalo is used in all Asian countries as a source of both milk and meat. Indian nationalism has to be built on the buffalo, which is exclusively Indian (Illaiah xxxi 2007).

In all these instances, the word 'brahminical' is used for the conventional diet and also for the institutional practices. Today, caste is often represented as a matter of cultural identity and community rather than inherited status and inequality (Gupta 2002). Those who are part of the activism highlight their ideology which connects them with their 'common' historical experience of discrimination and deprivation. According to Gramsci (1971) the dominant class maintains its position through the oppressed class's consent. This consent is achieved through hegemony. This cultural life includes some festivals, symbols and rituals where the centrality of the authority exists. Rituals have always been a crucial site of struggle, involving both claims about authority and struggle against (within) it. Rituals may be part of everyday life, but are fundamentally opposed to 'the everyday' (Haynes and Prakash 1991: 227) part. According to Dirks, ritual practice is genuinely dangerous and already has an element of subversiveness[19]; which has also to do with the politics of representation and misrepresentation (Dirks: 235).

Thus, the students started changing their attitude not just towards food but towards all other elements of campus life such as celebrating festivals and organising poojas, etc. In the past years in university campuses, rituals turned out to be a core arena of resistance by Dalit and OBC students (ibid. [Dirks] 228). These symbolic struggles against the existing discourse ie Hinduism. By opposing Durga Puja in campus, Dalit students raised a debate on the university as a secular institution. They call it a 'Hindu-ideology' which works through state power and every educational institution that reproduces it.

In 2013, OU organised a rally to pay homage to Naraka Shoora, who according to the students, was a great Dravidian warrior who was killed by Aryan invaders. EFLU Dalit students in 2013 questioned the Onam festival celebration on campus. 'Dalits and Adivasis work from dawn till dusk to fill your granary. Why should we celebrate your harvest festivals when it always left us landless, poor and deprived'?[20] To counter Onam, students highlighted Phule's story of 'Bali-Vamana' from his book Gulamgiri.

Joshi and Josh (1992: 79-80) argue that perhaps all power is cultural-ideological (1992: 80). In this process, Dalit students have challenged the dominant rituals and festivals which are part of Indian consciousness. In 1991, the first cultural group called UDSF emerged on campus and started celebrating Bheem Saptah (one week celebration to honour Dr Ambedkar). This practice was extended to include other historical figures from marginalised sections such as Jyoti Rao Phule, EV Ramsamy Periyar Naikar, Shahuji Mahraj, Birsa Munda, Mahatama Ayyankali, Sant Gadge Baba, Sant Ravidas, Sant Kabir and Gautam Buddha. Recently they have added Babu Jagdeo Kushwaha (Famous as Bihar Lenin). Other campuses followed suit. In the past decade, their voices are echoing a radical tone. To counter Mahatama Gandhi, the Father of Nation, they project Jyoti Rao Phule as the Father of Nation. They renamed Savitribai Phule as Krantijyoti Savitribai Phule (The flame of revolution) and celebrate her birthday as National Teachers' day and as Women's Liberation Day on 3 January.[21] Dalit voices aggressively and passionately advocate their appreciation for Savitribai. In Indian history, Savitribai Phule is the most celebrated ideal female leader for the depressed and backward majority masses. According to one respondent:

> It is the conspiracy of Manuvadi/Brahmanical ideals to keep the contribution of Savitribai Phule under the carpet so that the depressed and backward masses should not get enlightened and they remain mental slaves by worshipping unqualified Saraswati as a source of education. If this is not so, then where did she study? Why does Saraswati never speak even about the need to give education to women? How is it that the so-called source of education herself is an illiterate woman! In the real sense, the contribution of Saraswati-Vidya ki Devi (Goddess of Education) is nothing, and it is a pity that our educated student community follows it blindly!

In the education system, similarly other mythical characters such as Rama, Pandavas, have been projected as symbols of 'morality', 'humility', 'sacrifice', 'dedication', and 'peace', etc. In other words, marginalised students on campus raise their voice against the customary practices and they provide other ways to define these customs. Generally, in any society, deviation from a set of customary behaviours, is considered moral transgression. To challenge this, EFLU, Hyderabad students started 'Asura Week' in October 2013 to counter the Ganesh Chaturthi. They created a Facebook page, 'Asrua week at EFLU' and each day a group of Dalit, OBCs and Muslims and a few upper caste students painted their faces as Ravana, Hidimba, Shoorpnakha, Ghatotkach, Mahishasura, Baliraja, Mahabali, Hidmba, Shoorpanakha, etc as lower caste ideals. Various competitions were held for a week including painting, making slogans and drawing Rangoli in the name of mythical characters which are projected negatively in our society. This act inspired the Dalit-Tribals and Backward students at Osmania who came out with a pamphlet criticising the celebration of 'Vinayak Chaturthi/ Ganesha festival' in the name of 'liberal space of the campus'. This resulted in tension among the Hindu groups like ABVP who complained to the police. Some students were arrested and released after a few days. The author observed during these arrest police people asking the students: 'How would you family feel when they would know that their son wants to become Ravana?' and 'How can you be anti-social as a university student?' Durkheim (1961: 28) suggests that whoever resists the customary, runs the risk of defying morality. Further, he explains that the ideas of discipline and custom are interlinked. Discipline promotes preference for the customary and it imposes restrictions (ibid: 47). Thus, the counter-culture offered by marginalised students also challenges the notion of being 'moral' in our society. Joshi and Josh (1992: 84) argue that cultural hegemony is a mode of exercising power, which establishes relationship that are 'moral' and creates 'affective' obligation for the subordinated. Therefore, by worshipping negative characters or eating beef, the Dalit movement has a larger agenda to challenge the hegemony as well as the 'morals' and 'values' of the Hindu culture. It also believes in the integrated national development within this discourse. Illaiah explains this:

> The present Dalit-Bahujan struggle is to undo that structural process of underdevelopment. For that we need to change the philosophy of caste, colour, language, land, animals, birds, food and so on. We must deploy symbols that have opposite and corrective meanings, ideology and philosophy to that of Hindu Brahmanism. That is where the survival of this nation lies (Illaiah xxxi 2007).

Therefore, it is not just about food politics, but their movement is connected with the broader aspects where Dalits are entering into business, management, industries and offering employment to other Dalits business and also in terms of collective consciousness.[22] In this process of countering hegemony, language is another issue. Interestingly, Hindu culture which is preserved through Hindi and Sanskrit language need to be countered only with English language. Going beyond their local/regional languages, Dalit activism opts for 'English' language as the only way to liberate. Osmania University students celebrate the birthday of one of their activist professors as *Dalit-Bahujan English Education Day*. This would probably be the 'new' voices looking for an alternative to compete with the upper caste in education. In other words, the Dalit movement is realising that their pathways to the global knowledge goes via English.

This activism, in other words, offers a critical education, which exists beyond classrooms. The meaning of democracy is linked with their own life-world. Giroux defines democracy as the 'lived experience of empowerment of the majority' (1997: 268). This lived experience has a history of discrimination, exclusion, marginalisation and humiliation which exist with the identity of a Dalit. The negation of an identity shall be accompanied by retrieving our lost identities. And the most democratic of all our identities are our ethnic identities

(Thirumaavalavan 2004: 232). Instead of evolving into a people's movement, the Tamil movement became stagnated in opposing the hegemony of Sanskrit. The fundamental reason for this stagnation, according to Thirumaavalavan, was because they took up the opposition of Brahmanism and Sanskrit instead of dropping the Hindutava lifestyle (Thirumaavalavan 2004: 237). Lifestyle here means the way of living, dressing and consuming food etc. What Thirumavalan is suggesting is that this process should go in tandem because lifestyle itself can be a form of resistance. In case of Dalit student activism, there has been a limitation as they functioned within the framework of Hindu structure, unlike Ambedkar who rejected the entire structure and just focused on Hinduism. He did not demystify myths of Hinduism. There Dalit students' use of Ambedkar ideology consists of a lot of ambiguities. However, one cannot reach the conclusion about what exactly this ideology meant for them. Though a number of alliances are created in the name of ideology, the fact remains that ideology has been the fluidest (sic) aspect of Dalit politics. Anything could be the ideology if it could be shown to have the approval of Babasaheb Ambedkar (Teltumbde 2011). Thus, the student politics on campuses are in the stage of a struggle between identity and ideology. They are as divided as left parties on campus, and are thus, unable to adopt the larger goal of the ideology.

Conclusion

Academics can no longer retreat into their traditional sites such as the classrooms of universities or symposia as if these were the only public spheres available for engaging with the power of ideas and the relations of power (Giroux 1997: 267). Interestingly, few university campuses in India serve as sites for struggle in general and rise of the new forms of struggle with age-old issues in the campuses for over decades. The claim of the lower caste students on campus resulted in tensions for the students who are part of the hegemonic culture. But at the same time, it 'unlearns the undemocratic values and practices' (Thorat 2004) that prevailed in our educational institutions, and were historically rooted in consciousness through school education and are accepted and established as 'common sense'. The 'collective action' as Tarrow would state, becomes contentious when it is used by those people who lack regular access to institutions (Dalits and Backward students), who behave in a way that fundamentally challenge others or authorities. The process of democratising the public sphere of campus raises questions of identity and representation in a more pragmatic manner. Apart from claiming their identity and pride in food practices it was also an open invitation to accept or taste their food as Gundimeda (2009) puts it as 'at least re-assess the value of the denigrated action'.[23]

Secondly, why are the representation and assertion of the Dalit section recognised as 'negative', 'rustic' and 'uncivilised' or 'barbaric' acts by the dominant culture? The answer lies again in the in the notion of hegemony which has the power to convince the masses rather than just limiting it to the notion of 'purity and pollution'. The present Dalit student movement in particular and in general is trying to find its liberation by projecting a culture which ultimately strengthens the dominant culture (Hindu culture) as it draws clear-cut boundaries in the name of food or celebration which are hard to find in practical life in a Dalit life. Ideologically, Dalit student activism paid little attention to conversion to Buddhism (as Ambedkar did) but concentrated more on opposing the ritual aspects of Hinduism. No doubt, this created a critical consciousness among masses. But in a similar fashion, it creates another kind of hegemony as it starts off from the same vantage point of Hinduism. The paper raises the question whether or not we should consider it as part of Ambedkarite ideology which favours the rejection of Hinduism by adopting a whole way of consciousness ie Buddhism[24]. As caste, class and culture are overlapping categories in the present times of globalisation where a large section of lower castes have become part of the mainstream culture or the 'vegetarian hegemony'. Therefore, the views also face lots of reaction within lower caste students as, Gramsci claims that 'hegemony is always a contested process' (Morrow and Torres 1995: 262).

Thirdly, with the student activism, it is also the role of the university intellectuals' education needs to be questioned as whether or not this education is liberating us from the all those prejudices, a set point of view, and a fixed notion of one's identity. Does it empower us enough to question our own historicity and critique our own reality, in what Freire (1970: 453) calls as 'cultural action for conscientisation'.

Fourthly, why have intelligent people/ intellectuals at the universities even after being aware of the caste issues (and they were not intellectually limited or morally atrophied, according to Bowers 1997:13), kept ignoring the caste issue until the lower caste students raised it through their own platforms? This question applies to the already existing dominant left ideology in some of these campuses. Gundimeda (2009) and Pathania (2012) raised a point that in recent years the left parties have changed their original position on caste, and are now supporting caste-based mobilisations for justice. But the larger question we need to ask is that 'why even being a dominant force in campuses like JNU, left politics did not address the question of reservation (especially in faculty recruitment as a medium of maintaining social justice), or opposed *Durga Puja* on campus (or rather celebrating it). In other words, who is responsible for maintaining this upper caste hegemony in campuses.'[25] It is a question to explore why the Left could not take a lead in all those protests/demands for social justice. In fact, the 'politics of giving support' (inside or outside) needs further critical examination. Thus, counter-hegemony is also about exposing the left and the right wing student politics highlighting Ambedkar as the compulsion of their vote bank politics. Another pertinent question for the future would be to see how this counter-hegemony will garner support from the so-called civil society existing on campuses.

REFERENCES

Ambedkar, B.R., 2007. *Annihilation of Caste,* Critical Quest, New Delhi.

Andersen, Margaret L. and Taylor, Howard F (2013) *Sociology: The Essentials*, 7th edition, Califronia Wardsworth Cengage Learning, Belmont.

Apple, Michael W. and King, Nancy R., 1977. 'What Do Schools Teach' in *Curriculum Inquiry*, Vol. 6 (4) 341-358.

Asulkile, Thabit and J.A. Rogers, 2006. The Scholarship of an Organic Intellectual, *The Black Scholar*, Vol. 36 (2/3).

Benei, Veronique, 2001. 'Teaching Nationalism in Maharashtra Schools' in Christopher J. Fuller and Veronique Benei (eds.) *The Everyday State and Society in Modern India*, Hurst & Company, London, 199-222.

Bernstein, Basil, 1975. *Class, Codes and Control, Towards a Theory of Educational Transmission*, Vol. 3, Routledge and Kegan Paul.

Bourdieu, P., 1977. Cultural Reproduction and Social Reproduction In J. Karabe and A.H. Hasley (eds.) *Power and Ideology in Education*, OUP, New York, 487-511.

Bowers, C.A., 1997. *The Culture of Denial: Why the Environmental Movement Needs a Strategy for Reforming Universities and Public Schools*, State University of New York Press, Albany.

Brisson, Luc, 1994. *Plato the Myth Maker*, University of Chicago Press, Chicago.

Castells, M., 1997. *The Power of Identity*, Blackwell, Boston, MA.

Chaudhuri, Ajit, 1998. From Hegemony to Counter-Hegemony: A Journey in a Non-Imaginary Unreal Space, *Economic and Political Weekly*, January 30.

Chopra, Rohit, 2006. 'Global Primordialities: Virtual Identity Politics in Online Hindutva and Online Dalit Discourse', *New Media and Society*, Vol. 8: 187-206

Coben, Diana, 1998. *Radical Heroes: Gramsci, Freire and the Politics of Adult Education*, Garland Publishing Inc., New York.

Coser, Lewis A., 1967. *Continuities in the Study of Social Conflict*, The Free Press, New York.

Delpit, L., 1988. The Silence Dialogue: Power and Pedagogy in Teaching Other People's Children, *Harvard Educational Review*, 58(3) 280-298.

Demetrion, George, 2001. 'Reading Giroux through a Deweyan Lens: Pushing Utopia to the Outer Edge', *Educational Philosophy and Theory*, Vol. 33, No. 1.

Diani, Mario, 2000. Simmel to Rokkan and Beyond: Elements for a Network Theory of (New) Social Movements, *European Journal of Social Theory*, 3, 387-406.

Dirks, Nicholas B., 1991. 'Ritual and Resistance: Subversion as a Social Fact' in Haynes, Douglas and Prakash, Gyan (eds.) *Contesting Power: Resistance and Everyday Social Relations in South Asia,* Oxford University Press, pp. 213-238.

Durkheim, Emile, 1961 [1925], *Moral Education: A Study in the Theory and Application of the Sociology of Education.* New York, Free Press.

Editorials, *Economic and Political Weekly,* Vol. XLVII (17), April 28, 2012, p. 8.

Forgacs, David and Nowell-Smith, Geoffery (2014), *The Gramsci Reader: Selected Writings 1916-1935,* Aakar Books, Delhi.

Foucault, M., 1977. Intellectuals and Power in D.F. Bouchard (ed. & Trans.) *Language, Counter-Memory Practice,* pp. 205-217, Cornell Univeristy Press, Ithaca, NY.

Foucault, M., 1986. *Discipline and Punish: The Birth of the Prison,* Peregrine, Harmondsworth, England.

Friere, Paulo, 1970. 'Cultural Action for Conscientisation' *Harvard Educational Review,* 40 (3). 452-77.

Giroux, Henry A., 1997. *Pedgogy and the Politics of Hope: Theory, Culture and Schooling: A Critical Reader,* Westview Press, USA.

Giroux, Henry A., 2000. *Stealing Innocence: Youth, Corporate Power and the Politics of Culture,* St. Martin Press, New York.

Gramsci, Antonio, 1971. *Selections from the Prison Notebooks,* edited by Quintin Hoare and Geoffrey Nowell Smith, Introduction Publisher, New York.

Gramsci, Antonio, 1995, *Further Selections from the Prison Notebooks,* edited and translated by D. Boothman, University of Minnesota Press, Minneapolis.

Gramsci, Antonio, 1982, *Selection from Cultural Writings,* edited by D. Forgacs and G. Nowell Smith, translated by W. Boelhower, Lawrence and Wishart, London.

Gramsci, Antonio, 1978, *Selection from Political Writings, 1921-26,* translated and edited by Quintin Hoare. Lawrence and Wishart, London.

Gundimeda, Sambaiah, 2009. 'Democratisation of Public Sphere:

The Beef Stall Case in Hyderabad's Sukoon Festival', *South Asia Research*, Vol. 29 (2) 127-149.

Gupta, D., 2000. *Interrogating Caste: Understanding Hierarchy and Difference in Indian Society*, Penguin Books India, New Delhi.

Haynes D. & Prakash, G. (eds), 1991, *Contesting Power: Resistance and Everyday Social Relations in South Asia*. University of California Press, Berkeley.

Ilaiah, Kancha, 2007, *Why I am Not a Hindu*, Samya Publications, Hyderabad.

Jaoul, Nicolas, 2011. 'Casting the Sweepers: Local Politics of Sanskritisation, Caste and Labour' in Daniela Berti, Nicolas Jaoul and Pralay Kanungo (eds.) (2011) *Cultural Entrenchment of Hindutva*, Routledge, New Delhi, pp. 273-306.

Jodhka, Surinder and Murali Dhar, 2003. 'Cow, Caste and Communal Politics', *Economic and Political Weekly*, 38(3): 174-176.

Joshi, Shashi and Josh, Bhagwan, 1992, *Struggle for Hegemony in India*, Sage, New Delhi.

Levi-Strauss, C., 2008. The Culinary Triangle, in C. Counihan and P. Van Estrik (eds.). *Food and Culture: A Reader* (2nd ed.) Routledge, London, pp. 36-43.

Morrow, Raymond Allan and Torres, Carlos Alberto, 1995. *Social Theory and Education: A Critique of Theories of Social and Cultural Reproduction*, State University Press of New York, Albany.

Ogbu Lundy, Garvey F., 2003. The Myth of Oppositional Culure, *Journal of Black Studies*, 450-467.

Omvedt, Gail, 2004, Jyotirao Phule and the Ideology of Social Revolution in India, Critical Quest, New Delhi.

Pathania, Gaurav J., 2011. 'University as a Site for New Social Movements: A Study of Identity-based Student Activism at Jawaharlal Nehru University', Unpublished M. Phil. Dissertation.

Pathania, Gaurav J., 2012. 'JNU Speaks the Language of Lenin: Analysing JNU Student Union Elections', *Mainstrem Weekly*, Vol. L (40) September 22.

Rege, Sharmila, 2010. Education as Trutiya Ratna: Towards Phule-Ambedkarite Feminist Pedagogical Practice, *Economic and Political Weekly*, Vol. XLV (44) October, pp. 88-98.

Ribas, Vanesa and Raj Andrew Ghosal, 2013. States Make Movements, *Sociological Perspective,* Vol. 56 (3) Fall 2013.

Semmes, Clovis E., 1992. *Cultural Hegemony and African American Development,* Praeger, USA.

Stavarianakin, Anna, 2006. 'Call to Arms: The University as a Site of Militarised Capitalism and a Site of Struggle' in *Millennium: Journal of International Studies,* Vol. 35 (1) 139-154, Dec. 1.

Teltumbde, Anand, 2011. The Farce of Bhimshakti and Shivshakti, *Mainstream Weekly,* Vol. XLIX (30), July 16.

The Hindu Bans Non-Vegetarian Food in its Canteen and Dining Hall, Published on 15 April 2014. roundtableindia. co. in (Website accessed on 15 April 2014).

Thirumaavalvan, 2004. *Uproot Hindutva: The Fiery Voice of the Liberation Panthers,* Samya, Kolkata.

Thorat, Sukhdeo, 2004. Marginalised Group and Democratisation of Higher Education in Arun Kumar (ed.) *Challenges Facing Indian Universities,* JNU, New Delhi.

UNESCO 1992. Experts Meeting on the Integration of the International Education into Higher Education, Tunis 21-25 September 1992, Final Report. Newpapers on Higher Education, Meeting Documents, 3.

William, Eric, 1944. *Capitalism and Slavery,* University of Northern Carolina Press, Chapel Hill (Reprint Andre Deutsch, London, 1999), p. 7.

Wilson, James Q., 2003, James Q. Wilson on John Ogbu: Convincing Black Students That Studying Hard is Not 'Acting White', *Journal of Blacks in Higher Education,* Vol. 39, 85-88.

Watkins, E., 1989. *Work Time: English Departments and the Circulation of Cultural Values,* Stanford University Press, Stanford.

NOTES

1. Scheduled Castes, Scheduled Tribes, Other Backward Castes.
2. As a matter of fact, education is an important instrument used by the State to bring about changes among the Scheduled Castes. In 1931, the year in which the government decided to admit 'exterior caste' pupils in aided schools- the literacy rate among SCs was a mere 1.9 per cent. Reaching (Reacting) to this new measure, many schools managed by upper castes were

closed down and caste-Hindus withdrew their children. Broadly speaking, SC pupils have to go through three stages vis-a-vis their entry into schools: 1) admission to the school, without being allowed to enter the classroom; ii) permission to enter the classroom but being kept physically separate and iii) the absence of any visible discrimination. By 1961, the rate of literacy among SCs was 10.27 per cent and by 1991 it had risen to 37.41 per cent. Although theirs was still lower than the general literacy level (24 per cent in 1961 and 52 per cent in 1991), the increase in the literacy level of SCs is commendable, viewed from the baseline from which the change started.

3. David Forgacs (2014) *'Antonio Gramsci Reader: Selected Writings 1916-1935'* Aakar Books, Delhi.
4. Hegemony is not to be confused with domination or with consent manufacturing consciousness.

   Gramsci also pointed out that the ideology of the dominant fundamental group pervades all aspects of civil society, including the law, education, morality and culture in the widest sense and so it is in these areas, as well as in the military field, that the revolution must be waged in order to form a new 'historical bloc'— a bloc between structure and superstructure.
5. Gramsci rejected the simplistic idea of a purely instrumental class state expressive only of the interests of the dominant class (Coben 16).
6. According to the Gramscian point of view, the only way of socialist revolution to take place is for 'organic Intellectuals' to 'organise the cultural life of the people', thus producing a 'counter-hegemony' (Eagleton, 1994).
7. A key element of cultural hegemony is that progress for the subordinated group meant the uncritical assimilation and regurgitation of the (dominant/hegemonic) culture. Creativity, criticism, theorising, theologising – in short, reality construction-were left to the oppressor. Cultural hegemony tends to pre-empt intellectual production and material production; it negates self-development (ibid 3 –David Forgacs).
8. In August 2003, five Dalit men were lynched by a caste Hindu mob in Jhajjar district, Haryana (Jodhka and Dhar, 2003).

9. After Ambedkar, most of the radical thinkers contested the food culture as a part of anti-caste movement. e. g. the popular Socialist leader Jayaparkash Narayan (known as JP) and Lohia both focused on inter-dining and inter-caste marriage (Roti-Beti relationship) to eradicate the caste system. However, their movement was limited to North India.
10. From the interview taken on 10 January 2011.
11. Gundimeda (2009) also highlighted this aspect in his paper on University of Hyderabad.
12. On 20 March, 2012 TNM organised a talk 'The Politics of Food Culture: The Holy Cow and Unholy Swine' organised by The New Materialist at Koyna Hostel Mess Hall.

    On 17 August, 2012, TNM organised a talk 'Why beef and pork food festival in JNU?' at Satluj Hostel.
13. A Facebook retaliation states: If the beef eating party publicly in JNU holds the right to eat and drink without any bar, then we have the right to hit a mad dog with a red hot bullet. One must not be spared to live long.

    To see more: http://hinduexistence. org/2012/09/20/delhi-hc-banned-beef-pork-festival-at-jnu-upon-the-petition-of-rashtriya-goraksha-sena/(website accessed on 14 August 2014). http://hinduexistence. org/2012/09/11/strong-hindu-retaliation-will-curb-the-illegal-beef-party-in-jnu/.
14. 17 March 2012, from a joint pamphlet by TSA, DAMBSA, PDSU, BSF, and TVV.
15. In the Telangana region, although Madigas are one of the socially oppressed and politically powerless castes, they are one of the largest. During elections, their votes can change the fortunes of candidates. One way of gaining support from Madigas, both inside and outside the campus, is backing their caste-based issues.
16. From the poster titled 'Down with Food Fascism: Condemn the Brahmanical EFLU Student's Council' jointly published on 28 Mach 2014 by DAMBSA, TSA, SIO, PDSU and MSF)

    A famous Telangana poetess Gogu Shyamala wrote her poem 'Beef, Our Life, Our Culture' published in Anveshi Broadsheet on 10 May 2013.
17. *Anveshi Broadsheet on Contemporary Poltiics*, Vol. 1 (4) 2013.

18. *Mumbai Mirror*, Saturday 9 August 2014. 'Beef and Pork Politics Divides TISS students'.
19. Part of the subversiveness, according to Dirks, has to do with what we have considered the constant possibility of 'conflict, fission, paralysis, and hermeneutic if not agonistic explosion'.
20. A joint pamphlet published by DAMBSA, TSA, PDSU, BSF, and TVV at EFLU on 15 August 2012.
21. A poster jointly published by DABMSA, TSA, PDSU and SIO on 1 January 2013.
22. To compete with the dominant business association FICCI, they started their own DICCI. They are a global network of businessmen and scholars to support and spread the Ambedkarite movement.
23. Famous Dalit writer Om Prakash Valmiki made a similar claim while commenting on whether Dalits should write autobiographies: 'Every section of society should write their biographies. Do upper castes of India have any idea what happens in lower castes' private sphere and life-world? If we are taught everything about upper castes' lifestyle, culture, festivals and language in our school text-books, then upper caste should also know about us. This is the democratic process of education system'.
24. However, the paper does not intend to suggest that these campus activities are wrong but it questions their ideological stand.
25. In 2009, BSF issues a pamphlet titled 'Pardafassh' (expose) which highlights the almost nil representation of SC/ST/OBC faculties on campus.

10

Exclusion of Dalit Issues in Social Sciences

Vivek Kumar

Introduction

This chapter tries to highlight the exclusionary nature of Indian social sciences with respect to Dalits of Indian society. It is my contention that different social science subjects like, history, economics, political science, sociology, psychology, and to a large extent mainstream Literatures etc have neglected the existential and experiential realities of Dalits. Their icons, movement, labour, world view, their historical evolution etc have been either totally blacked out or partially discussed or erroneously analysed in the annals of Indian social sciences. With regard to erroneous understanding of issues of Dalits, the paper tries to highlight the misunderstanding in understanding the issues of Dalits by the so-called upper caste social scientist with specific examples. The chapter analyses how Indian social scientists commit factual errors while discussing the issues about Dalits in their analyses. Moreover, their subjective analyses have not been able to capture total realities of the structures and processes which affect the Dalit community. In the same vein, this paper records the impact of blackout and erroneous analysis of Dalit issues, in the annals of Indian social sciences, on the psyche of Dalit social scientists. A natural corollary to the main issue discussed in the paper is how objectively Dalits as a category has been conceptualised in the Indian social sciences.

Whether there exists a definition of this category or not? The nature of language used to define and describe this category in Indian social sciences itself underlines exclusion of Dalits in the social sciences. In this context, the paper tries to evaluate how condemnation, stigmatisation and thereby reductionism of Dalits take place within the Indian social sciences.

Apart from discussing exclusion of Dalits from Indian social science discipline, the chapter discusses the causes of the same as to why Dalits have been excluded from the social sciences. If there has been so much exclusion then whether Dalits have been passive recipients of this culture or not? To analyse this question the chapter records the nature and type of academic assertion of Dalits in social sciences. This chapter asks what the characteristics of this academic assertion of Dalits are? We will try to capture these characteristics by analysing how Dalit social scientists have contested the concepts and perspectives through which so-called upper caste social scientists have analysed Indian society. In this context, we will observe in passing how Dalit social scientists have questioned the validity of concepts like – caste, class, village, Hindu social order and *Sanskritisation*. As a part of the academic assertion of Dalits this chapter will probe the merits of the so-called upper castes as analysed by the Dalit social scientists. Can there be an alternative pedagogy of the Dalits social scientists? And whether or not Dalit literature has shown the way to the so-called upper caste social scientists to make Indian social sciences more objective, inclusive and effective? In this context, taking specific clues from the practice of social sciences in the State and Central universities alike, this paper would like to capture the inter-related and inter-connected processes, related to Dalits and their issues in Indian social sciences. On a cursory observation we have found processes like 'Cognitive black out', ,' Forced Availability', 'Pseudo Inclusivity, 'Lack' of Reflexivity', 'Chequered Accessibility' 'Ad-hoc-ism and Optional- ism' and 'Perpetuation of Hegemony'occurring regularly in the disciplines of social sciences in India.

Understanding the Misunderstanding of Dalits

Let us begin with a few examples, which verify empirically the nature of erroneous understanding of the Dalit issues by the so-called upper-caste social scientists. Also we will analyze how this knowledge production hegemonises the minds of Dalits who in turn produce erroneous literature about the Dalits.

In 1999, a high profile university professor, who has extensively worked on issues relating to caste 'after my presentation at a seminar on 'Dalit Identity' asked me, 'What is the difference between Jai Shri Ram and Jai Bheem, as both are religious symbols?' I had to explain to the learned professor that the Jai Bheem which was referred to by me is not the Bheem of Mahabharata rather it is the first name of Bheem Rao Ambedkar which has now become the greeting symbol of Dalits. This was not the only mistake this Professor committed regarding Dalit issues. A few years after this incident I was reading an article written by the same professor published in *The Annual Review of Anthropology* from the UK–This time he committed a number of mistakes in analysing the issues related to Dalits and their icon. The professor wrote, 'In any event, roughly 17 per cent of seats in government educational institutions and in the public sector were reserved for Scheduled Castes'. This is wrong. It is only 15 per cent. The astonishing part is that it is a constitutional provision, then how can he commit such a blunder?

In the same article the same professor committed another blunder. He wrote, 'The Republican Party was founded by the legendary Babasaheb Ambedkar in 1957. He later led his people to reject Hinduism and embrace Buddhism instead.' The fact is that Babasaheb Ambedkar converted to Buddhism on 14 October 1956 and passed away on the 6th of December, 1956. Then how could he establish the Republican Party of India in 1957? The most worrisome aspect of this factual mistake is that the learned professor has quoted Zelliot (1970) to substantiate his point about Babasahebs's conversion and formation of Republican Party of India. I cross checked the fact from the original source Zelliot (1970) which is an article published by her in the volume *Caste in Indian Politics* edited by Rajni Kothari. I found Zelliot (1970) had written something very different. According to her, 'Dr Ambedkar died on December 6, 1956, two months after the conversion movement...The Republican Party was not formally organised until October 1957' (Zelliot 1970: 59). The question is that if a professor can commit such factual mistakes then how should we believe that he would be objective in his analytical description about the Dalits? Let us comprehend the following example to prove our point regarding his objectivity in the subjective description about Dalits.

The professor while quoting Zelliot (1970) in the same article has argued that, 'Ambedkar's conversion was a highly symbolic political act'. However, when I enquired about Zelliot's position I did not get any such fact in Zelliot (1970). After a little more research I came across one of her articles written in 1968 and later on published in her book, 'From Untouchable to Dalit' in 1992. In this article, she has narrated a completely different position with regard to Ambedkar's conversion to Buddhism than what has been quoted by the professor. Her following words are enough to explain to us that how this social scientist has misled readers about the Dalit society and got unknowingly involved in the process of reductionism of a Dalit icon. She has written, 'Those of us who have worked on Buddhist movement are often asked, both from Indians and Westerners; 'Is it just a political stunt'...? Our answers generally take the form of other questions, 'What possible political advantage does conversion offer'? Conversion to Buddhism immediately cuts off...deserving ...Governmental benefits, all those official, political and social privileges afforded by the Government of India to untouchable castes. Ambedkar's delayed conversion came long after the period of combining the conversion idea with political expediency, and by then reference to conversion as a political threat had lost it significance. Instead, it had reference to the great Asian Buddhist world, the reputation of Buddhism as an important religion both in India and the West and the possibility of Buddhism as a moral force' (Zelliot 1992:

195). The question is that how can the learned professor be so selective and hide the full facts delineated by Zelliot (1992)? However, this subjective analysis becomes even more selective if we ask why the aforesaid social scientist did not quote Ambedkar's own version about his religious conversion, which is now readily available to one and all (see Ambedkar 1989: 403-76). In this manner we can observe how Indian social scientists have highlighted only a partial picture of Dalit society in the production of their knowledge.

Some so-called upper caste social scientists have produced an erroneous empirical and subjective analysis of Dalits society and their icons. At the same time a few Dalit social scientists have produced such material that has on the one hand privileged the so-called upper-caste social scientists and on the other hand stigmatised and condemned Dalits in general and Dalit social scientists in particular. In this context the following lines of a political science professor are self-explanatory. According to him, 'In India social... groups like Dalits who did not form part of the organic labour process ultimately failed to develop an intellectual capacity to reflect... generation after generation, they were pushed into occupations that were completely devoid of any possibility of innovation and imagination and hence were not impregnated with any possibility of knowledge'. However, this statement belies all canons of philosophical and empirical explanation of evolution of consciousness, reflexivity, and thereby knowledge among individuals or groups in whatever condition they are forced to live. This can be argued firstly, on the basis of Descartes preposition of possession of critical reasoning by every individual. Secondly, it can be done with the help of Durkhiem's notion of necessity of conceptual ordering of natural and social order for his survival by individuals. And thirdly, no Dalit caste survived exclusively and solely on one and only one occupation.

To begin with what was distinctive about the rationalism of Descartes was the democratic and individualistic form which the demand for rational defence took. At the very start of 'Discourse on Method' he suggests that, 'the power of judging rightly and separating what is true from what is false (which is generally called good reason) is equal by nature in all men'. All men, it follows, have the power to submit any established doctrine to the test of critical reason (Descartes 1964). Further, according to Durkheim, 'Man cannot live among things without forming ideas about them according to which he regulates his behaviour... Some form of conceptual ordering of the natural and social order is indispensable to material and social survival. They tell us of the danger, usefulness, edibility, etc of things...Not only are they within us, but since they are the product of repeated experiences, they are invested with a kind of ascendency and authority, by dint of repetition and the habit which results from it' (Durkheim 1895 (2014: 29-31)). Therefore, it is totally wrong to argue that Dalits were/are devoid of any capability of innovation, imagination and knowledge as it was produced because of practical use and in direct interaction with the natural world. Each, Dalit caste had its own knowledge although it was qualitatively different from upper-caste knowledge. Moreover, no Dalit caste survived on one occupation as most of them were associated with agricultural labour—ploughing, sowing seeds, weeding and harvesting the crops. Most of them still perform these jobs. How can they do all this without reflexivity? Furthermore, they had their own lifeworld, value system, art form, songs, ways of recreation, dietary practices and knowledge of dealing with nature. Why is all this accumulated wisdom not treated as knowledge?

These aforesaid examples highlight the production of erroneous knowledge about the Dalits by the so-called upper caste social scientists and a Dalit social scientist. We will now try to understand the nature of Indian social sciences in India with special reference to Dalits.

Economics and Dalits

The Indian economists on the one hand have failed to record the causes of the relative poverty and inequality between Dalits and the so-called upper castes; on the other they have not taken note of the contribution made by the Dalit labour in running the economy of the country. Akerlof (1976) and Scoville (1991) have argued that caste economy causes an inherent immobility of labour between occupations and creates caste-based segmentation in labour markets. Further, caste system imposes penalties on workers, employers, and customers for violating caste rules for employment, which segregate workers into their specific caste-based occupations. But there are hardly any studies by any Indians scholar in this regard. Moreover, as far as the recognition of contribution of Dalit labour is concerned, from the midwifery role played by Dalit women, who help majority of women to deliver their babies and thereby help the development of next generation, to the landless agricultural labour who help to grow enough food material in the fields to feed the Indian population, all belong to Dalit community. From sweepers and the hide cleaners to factory workers who toil to help the Indian production systems belong to Dalit community. If we quantify the labour of these people then we would not allege that Dalits are professing a selfish agenda. Rather they are contributing much—much more to the State than what they are getting. Why have then Indian economists failed to recognise and record the contribution made by the Dalit labourers in the building and running of the Indian economy?

Moreover, economists have applied the concept of 'class' to measure the economic status of the people in general. In most of the cases, the concept of class is exclusively related to economic and secular educational status of individuals without any association of social aspects like castes and religion although, caste and religion play a dominant role in deciding the economic status of individuals and groups in India. As religion and caste play a dominant role in the establishment of social status of an individual or group it is difficult to analyse the real social status of poor Brahmins and poor Dalits through the concept of 'class'. Though there is a general understanding that all the poor are equal it can be easily argued that the poor of the so-called upper castes and the poor of the so-called lower castes are not equal because of the role played made by religion and caste in the crystallisation of their classes. Hence, we can objectively argue that the causes of poverty of Dalits and upper castes are different and depend on their structural location in the social structure. Then it becomes obvious that structural location of the individuals also decides their various types of-economic, social and political, networks and relationships with the other groups. For instance, a penury stricken Brahmin comes and begs but he possesses the power to bless the donor. On the contrary, a cobbler, belonging to an ex-untouchable caste, who polishes shoes with his labour or a sweeper who cleans the excreta is treated with contempt and usually people throw money at them lest their touch defiles the people belonging to the so-called upper castes. Likewise, the richest of rich industrialists goes and bows at the feet of a poor Brahman priest in Kashi (Varanasi) or Haridwar. Why? It is so because in India only purchasing power does not give you class. Even religion gives you power. Similarly, a Rajput or a Kshtriya landowner will never plough his land even though he is economically broke because he will lose his high caste status. Yes, now with the advent of tractors, things have changed but even now not many Kshatriyas can afford to have tractors. On the contrary a hard working Dalit will not be allowed to open an eatery shop in the countryside even today. This proves the point how caste affects the economic activity in the Indian society. Yet economists on the basis of the argument that, 'economic behaviour was the reflection of a universal individualist psychology rather than of socially constructed institutions' (Wallerstein 1996 et. al: 17) treat all the poor as equal and formulate universal laws and policies for poverty alleviation. The result is that the poor Dalits are left in the lurch while the poor of the so-called upper-castes appropriate all the benefits.

Political Science and Dalit Issues

Political scientists have failed to record and observe objectively the qualitative and quantitative aspects of participation of Dalits in the Indian political spheres. They have failed to record that in political life, Dalits as a group have been most dedicated to democratic processes of Indian polity. From casting their votes for electing a democratic leader to holding a democratic demonstration under the Constitutional rights it is Dalits who respect Indian democracy much more than any other group. This can be argued on the basis of observed reality that they have seldom involved themselves in looting the votes of others (better known as booth capturing) or engineering a defection in other political party(by alluring elected candidates). Secondly, Dalits have themselves revealed that they love constitutional democracy the most because it is a gift of their Babasheb Ambedkar. Babasaheb Ambedkar has given the formula of 'one man one vote and one vote one value' which in turn has given Dalits equality. Today, 'a ruler is born not from the womb of a queen rather he/she is born out of the ballot boxes' they flaunt. Hence the Dalit society, movements and icons have a much larger agenda of nation building through the maintenance of Indian democracy. It is the Dalits who have taken the Indian democracy really close to the masses. In fact they have stopped the Dalit masses from joining hands with Naxal Movements by involving them in the democratic politics. For doing the same, they have formed their own political parties and have also joined the other political parties led and dominated by the so-called upper castes.

It is in this context the political scientists have not been able to understand the basic nature of Dalit politics. They treat Dalits politics as a monolithic whole. That is why they have reduced Dalit politics only to politics of Bahujan Samaj Party or politics of Kanshi Ram and Mayawati. The division of Dalit politics is based on empirical data. The Dalit political leadership and movement can be divided into dependent and independent Dalit political leadership (Kumar 2002). On the one hand the mainstream social scientists have not highlighted the marginalisation of Dalits in the mainstream political parties like Congress and BJP. On the other hand, the contributions of 'independent Dalit leadership' and 'independent Dalit political parties' like Independent Labour Party, Scheduled Castes Federation, Republican Party of India, Dalit Panthers, Bahaujan Samaj Party etc have also been ignored by the mainstream political scientists. However what is noteworthy is that mainstream political scientists have not failed to stigmatize the 'independent Dalit politics' as divisive in nature, spreading the venom of caste division, which is detrimental to the peace and amity of the society. Further, the political scientists have not taken note of limitations of democracy which have proved detrimental for the development of Dalit movement. In the same vein, mainstream social scientists have completely failed to analyse and highlight the positive contributions of 'independent Dalit political parties'. For instance, they have failed to analyse objectively the contributions made by 'Bahujan Samaj Party' (BSP) in the most populated and hierarchically divided state of Indian society that is Uttar Pradesh (UP). How the BSP has broken the political monopoly of the so-called upper castes in the UP politics has been totally neglected. Even when Dalit social scientists have highlighted these positive achievements of BSP (see Kumar 2006) the mainstream social scientists have not even bothered to take note of the same. Those who have done a little analysis a sympathetic, based mostly on secondary sources and hence it is partial. Under this academic type of exclusionary practice one cannot expect an objective analysis of political processes taking place in Indian society.

Sociology and Dalit Issues

Sociology as a discipline has completed a hundred years in India. However, even today the practice of sociology has not incorporated Dalits and their issues effectively like any other subject of social sciences. The most glaring exclusion of Dalits comes to the fore when we analyse the description of basic institutions of Indian society like—caste, village, religion, education, and economy. The Indian sociologists have discussed these institutions without taking into account, how individuals in these institutions have excluded and discriminated against the Dalits. Most of the institutions have been analysed and described with the help of a functionalist perspective. The functionalist perspective only tells us how different parts of an institution combine into the maintenance of the whole. Not even in one institution the unequal power relationship has been analysed by Indian sociologists. The second level of exclusion of Dalit issues occurs when the upper caste sociologists go to the field to collect data. More often than not so-called upper caste sociologists collect data while living in upper caste localities. Their identity and locality in which they stay, for collecting data lead to production of a biased field study. This leads to negative construction of Dalit images. That way the subject matter of sociology is carved out with the centrality of Hindu social order and caste. Dalits, their world view, and movements become marginalised on their own.

It is a well-known fact that Dalits have their own vibrant culture and literature. The Dalits have their own folk songs and dance and art forms but all have been blacked out by the caste Hindu sociologists. Gough has argued that there are differences between the cultures of untouchables and Brahmins. According to her, there is an implied confrontation between the inhibiting 'culture' of the Brahmins and the free 'nature' of the untouchables. Both differ in their attitudes towards sexuality, and aggression towards elders and peers. Engaged in the practical business of earning a living through manual labour, the low castes care more for health and prosperity in this life (Gough 1956: 846). In the same vein, Parvathamma (1978) argues that although occupational change and social mobility are linked, Srinivas in his study does not indicate any mobility for lower castes in the area of occupational mobility. For Dalits, Srinivas has only one mode of mobility that is Sanskritisation which according to her is a concept loaded with Brahmanical mobility. Oommen eloquently portrays the same fact that, 'There has been a cognitive black-out in Indian social science, until recently, as far as knowledge regarding the life-world of *Dalitbahujans*. The fact that the life-styles of upper castes and *Dalitbahujans* vary dramatically in terms of food habits, worship patterns or gender relations is tacitly acknowledged. But instead of squarely recognising these variations and explaining why they exist, the dominant tendency in Indian Sociology, at least until recently, has been to suggest that the *Dalitbahujans* are abandoning their way of life in favour of the life-styles of caste Hindus. This is what Sanskritization is all about. In this perspective, not only the norms and values of caste Hindus are privileged but they are also christened as norm-setters and value-givers for the society as a whole. Conversely, the norms and values of *Dalitbahujans* are knocked out, ignored, stigmatized and de-legitimized' (Oommen 2001: 21).

Further, a good number of studies conducted by Indian sociologists in the post-independence period have only tried to investigate whether constitutional measures have served to reduce the social disabilities or social discrimination of Dalits or not (Beteille 1969; Abbasayulu 1978; Malik 1979). There has not been any quantitative or qualitative analysis of the processes of exclusion and deprivation of the Dalits in Indian society in general and the Hindu social order in particular by the Indian sociologists. They have failed to record the impact of social, economic, and political exploitation on the Dalit communities. No sociologist has bothered to evaluate that how it has resulted in loss of cultural capital and hence the subjugation of Dalits generation after generation. Similarly the mainstream sociologists have failed to evaluate the exclusion of the Dalits from the modern institutions of democracy like judiciary, polity, bureaucracy, industry, academic, civil society (NGOs & INGOs), and media as industry. These institutions should be evaluated with their regional and local offices. Although, it has been accepted by a number of sociologists that the aforesaid modern institutions of democracy have deep anchoring in the traditional social structure of Indian society ie caste (Singh 1994: 129-158). Yet, sociologists have failed to accept that these institutions which were supposed to function on universalistic principles are influenced by particularistic values of caste. These institutions function most of the time on the basis of primordial identities and the so-called upper castes dominate in these institutions. The monopolisation of institutions of governance by the caste Hindus and the marginalisation of Dalits from the same institutions is an empirical fact (Kumar 2007a). This also bears testimony to the fact that there exists rampant discrimination against the Dalits in these institutions. Otherwise Dalits would not have been substantially underrepresented in the higher echelons of the institutions of governance, production and education. However, all this has never caught the imagination of the mainstream Indian sociologists. Similarly, the evaluation of the role of caste in the modern market and media in Indian society has not attracted the mainstream sociologists.

History and Dalit Issues

It has been argued by Ankersmit that history texts consist of many individual statements made by historians after careful selection. But the historians would not write many more 'true' statements which they could have written. The result is that a certain 'picture of the past' (an icon) is fabricated (Jenkins 1995: 20-21). In the Indian context Guha noted this selectiveness of Indian historians. He argues that, 'The historiography of Indian nationalism has for a long time been dominated by elitism-colonialist elitism and bourgeois nationalist elitism...Both these varieties of elitism share the prejudice that the making of the Indian nation and the development of the consciousness-nationalism-which informed this process were exclusively elite achievements... The history of Indian nationalism is thus written up as a sort of spiritual biography of the Indian elite" (Guha 1982: 1-2). Similarly Sumit Sarkar (2005: 359) has argued, 'Historiographical elision has been most powerful in respect of caste'. Mukherjee (1988: 12), emphasises, 'Some amount of hesitation and reluctance is noticed among Indologists and historians to study the past history of the untouchable'.

It is in this context we can observe that the historians have blacked out the Dalits and their contributions to the annals of Indian history. For instance, we do not read anything about the Dalit—poets, saints, social reformers, or even army men in the history textbooks taught at various levels of education. Nobody knows how the Chamar Regiment and the Mahar Regiment functioned and what were their exact contributions to the development of the country. It would be interesting to know how Majhabi Sikhs functioned as sepoys in a Sikh regiment. Cohen (2004: 59) writes,... 'Mahars, an untouchable caste of present–day Maharashtra. They were a sizeable portion of the armies of the Mahratta chieftain Shivaji... Heavily recruited in the pre-mutiny years, the Mahars constituted a fifth to a quarter of the entire Bombay Army'. But all these facts are missing from the history books in India.

Similarly the history books have blacked out a number of social reformers and saint poets of the Dalit communities from the mainstream historical and intellectual discourses. The case of Ambedkar is testimony to the above fact. In this context Viswanathan writes, 'The privileging of Gandhi as an emblem of nonpartisan feeling has, as its inverse, the demonisation of Ambedkar as a purveyor of sectarian politics. The view that 'the national hagiography in India has rarely conceded space for Ambedkar alongside Gandhi' is borne out by amazing excision of Ambedkar from several well known literary works about untouchability'(Viswanathan 2001: 220). The intellectuals and general masses alike have reduced him to the status of a Dalit leader. At the most, a few of the so-called progressive individuals call him a Constitution maker. In the process, social scientists have wilfully forgotten his role as a nation builder. So extreme has been the negation of these social reformers that Dalit politics led by Kanshi Ram and Mayawati had to construct the forgotten histories of these social reformers. The pantheon of Dalit leaders, which included Jotiba Phule, Narayana Guru, Chatrapati Sahuji Maharaj, E.V. Ramaswamy Naicker (Periyar) and Ambedkar and their important contributions do not form part of public memory. Historians never discussed them in their writings. Therefore it was left to a political party to popularise these leaders at the pan-Indian level ignoring their regional origins.

In the same vein, historians have written about and analysed social movements led by Raja Ram Mohan Roy and Dayanand Saraswati as reformist and revivalist movements. But the movement led by Narayana Guru has been completely sidelined. These movements have also raised significant issues realted to human rights of Indians. The most important aspect of these movements was they did not claim any position for the groups they were leading, within the Hindu social order. Therefore, this was in reality a third stream of social movements during 1840s and after that. It is a fact that such types of social reform movements were present in every part of India—East, West, North and South. However, the Indian historian wilfully neglected all this leaving it to historians, anthropologists and sociologist like—Zelliot, Lynch and Omvedt to come and record these events.

Psychology and the Dalit Issues

The neglect of the Dalit issues by the psychologists needs mention here. The psychologists have failed to understand the construction of consciousness of Dalit individuals and different groups within the Dalit society. The psychologists need to look into the aspects of construction of consciousness of Dalit groups, Dalit youths, Dalit women etc. For instance if we try to understand the Dalit women, then we come to know how she is different from the general caste women. In fact it has been argued by a number of Dalit activists that if the general caste women are doubly exploited on the basis of class and gender then the Dalit women are triply exploited on the basis of class, gender and caste. And therefore the construction of consciousness of Dalit women is qualitatively different from general caste women. Similarly we can see the difference between the general caste youth and Dalit youth. Why is it necessary to understand the psychology of Dalits? The answer is simple. If we understand the psychology of the Dalits then we will be able to understand the difficulties faced by them in the process of their integration in the mainstream of society. It is a fact that Dalits face lots of difficulty in getting integrated in the mainstream of the society, as has been rightly brought out by Kulke. He argues, 'The consciousness of having repeatedly to suffer discrimination and of belonging to a group that is branded 'untouchable' manifest in the form of latent psychological barriers which hinder the efforts of socially mobile

'Scheduled Caste' members towards social integration. Frequently, this consciousness is not even based on direct personal experience but rather on unconscious group solidarity or the conscious effort to detach and free oneself from the group of origin is very difficult for socially mobile (Scheduled Caste) members' (Kulke 1983: 141). But all this has not become part of studies done by Indian psychologists.

Language of the Social Sciences and Exclusion of Dalits

Besides, exclusion or black-out of the issues of Dalits in different social science subjects and exclusion of Dalits from Indian social sciences can also be empirically observed by the nature of language used for them, their icons, movements and their labour. The language used for their identity is stigmatising and contemptuous. The Indian social scientists have not been able to evolve a politically correct language to describe the Dalits, their icons, movements, lifestyles, worldview in one word, whole community. The social scientists use the same stigmatised identities like 'Lower Castes', Exterior Castes', 'Untouchables', 'Harijans' etc for the Dalits which were used a century ago. A few social scientists have now started using the term Dalit for them. As against the usage of stigmatised identity of the Dalits the Indian social scientists have used refined language for the castes located higher in the caste hierarchy like—Upper Castes, twice-born etc. This whole language discourse appears partisan and attaches stigma to the Dalits and charisma to the so-called upper castes. When questioned, the Indian sociologists have argued that they do it for objectivity. How can they act as policemen of the subject? They state that they are using the same identities or terms which are used by Dalit themselves. However, the objective reality is different. We all know that Dalits have been identified by different nomenclatures at the grassroots such as *Chandalas, Hinajatians, Avarnas, Asprashya, Antyajas, Achhuts, Pariahs, Namsudras, Panchamas* (the fifth class or category of the four varnas), etc. These identities had stigma, segregation and contempt writ large. These can be called as negative social identities of the Dalits heaped on them by the sacred texts of Hindu society. Had the Indian sociologists been objective they should have used respectable categories rather than the generic terms like lower castes, untouchables etc.

Further, another objective reality about the usage of an identity for the Dalits is that they were also known by their traditional identities in the local regions like—Chamars, Mahars, Mangs, Holiyar, Pulayas, Pasi, Dhobi, Chakkliyar etc to name just a few. However Indian sociologists do not use the exact names of the Dalit castes for maintaining objectivity. Instead, for their convenience they propagated a generalised and common identity for the Dalits ie lower castes or untouchables etc. In this regard the Indian social scientists have also not revealed the fact that Dalits have been uncomfortable with these identities. With the gradual awakening for self-respect among them they have intensified their hatred against these names, and consequently they demanded changes in their caste names. To assert their aboriginal lineage they adopted the appellations like Adi-Hindu, Adi-Dravida, Adi-Andhra, Adi-Karnataka, Adi-Dharmi etc towards the close of the nineteenth century and in the beginning of the twentieth century.

Indian social scientists in general and sociologists in particular have also failed to record efforts of various actors to give different identities to Dalits in past. For instance, the term 'depressed classes', was used for these castes either by the missionaries or the social reformers. However, the identity of the 'Depressed Classes' or the 'Untouchables' as depressed classes could not last long. There classes led by B.R. Ambedkar, Babu Khem Chand, M.C. Rajah and R. Srinivasan in the South, etc. asserted that the term depressed classes should be categorically defined as a few other non-dvija castes Hindus were also being identified under that nomenclature. Later, Ambedkar refuted this identity for the 'Untouchables' and urged, 'We would like to point out that the existing nomenclature of Depressed Classes is objected to by members of the Depressed Classes who have given thought to it and also by the outsiders who take interest in them. It is degrading and contemptuous' (Gupta 1985:26). Ambedkar suggested five alternatives—the 'non-caste Hindus', the 'Protestant Hindus', the 'non-conformist Hindus', the 'Excluded Castes,' and the Exterior Castes' to be considered for the selection of a better denomination for the Untouchable communities (Gupta 1985).

Against the assertion of Dalits for usage of a dignified identity, the Indian social scientists used to use, for long, the term Harijan for the Dalits as if it was a neutral and universal identity of the Dalits. When probed why they use this identity, a number of social scientists revealed that it was so because the people in their locality address them with this name. Secondly, many Dalit groups also identify themselves with this identity. However, the social scientists fail to highlight the most important role played by Gandhi in popularising this identity in the beginning of the 1930s although he did not coin the term. It is a general misconception that the term ' Harijan' was coined by Mahatma Gandhi. In fact, it was originally used by Narsinha Mehta, a Gujrati poet-saint of the Bhakti tradition in the medieval period (Gupta 1985: 30). Gandhi himself accepted this in one of the issues of weekly *Harijan*. He argued that, 'It is not a name of my coining. Some years ago, several untouchable correspondents complained that I used the word "Asprishya" in the pages of Navjivan. "Asprishya" means literally untouchable. I then invited them to suggest a better name, and one of the "untouchable" correspondents suggested the adoption of the name "harijan", on the strength of its having been used by the first known poet–saint of Gujarat (*Harijan*, 7 February, 1933, p. 7). After this Gandhi with the help of Congress popularised this term at pan-India level. Though, Gandhi popularised 'Harijan' as the identity of the Dalits, the members of the 'Untouchable' castes, especially the educated and politically conscious ones did not take to the given identity of 'Harijan', kindly. They wondered how this nomenclature could solve their real problems. Till date the term is hated and despised by the Dalits. Lynch, has stated that, 'Literally the word means 'child of God' but figuratively its connotations are quite different. My Jatav informants showed dislike—at times an intense dislike, for the word. They felt, it connoted the idea of being a bastard and also brought to mind patronising upper caste benevolence' (Lynch 1974: 128).

The then Government carved an identity—the 'Scheduled Castes' for the Untouchable castes as these were put in a Schedule (list) for the purpose of providing Constitutional safeguards to them under the new Constitution of the British Government in India, 1937. Since then Scheduled Castes or SC has become their Constitutional identity. However, again social scientists had to use this identity for Dalits in their discourse. After independence with increased assertiveness among Dalits they started claiming a new identity since 1970. This identity is 'Dalit' identity. A feeling of pride and contentment is associated with identity of Dalits. It is so because they feel that their identity was coined by 'Dalits' themselves. In mid-1970s again the Dalit leaders coined a new identity in the name of 'Bahujan' with the emergence of Backward and Minorities Communities Employees' Federation (BAMCEF) and the rise of Bahujan Samaj Party. Hence we see that there has been a long movement by the Dalits for their dignified identity and yet the Indian social scientists have only used their stigmatised social identities for their academic discourses in their respective disciplines. Is it a case of value neutrality or biases?

While the world over, there is a move to use consciously or deliberately politically correct terminologies to describe erstwhile stigmatised collectivities like Negroes are called Blacks, prostitutes are now being referred to as sex workers, the handicapped as physically challenged, and the aged as senior citizens etc to name just a few. However, Indian Social scientists are still stuck with the stigmatised identities for the Dalits. What is the social significance of using politically correct language for erstwhile stigmatised collectivites in the academic discourses? The significance is that the construction of language depicts the attitude of the people towards the stigmatised collectivities. A positive identity or value neutral identity in place of a negative identity helps to relate people with stigmatised collectivity on more cordial planes. Hence there is need to carve out a neutral language for the Dalits without any suggestibility which will make people more conscious in the orientation towards them.

Exclusion through Reductionism and Stigmatisation

Dalit society, its movement and its icons have been captives of the process of reductionism and stigmatisation in the spheres of Indian social sciences. Indian social scientists have generally projected Dalits as dirty, drunkards, devoid of any merit, good for nothing, burdens on this earth, and as a category professing an agenda of selfish demands. Some social scientists have projected this category as one which is seeking privileges from government like reservation or special legislations or compensation against atrocities committed on them by the so-called upper caste Hindus. Another section of them try to observe and study Dalits through statues of Babasaheb Ambedkar, feeling uneasy as the statues remind them of their presence in the centre of their city. Academics try to analyse Dalit society when the conscience of some social scientist is pricked by an audio or video news item of mass killing of the members of the Dalit community or the rape of Dalit women.

To prove our point of reductionism we can take an empirical example. This example can be drawn from the fact how social scientists have reduced the whole gamut of Dalit movement to the political movement led by Bahujan Samaj Party (BSP) and its leaders like Kanshi Ram and Mayawati. Although it is a fact that politics is just one facet of the total repertoire of Dalit movements we can observe empirically at least seven shades of Dalit movements in Indian society. These are—socio-religious reform movements, political movements, literary movements, movements of Dalit employees', womens movements, NGO movements and diaspora movements. However, other movements are wilfully forgotten and reduced to Dalit political movements. Further this, reductionist approach of Indian social scientists about the Dalit movement comes to the fore when the political movement of Dalits is criticised by the mainstream social scientists as 'divisive and casteist' in nature, 'spreading poison of caste' and possessing no positive agenda for Indian democracy.

The cumulative impact of this reductionism of Dalit society, its movements and its icons has been that Dalit society has been reduced to an appendage of Hindu society in general. It has been accorded a peripheral position in the academic discourses. Most of the intellectuals, researchers, media persons etc would argue that though democracy has given so much to Dalits, they keep on demanding more and more. That is why they call Dalits in a sarcastic tone by using the euphemism—'*Sarkari Brhamans*' (Government Brahmins) or Dalits as '*Sarkari Damad*' (sons-in-law of the Government). It is a fact that this negative identity has crystallised, in less than fifty or sixty years, specifically after the commencement of the policy of protective discrimination enshrined in the Constitution. Prior to this, in the ancient and medieval India even the existence of Dalits, as human beings, was not accepted. Hence, we can argue that there is a linear movement of the Dalit identity in the Indian social sciences ie from denial of existence in the Hindu social order (*Purushsukta* tenth chapter of *Rigveda* denies their existence in the *Varna-Ashrama-Dharma* scheme) to a stigmatised identity.

Causes of Exclusion of Dalits in Indian Social Sciences

The first and foremost reason for this exclusion is that most of the social scientists in India are drawn from the so-called upper caste background. Department after Department of social sciences is dominated by the practitioners belonging to twice-born castes. Considering these facts about the reductionism of Dalit society, its movement and its icons, in the Indian social science, one is forced to ask why at all do these negative constructions and reductionism of Dalits occur? Why does stigmatisation of Dalits take place even in the computer age of twenty-first century? Why is there so much of indifference on the part of students of social sciences to objectively analyse and describe the existential and experiential realities of Dalit lives, and their worldview? There may be many reasons for this attitude of the social scientists but here we can identify some of the most common reasons. One, the social sciences in India have been preoccupied with answering European criticism of Indian society and culture. In doing so they have involved themselves in the process of 'academic nationalism'. That means the Indian social scientists without evaluating their own society objectively and critically have justified the decadent and degenerate part of our culture and tradition. Secondly, the hierarchical nature of the Indian social structure is also replicated in the spheres of academics as well. Departments in most of the Universities are dominated by the so-called upper castes who never bothered to study the erstwhile excluded collectivities like Dalits. In this context, it is pertinent to ask how many leading social scientists have done a study in the localities where Dalits live. The answer is not even one. The third reason is that the structural location of the social scientists never allowed them to evaluate objectively the whole structural and cultural lives of Dalits, who account for a quarter of the nation's population. Another view can be the lack of perspective—how many studies have taken place from the perspectives of Dalits to understand the basic institutions of the Indian society like caste, village, etc? Not many or not even one? If we accept the proposition that there is a lack of objectivity and perspective with regard to understanding of Dalit issues in social sciences then a destructive and negative understanding of Dalits in the social sciences is a foregone conclusion. A caveat is put here that one is not asking the social scientists to eulogise the Dalit society, its movements and its icons but only emphasising that objectivity in the social sciences demands the recognition the real nature and contributions of Dalits in the development of Indian society and democracy.

Academic Assertiveness by Dalits in Social sciences

Contestation against Concepts

This chapter underlines the fact that although historically there has been exclusion, reduction and stigmatisation of Dalits in Indian social sciences, of late, there have been definite assertiveness by the Dalit masses in general and social scientists born in the Dalit community in particular. The increased numbers of Dalit teachers in Indian universities and colleges have further amplified this assertiveness. Foreign scholarships in higher education, for Dalits, have further augmented this process. Even though, all of them are not equally assertive, some of them have produced substantial literature in the sphere of social sciences which has raised a number of questions regarding the exclusionary nature of Indian social sciences. The Dalit assertiveness in the academic sphere has led to the development of a new perspective in social sciences which questions the existing wisdom of the Indian social scientists. At the outset, categories and concepts evolved and developed by the so-called upper caste social scientists through which Dalits and their society have been understood till now have been contested and challenged by the social scientists born in the Dalit community. The concepts like—village, caste, Hindu social order, class, Sanskritization have been deconstructed by different social scientists belonging to Dalit communities. For instance, Kumar (2010 & 2014) has contested the use of the euphemism 'Hindu social order' as an academic category to define Indian society. According to him, this euphemism is an artificial construct. This construct is the handiwork of the so-called upper-caste social scientists, in connivance with their colonial masters. They have carved it out by deliberately intermixing two terms which have been temporally dissociated from each other for more than two-and-a-half millennium. By intermixing elements of Rig-Vedic text which dates backs to 1500 BC and the term Hindu which goes back to onlyAD 8th century they have carved out the euphemism 'Hindu Social Order'. Secondly, the concept of Sanskritisation which replaced the earlier term Brahmanisation has been contested as an example of totally biased observations and social construction. This emerges from the social background of the author itself. Moreover, there is no such concept of pure culture (Parvathamma 1978, Kumar 2010). Similarly, the way caste has been understood in sociology has been challenged by Kumar (2014) and long back by Babasaheb Ambedkar in the year 1916. It has been challenged on the ground that it does not capture the total reality subsumed under this institution. The concept of caste as used has hidden a number of characteristics which should have been intrinsic to it. It has also been challenged on the basis of the history of the term of caste as it came into existence only in the beginning of fifteenth century with the arrival of the Portuguese. Therefore the question arises what were the terms used by the Indians to understand this institution before fifteenth century? The answer is *Jati* or *Jat*. These capture the total functions performed by a group of persons called *Jati* or *Jat*.

The entity village has been contested since long. Ambedkar had described it as a den of ignorance and the very negation of a republic. If it is a republic, it is a republic of the touchable, by the touchable and for the touchable. The untouchables have no rights... They have no rights because they were outside the republic. However, Indian social scientists have defined Indian villages through a functionalist perspective. That means the Indian village is a functional category with each caste contributing to the maintenance of the village structure. *Jajmani* relations, in the village, were hailed for their economic interdependence hiding the exploitation and unequal power distribution between Dalits and the so-called twice-born castes. Thanks to the assertions of Dalit youths with their autobiographies, which started appearing from the year 1990 onwards the functionalist image of Indian villages has been deconstructed. Starting from the village locality, where the Dalits live and where the so-called upper castes live, to the ownership of land and services rendered by the ex-untouchable to the so-called upper caste there exists complete domination of one community over the other. The ex-untouchables find themselves excluded in every sphere of the life. Such is the reality (Valmiki 2003, translated from Hindi).

The concept of class (Kumar 2010) has been contested because there cannot be such pristine and pure institutions in India. It is so because; people are first born in a caste. The caste gives them the cultural, social, and symbolic capital which is then converted into different categories called classes. These classes are defined in social sciences on the basis of the economic, educational and professional achievements which are considered to be secular in nature but are not. However, the moot question is that whether Indian social scientists have been able to evolve a scale which can measure how much contribution the caste makes into the making of a class? How much do caste networks, social and ritual status of the individual help him to gain the present status which is called as class? These facts are still not measurable. Unless and until social scientists evolve such a scale any attempt to analyse social reality in India on the basis of class will be erroneous.

Evaluating 'Merit' of the other Side

It is a ritual that whenever the Dalits ask for reservation in the education system the upper castes raise a hue and cry that the Dalits are devoid any merit and if they are given reservation in the education system then the standard of the reservation will go down. Therefore Dalits have questioned first the concept of 'merit' itself. They ask, 'What is the sociological and Constitutional definition of the term merit? If not, then are the marks scored in an examination the only criterion to measure the 'merit' of an Individual? Moreover, in some exams proficiency in language is taken as 'merit'. This is too elitist because in an exam marks can be awarded differently by changing the yardsticks. Also one can learn a language because of family background and by practice if you are financially secure.

Secondly, they have raised the issue to assess the 'merit' of the so-called upper castes who do not have any reservation enshrined in the Constitution of India. One cannot deny that the so-called upper castes enjoy enormous benefit and patronage of their caste brethren and religion etc in every sphere of life. Hence, Dalits wonder, are the communities, who do not avail of Constitutional reservation, necessarily meritorious? Dalits have tried to evaluate their 'merit' via the status of people in the ancient Indian society which was based on traditional social structure. The Brahman, Kshatriya and Vaishya Varna, assigned with particular functions, were said to be initially open but became closed later (Dumont 1970: 69). In an interview in a

North Indian village a Dalit revealed something which has not been revealed by social scientists who really boast about the concept of 'merit' in the annals of social sciences. According to him, 'The Brahmins had the privilege of teaching, the Kshatriyas of protecting all creatures, and the Vaishyas of living by trade and commerce. However, if the Brahmins were so meritorious then why is it that still half of the country's population is illiterate? If the Kshatriyas were so meritorious then why could they not defend our borders? The Tartars, the Mughals, the British, etc all defeated and subjugated us. Similarly, if the Vaishyas were so meritorious then why is the trade and commerce of India in a shambles? In the same vein, if Arjuna of *Mahabharat* was so meritorious in archery then why did Dronacharya (a Kshatriya guru of Arjun) have to unjustly demand Eklavya's thumb'.

Not only for the ancient and medieval periods, Dalits also want to understand the standards of 'merit' of the so-called upper castes but also in the modern society. They try to invoke some indicators to measure these standards. These indicators are HDI (Human Development Index), Corruption Perception Index, NPA (non-preforming assets) of the banking sector, Indian universities' performances at the international levels, sports etc, to name just a few. These indicators have been taken with the rationale that institutions on the basis of which these indicators evolve either have been totally monopolised by the so-called upper castes or at least they over-dominate in them. The institutions are in the spheres of governance, production, education, etc.

In the aforesaid context, if we first take a look at the present Human Develop Index (HDI) of India. In terms of HDI, India is placed at the 127th position in the group of 174 countries. Similarly, in the 'Corruption Perception Index' for the year 2004, India ranks the 90th in the group of 146 countries (*Transparency International India Report 2004*). Above all, the external debt of India is a whopping of Rs 5,11,861 crore (*Economic Survey 2003-4*; p. 128). As all the meritorious economists and administrators who are managing the affairs of the country without any reservation, why is the situation so bad? The situation in science and technology, which is considered a realm of high specialties and, hence, kept out of the bounds of reservation, is also not very encouraging. In this regard, 'Professor Nian Chai Liu and his colleagues at the Shanghai Jio Tong University in China spent two years collating and analysing the output of 2000 universities worldwide and ...published their results by ranking five hundred universities. Only three universities/institutions from India figure in the top 500- Indian Institute of Sciences-at No. 260 and the Indian Institutes of Technology at Kharagpur and Delhi at Nos. 459 and 460 respectively' (Dinesh 2004).

In this context, it will be worth taking a look at the merit of the doctors working in the most prestigious hospitals of the country. If the Indian doctors and medical specialists are so meritorious then why is it that most of the VVIPs, including the ardent supporters of *Swadeshi,* run away to foreign countries for the simplest of their illness? Here, it will be interesting to measure the merit of the professionals passing out from the various private colleges of courses in engineering, medical, management, etc where a seat for admission can be bought for some lakhs of rupees. In the event we know that the marks scored in qualifying examinations do not matter. Whether you have secured 50% or 60% it doesn't matter. The only criterion is that whether you have the purchasing power or not for that seat. Here, in this case no one raises the issue of lowering of 'merit' in the professional and technological institutions. Further, what about our sports in which there has never been reservation? A nation of 125 crore population has not been able to produce meritorious sports persons to win gold medals in Olympics, except in hockey and one in shooting. Similarly, is it really a case of meritocracy that the progeny of film stars are given chance to act and sing in the film industry even though they may not have any professional training and experience? Are all these not instances of 'pedigree reservation'rather than merit. Then, the point to be noted is that most of such meritorious personnel reach certain levels of achievement because of their access being facilitated by their life chances, a fact highlighted by Bowles and and Ginits (1976).

Social Sciences and the Pedagogy of the Dalits

If there is such exclusion of the Dalit issues in the social sciences is there a way out? Here Paulo Freire can be taken as the starting point, who argues for the development of 'Pedagogy of the Oppressed'. He opines, 'a pedagogy which must be forged not for oppressed (whether individuals or peoples) in the incessant struggle to regain their humanity. The pedagogy makes oppression and its causes object of reflection by the oppressed, and from that reflection will come their necessary engagement in the struggle for their liberation. And in the struggle this pedagogy will be made and remade' (Freire 1993: 30). But what is important about this pedagogy is that, 'those who recognize, or begin to recognize, themselves as oppressed must be among the developers of the pedagogy. No pedagogy which is truly liberating can remain distant from the oppressed by treating them as unfortunate oppressors. The oppressed must be their own example in the struggle for their redemption' (Freire 1993: 36). It is not that 'pedagogy of the oppressed' is a new thing for the Dalits, yes the Dalits had started writing their own pedagogy long back when they started writing their own literature.

Has Dalit Literature Shown the Way?

Serious critiquing is a sine qua non for any literary work of significance. Dalits claim that the literature of the dominant group or so-called upper castes is petty and false and over-powered by romanticism. Another fact about the so-called mainstream literature or writing has been that it was excessively individual and also urban-based. It ignores the social reality of appalling poverty and oppression of the Dalits. It has been stated that high caste Marathi literature is artificial and false, 'like paper flowers'. The same has been underlined by Wankhade that, 'A Marathi writer's understanding of life is restricted by his birth and upbringing in a particular caste and class and he is unable to get out of his own little pond. He has never seen that outside there is a vast world—a suffering, distressed, struggling, howling world, burning with anger from within like a prairie fire.' In the same vein Devy argues that, 'when Dalit literature started emerging in the 1960s, Marathi literary taste dominated by a narcissistic tendency that foregrounded formalistic, non-confrontationist, and titillating works. One of the central debates in that era was focused on an 'art for art's sake' or art for life's sake kind of issue' (Devy 2003: xx).

To counter the total exclusion of the Dalits, their movement, icons, experiences, worldview etc Dalits were forced to write their own experiences. The process assumed such a proportion that it took the shape of a movement and thus the Dalit literature movement was born in 1960 in Maharashtra. But the irony is that as soon as the Dalit literary movement started taking root, the mainstream writers belonging to so-called upper-castes, who had avoided writing on the issues of Dalits, started criticising and discarding the Dalit literature as propagandistic, univocal and negative. Dalit autobiographies, a source of authentic experiences, were rejected on the flimsy pretext such as they were not structured; they were artless outpourings of Dalit writers' unmediated experiences and had become repetitive. Replying to the objections raised by the mainstream literary figures, Dalit writers try to highlight the unrepresentative nature of mainstream literature, the total blackout of the experiential and existential reality of Dalit lives, the insensitiveness towards their absolute exclusion, oppression and deprivation from the mainstream literature. Dalit writers ask, 'Why have they been silent on the exploitative nature of social, political, economic and educational institutions of Indian society?' To answer these questions the Dalits have lifted their pens. That is their literature which is produced out of their experiences. It is coming out from the locales where they have lived and suffered because of the social order. That is why it can be argued that there is qualitative difference between literatures produced by the Dalits and the so-called upper castes.

Today Dalit literature is coming out in abundance in every mode and language in the form of a movement. It is exposing and deconstructing the existing socio-political images established by the earlier writers or were not touched by them at all. The Dalit writers and intellectuals argue that as the Dalits are in majority in the coming days their literature will become the mainstream literature and if this phenomenon starts happening in every social science subject then the texture of Indian social sciences will change. This will in turn relegate the existing subject matter of social sciences written by the so-called upper caste to the periphery. Now the moot question is we can incorporate this Dalit literature, produced by Dalit themselves, in the social sciences. If we can, then how much can be taken as objective?

From Blackout to Reproduction of Hegemony

It is true that Dalits form part and parcel of manpower which runs the economy, polity and society. However, their contribution has been never recorded by the social scientists whether economists, political scientists, sociologists, historians, or psychologists etc. However, four simultaneous processes ushering in the Indian society have forced Indian social scientists to throw some light on the nature and scope of the exclusion of Dalits depicted in the subject matter of sociology. These four processes are as follows. The first is, the process of democratisation of the society on the basis of Constitutional rights. Secondly, equipped with these Constitutional rights there is Dalit assertion in every realm of Indian society whether it is in religion, politics or culture etc. The third is, the role of market in creating a buyer for the Dalit literature written both by the Dalits and non-Dalits. Lastly, we have the process of globalisation with its information revolution and increased role of supra-institutions like UNHRC and different Social Forums—like the world, European and Asian social forums. All these processes along with the academic assertions of Dalits have given Dalit issues greater visibility. However, the exclusion of Dalit issues in the annals of social sciences continues unabated. This exclusion of the Dalits from the curriculum of social sciences in India can be understood through the six simultaneous processes taking place in the disciplines of social sciences. These six processes are -

Cognitive Blackout

Forced Availability
Pseudo Inclusivity
Lack of Reflexivity
Chequered Accessibility
Reproduction of Hegemony

At the outset the exclusion of Dalits in the discipline of social sciences takes the shape of 'Cognitive Blackout' (Wankhede 1992). It is so because Indian social scientists have failed to underline the fact that there are structural and historical differences between the society and the culture of so-called upper-castes and the so-called Dalits. We have observed in our analysis how Dalit icons, movements, labour, world view injured psyche and in a world where the whole Dalit society has been blacked out form the subject matter of social science disciplines ie economics, political science, history, sociology, and psychology. To add to these if we take specific example of cultural aspects of Dalit life then we observe that their culture, their folk tales, songs, dance, music, art of taming wild animals, birds, and their food habits etc have all been blacked out specifically from subjects like history and sociology. Even today cognitive black out is maintained when no differentiation is done between the poor of a Dalit community and that of the so-called upper-caste in economics. There is no discussion in Indian social sciences regarding the loss of social, cultural and symbolic capital suffered by Dalits in Indian society. Only a few social scientists have raised these issues concerning Dalits. For instance, a few social scientists have highlighted the differences between the cultures of Dalits and Brahmins. According to Gough, there is s clear conflict between the inhibiting 'culture' of the Brahmins and the free 'nature' of the untouchables. Both differ in their attitudes towards sexuality, and aggression towards elders and peers. Engaged in the practical business of earning a living through manual labour, the low castes care more for health and prosperity in this life (Gough 1956: 846). Parvathamma (1978) and Kumar (2010, 2014 a) have also highlighted their differences between the so-called upper castes and Dalits.

However, Indian social scientists have blacked out all these differences. That is why Oommen has eloquently portrayed that, 'There has been a cognitive black-out in Indian social science, until recently, as far as knowledge regarding the life- world of *Dalitbahujans* goes. The fact the life-styles of upper castes and *Dalitbhujans* vary dramatically in terms of food habits, worship patterns or gender relations is tacitly acknowledged. But instead of squarely recognizing these variations and explaining why they exist, the dominant tendency in Indian Sociology, at least until recently, has been to suggest that the *Dalitbahujans* are abandoning their way of life in favour of the life–styles of caste Hindus. This is what *Sanskritization* is all about. In this perspective, not only the norms and values of caste Hindus are privileged but they are also christened as norm-setters and value-givers for the society as a whole. Conversely, the norms and values of *Dalitbahujans* are knocked out, ignored, stigmatized and de-legitimized' (Oommen 2001: 21).

Forced Availability

What needs to be highlighted in this context are that the availability or inclusion of Dalits in the research and teaching jobs is not natural. It has been forced via external agencies. Five important agents which have forced Indian social scientists to include them in their research and teaching are, firstly Dalit movements and assertiveness, second, social scientists drawn from USA, UK and European countries, third, the market, fourth, the social science research funding by ICSSR, ICHR, etc., and fifth, the increased number of Dalit scholars that is research scholars and teachers.

The Indian social scientists practised academic untouchability with the Dalit community; however, by 1970s Dalit political and social movements started raising their voice at times democratically and sometimes violently (see Kumar 2002, 2007b, 2014). This forced the social scientists to include them in their research. Second, we can observe around this period a number of American historians, anthropologists, sociologists and a few economists who started conducting their research on Dalits. This, in turn forced the Indian counterparts to take up research in these areas. For instance, Lynch (1969), L. Hardgrave Jr. (1969), Zelliot (1970), Omvedt (1976), and Michael Moffatt (1979), published their works on the basis of their fieldwork done on Dalits. In fact, these researches became the founding material for research for generations to come.

The third reason that forced Indian social scientists to take up nominal research on Dalits is that Indian Council for Social Science Research (ICSSR) specifically asked a few social scientists to take up Dalits as research subjects. One very senior social scientist revealed that during 1970s nobody was ready to take up research on Dalits. Therefore, ICSSR had to sponsor a number of studies. If we take the specific example of sociology as a social science subject then we will find that this subject got established in the universities in 1914 in India. Since then it took 56 years that is till 1970 for sociologists to take up some kind of research on Dalits. However, a cursory look at ICSSR the sociology trend report would reveal that the researches on Dalits were related to their poverty, illiteracy, atrocities against them and untouchability. It was as though the Dalits did not have any other socio-cultural indicators.

The fourth reason for the forced availability is the market. Especially in contemporary times, literature related to Dalits has led to the emergence of a market. With the onset of globalisation and liberalisation, the issues of Dalits, especially violation of Dalit human rights have got greater visibility at the national and international forums. Information revolution internet-websites and cable TV have further given the issues of Dalits international visibility. Supra-institutions like United Nations Human Rights Committee, World Social Forum, European and Asian Social Forums have given them a vocabulary which is helping them to relate to other such movements and hence they have got greater visibility. With such wide publicity and visibility, the Dalit issue has now got a market. People want to buy and read new literature on Dalits. That is why more and more so-called upper-caste social scientists get attracted to write on the issues without having any organic relationship with their subjects.

Last but not least the increasing number of Scheduled Castes, Scheduled Tribes and Other Backward Class teachers and students in higher education has also promoted the availability of research and training facilities pertaining to the Dalit issues. The students do not now hesitate to work on issues of Dalits. And the availability of Dalit teachers in the university system has facilitated the research on the Dalits. A few teachers have taken the initiative to organise seminars and conferences on the issue and have made available projects for research also. All these processes have given Dalit issues in social sciences, great visibility, though it is of the forced variety.

Pseudo Inclusivity

If after cognitive blackout Dalit assertiveness and the intensity of Dalit movement along with academicians of Dalit society and other processes have caused the 'forced availability' of Dalit issues in the social sciences it has become a reality, this inclusivity is pseudo and such attention in nature. For instance, nowadays it has become a ritual to include a chapter on the issue of Dalits towards the end of a book. In seminars and conferences toward the end of the seminar or conference there may be a seminar on the Dalits and related issues. In the syllabi of sociology or political science or history we have observed that in the curricula towards the end, we would have one topic on Dalits. By the time we reach that part of the course the semester might have ended and hence you can discuss that topic nominally or leave it untouched. SC/ST/OBC students of a few universities are on record that Jotiba Phuley, Babasaheb Ambedkar, Periyar etc are never taught as independent thinkers or social reformers. Their social thought becomes part of the discussion only in reference to Gandhi, Tagore, Vivekanand, Nehru, Tilak etc to name just a few. They are discussed only in passing. Hence, they are included yet not included. This is what I call 'pseudo-inclusivity' in social science practice.

An added aspect of pseudo-inclusivity is optionalism. A topic related to Dalits is included at the end of a course outline which gets taken up towards the end of the course; however, the more serious issue is that students and teachers can get away with it. The *modus operandi* is simple. The topic can be asked as an optional question in the exams. This is a compromised condition that is for the public you have included a topic or issue in the course outline but when it comes to actual engagement with the topic, the teachers and students skip it by making it an optional topic for the exams.

Lack of Reflexivity

There is a very thin difference between 'pseudo-inclusivity' and 'lack of reflexivity'. In a way they are interconnected and interrelated. However, in my opinion, the lack of reflexivity occurs once inclusivity takes place. It is related, to the treatment given to the Dalits subject matter or issues in the classroom. What is the nature and level of engagement of teacher and researcher with the Dalit issues? How does one teach and reflect on the issues in the classroom and his/her research? Lack of reflexivity of social scientists come to the fore as soon as we observe a teacher's and researcher's reductionist approach toward Dalit society, its icons, movements, polity and its worldview. They approach Dalit issues only through poverty, illiteracy, untouchability and atrocity as relevant to social and cultural aspects of the Dalit society. The teachers adopt a reductionist approach in the classroom and so do the researchers. For instance, their icons are reduced to Dalit leaders or ideologues as if they were not engaged with the total humanity. They never become universal speaking on behalf of everyone. They are reduced only to Dalit lifeworld. Secondly, reductionism of whole Dalit society can also be witnessed when the researchers and course teachers reduce the whole Dalit society to an entity without any worth or merit, without taking into account of their contribution to the society, their labour, their participation in democratic processes etc. The social scientists have declared them as a Constitutional Category surviving on the affirmative action and welfare policies of the State.

The lack of reflexivity of Indian social scientists can be further empirically demonstrated with the help of many other examples apart from those discussed above. The first and foremost issue is associated with a comprehensive definition of the Dalits. A definition of the collectivity is *a sine qua non* to be treated seriously. In different subjects very tentative definitions have been used of this group (Kumar 2005, 2010). The social scientists have used the term 'Dalit' for poor people, tribals, women and ex-untouchables simultaneously without reflecting on their differences. These differences can be traced easily on the basis of their structural location and therefore the exclusion they suffer. This disengaged attitude creates confusion among researchers and policy makers.

Further, the usage of contemptuous language for Dalits also tells us about the lack of reflexivity of the social scientists. We have observed how in the name of objectivity Indian social scientists have called Dalits as 'lower castes' while they call others as upper castes. The result is that this language further reproduces the stigma for the Dalits in academics and charisma for so-called upper castes. Usage of a neutral language for the erstwhile stigmatised collectivities is an important aspect of reflexivity of social scientists in any society. We have observed that the world over there is a move in the society and thereby in academics, to use sophisticated language for prostitutes, the handicapped, elderly persons etc. They are now referred to as sex-workers, differently-abled and senior citizens respectively. However, Indian social scientists without analysing the social reality address Dalits as 'lower castes', 'Harijans' or sometimes even 'untouchables' in their academic discourse. The moot question which can be raised here is why at all we need neutral or sophisticated language for the erstwhile stigmatised collectivities. The answer is because a more sophisticated or even neutral language lessens the intensity of prejudices of the so-called upper castes against the so-called lower castes. It helps to sponge the stigma attached to them to a certain extent. And last but not the least, it speaks volumes of the sensitivity and reflexivity of the whole society in general and social scientists in particular towards the erstwhile stigmatised communities.

Chequered Accessibility

Once, the subject matter of social sciences gets nominal representation because of external forces, and their pseudo-inclusivity there arises another problem of availability of relevant material to be discussed in the classroom or the relevant topic for research. Indian social scientists regularly complain that they want to teach the issues related to Dalits but there is no standard text which is theoretically and methodologically objective enough to be taught in the classroom. However, two points should be kept in mind before we take this problem at its face value. One, these questions are not raised when it comes to teaching the issues and icons of the so-called upper castes. Second, who decides which text needs theoretical and methodological standards? And what are the characteristics to decide the same? However, one fact about the chequered availability of relevant material is that Indian social scientists prefer the relevant material related to Dalits written and produced either by so-called upper caste or by a foreign author. The references, bibliographies and indices of the different articles and the books respectively would amply prove the point. A corollary to this fact is that books and articles written by Dalits on Dalits are seldom referred to as standard textbooks.

Reproduction of Hegemony

The aforesaid processes of cognitive blackout, forced availability, pseudo-inclusivity, lack of reflexivity and chequered availability are the processes which should not be treated as ends in themselves. Rather they are means to an end or ends. That end is reproduction of hegemony of the so-called upper castes in the discipline of social sciences. The practice of social science establishes the worldview, social structure, icons, movements and other values and processes of the so-called upper caste society. At the centre of every analysis these are the elements traits which are then treated as national or universal. For instance, their icons are treated as national icons, their movements are national movements, and their values are universal values. In turn the icons, movements and values of the Dalit society are relegated to the periphery representing only a cross-section of the society. They are considered to be parochial in nature. This process further enforces exclusion or retards the process of incorporation of the Dalits and their issues in the disciplines of the social sciences.

In this process of reproduction of hegemony of the so-called upper castes the social sciences in India have lost their affectivity as an agent of emancipation of the suffering masses in a hierarchical and caste-ridden society like India. In this society, two hundred and fifty million Dalits and Adivasis have been exploited for millennia. From principles of universal psychology in economics, individualising laws of history and the functionalist perspective of sociology etc Indian social sciences have not been able to evolve affective subject matters or curricula which can help Indians in general to move beyond their caste, class, region, religion and other primordial identities. With the help of the subject matter of social sciences and the sanitised language used to define the heinous social reality suffered by Dalits and Adivasis, the general practitioners of Indian social sciences have not been able to give answers to the existing problems of the masses. Rather, it reinforces their hegemony because they use the same perspective and framework whose sources of foundation are values and worldviews of the so-called upper caste. Hence, it can be argued Indian social sciences lack a substantial emancipatory agenda for a progressive society. It is still steeped in status-quoism and reproduces Hindu hegemony.

Conclusions

The exclusionary nature of practice of social sciences has been analysed in this paper on the basis of empirical data extracted from different subjects of social sciences like—economics, political science, history, sociology, psychology and other sources. On this basis we can observe that the exclusion of 'Dalit issues' viz. their icons, movements, worldview, art, culture, folk-tales, song forms, music, taming of and interaction with wild life, and contribution of their labour in running the economy, polity and society etc have been excluded from the disciplines of social sciences. Further, this exclusion of Dalits from the disciplines has taken different forms. Apart from 'cognitive blackout' there has been the practice of stigmatisation, condemnation and reductionism of Dalit society, their icons and their social and political movements. We have specifically, in this context, analysed how Dalit icons and political movements have been reduced as parochial in their interests and thereby divisive in nature. Their icons and movements never acquire independent and universal status (that is in the interest of the majority community). Rather they are always cited with reference to the so-called upper caste leaders and movements led and dominated by them. Exclusion of 'Dalits issues' in the practice of social sciences takes the shape of erroneous explanations and interpretations of empirical and subjective facts about Dalits. The worst form exclusion is that the social sciences knowledge has impacted a few Dalit social scientists negatively. That is they produced theoretically and methodologically erroneous interpretations of the facts related to Dalits and their labour. However, this type of knowledge cannot be sustained epistemologically but it does create confusion. Last but not the least, the language of social science itself depicts social exclusion because it invokes the same old contemptuous and stigmatised identities for Dalits in its analysis.

In the same vein, the paper has also inquired into the causes of exclusion of 'Dalit Issues' from the practice of social science disciplines in India. We have found domination of the so-called upper-castes in the disciplines as one of the reasons for the exclusion. Second, the locale from where the primary data collected is another reason. Usually, the data is collected from the so-called upper castes localities in urban areas. Third, the cause of this exclusion is the lack of effective language in social sciences which can sensitise the masses and detach the so-called upper caste social scientists from their caste, class, linguistic and religious identities. The fourth cause of exclusion is the laws and perspective used by Indian social scientists for analysing

Indian society. For instance, the universal laws of economics are based on 'universal psychologism' which has not been able to take social hierarchy and religious legitimacy for the same as the primary reason of social exclusion of Dalits in India. Similarly the, 'functionalist' perspective in sociology has not been able to capture inherent unequal power relations in the village society.

Further, the paper has also analysed how Dalits have responded to the exclusionary processes in the practice of Indian social sciences. To begin with, Dalit social scientists have questioned the conceptualisation about the Indian society by the so-called upper caste social scientists. Specifically, they have questioned the concepts of caste, class, village, religion and social change through Sanskritisation. The concept of 'merit' has been questioned at two levels, one, at the level of epistemology and second, at the level of evaluation of merit of the other side. The epistemic question is sources, foundation and means of measurement of merit in a hierarchical society like India are not clear. For evaluation of merit on the other side Dalit social scientists have taken an evolutionary perspective. They have taken modern indicators like—income, education, military power, performance in science and technology, quality of educational institutions, sports and corruption. These indicators pertain to the nation as a whole. They have wondered over what is so meritorious about the other side that they lampoon and scoff at the Dalits. Academic assertiveness of Dalit social scientists goes on to ask if there is a way out from this biased practice of social sciences. The answer they give is 'pedagogy of the oppressed'. Another way out is to democratise the practice of social sciences by incorporating Dalit literature in its subject matter and more social scientists from Dalit background.

Last but not the least, this paper has investigated how even after sixty-seven years on independence and democracy, the process of globalisation and information revolution the practice of Indian social sciences has not changed substantially. Its practice for Dalits ranges from 'cognitive blackout' to 'reproduction of Hindu hegemony'. Hence Indian social sciences lack an emancipatory agenda for a hierarchically arranged, caste-ridden, illiteracy and poverty infested society. Therefore, Dalit social scientists make a plea to make it more inclusive. If Indian social sciences have to play an emancipatory role, if it has to have rigour and affectivity in Indian society, which has its own unique nature, and then it has to be inclusive.

REFERENCES

Abbasayulu, Y.B., 1978, *Scheduled Caste Elite*, Booklinks Corporation, Hyderabad.

Akerlof, George, 1976, 'The Economics of Caste and of Rat Race and Other Woeful Tales', *Quarterly Journal of Economics*-XC-4 (November).

Ambedkar, B.R., 1991, 'What Congress and Gandhi Have Done to the Untouchables', 'Mr Gandhi and the Emancipation of Untouchables', *Dr Babasaheb Ambedkar Writings and Speeches*, Vol. 9, Education Department, Government of Maharashtra, Bombay.

———, 1989, *Dr. Babasaheb Ambedkar Writings and Speeches*, Vol. 5, Education Department, Government of Maharashtra, Mumbai.

———, 1982, Ibid., Vol. 2.

———, 1979, Ibid., Vol. 1.

Beteille, Andre, 1969, *Caste: Old and New*, Asia Publishing House, Bombay.

Bowels, S. and Gintis, H., 1976, *Schooling in Capitalist America*, Routledge & Kegan Paul, London.

Briggs, W., 1920, *The Chamars*, Low Price Publications, Delhi.

Chauhan, Brij Raj, 1967, 'Special Problems of the Education of the Scheduled Castes' in *Journal of Higher Eduction*, UGC, New Delhi.

Cohen, Stephen P., 2004, *The Indian Army: Its Contribution to the Development of a Nation*, Oxford University Press, New Delhi.

Descartes, Rene, *Discourse on Method*, translated by Wollaston, Harmondsworth, Penguin, London.

Devy, G.N., 2003, in Introduction to Sharankumar Limbale, *The Outcaste: Akkarmashi*, translated from Marathi by Santosh Bhookar, Oxford University Press, New Delhi.

Dinesh, K., 2004, *The Times of India*, New Delhi.

Dumont, Louis, 1970, *Homo Hierarchicus: The Caste System and its Implications*, Oxford University Press, New Delhi.

Durkheim, Emile, 1895 (2013), *Rules of Sociological Method*, Free Press, New York.

Freire, Paula, 1993, *Pedagogy of the Oppressed* (Translated by Myra Bergman Ramos), Penguin Books, New Delhi.

Gore, M.S. (ed.), *The Sociology of Education in India*, National Council of Educational Research and Training, New Delhi.

Gough, Kathleen, 1956, 'Brahmin Kinship in Tamil Village', *American Anthropologist*, 58: 826-53.

Guha, R. (ed.) 1982, *Subaltern Studies–I, Writings on South Asian History and Society*, Oxford University Press, Delhi.

Gupta, S.K., 1985, *The Scheduled Castes in Modern Indian Politics: Their Emergence as a Political Power*, Munshiram Manoharlal Publishers Ltd., New Delhi.

Hardgrave, L. Jr., 1969,*The Nadars of Tamilnad: The Political Culture of a Community in Change*, University of California, Berkeley, CA.

Jenkins, Keith, 1995, *On 'What is History': From Carr and Elton to Rorty and White*, Routledge, London and New York.

Kulke, E., 1983, 'The Problem of Educated Middle Class Harijans', in John P. Neelsen (ed.), *Social Inequality and Political Structures*, Manohar Publications, New Delhi.

Kumar, Vivek, 2014 a, 'Dalit Studies: Continuities and Change' in Y. Singh (ed.), *Indian Sociology (Volume 3): Identity, Communication and Culture* (ICSSR Research Surveys and Explorations), Oxford University Press, New Delhi.

———, 2014 b, *Caste and Democracy in India: A Perspective from Below*, Gyan Publications, New Delhi.

———, 2010, 'Teaching Caste and the Hindu Social Order: Dalits in Indian Sociology' in Maitrayee Chaudhuri (ed.), *Sociology in India: Intellectual and Institutional Practices*, Rawat Publications, New Delhi.

———, 2007a, Governance and Development in the Era of Globalization: Understanding Exclusion and Assertion of Dalits in India, in Kameshwar Chaudhary (ed.) *Globalization Governance Reform and Development in India*, Sage Publications,

New Delhi.

———, 2007b, Bahujan Samaj Party: Some Issues of Democracy and Governance in Sudha Pai (ed.) *Political Process in Uttar Pradesh: Identity, Economic Reform and Goverance*, Pearson Longman, Delhi.

———, 2006, *India's Roaring Revolution: Dalit Assertion and New Horizons*, Gagandeep Publications, New Delhi.

———, 2005, 'Situating Dalits In Indian Sociology', *Sociological Bulletin*, Special issue on South Asia, Vol. 54, No. 3, September-December, New Delhi.

———, 2002, *Dalit Leadership in India*, Kalpaz Publications, New Delhi.

Lynch, Oven M., 1969, The *Politics of Untouchability: Social Mobility and Social Change in a City on India*, Columbia University Press, New York.

Lynch, Oven, M., 1974, *The Politics of Untouchability*, National Publishing House, Delhi.

Malik, Suncila, 1979, *Social Integration of Scheduled Castes*, Abhinav Publications, New Delhi.

Moffatt, Michael, 1979, *An Untouchable Community in South India:Structure and Consensus*, Princeton University Press, New Jersey.

Mukherjee, Prabhati, 1988, *Beyond the Four Varnas: The Untouchables in India*, Indian Institute of Advanced Study, Shimla and Motilal Banarsidas, Delhi.

Nadel, S.F, 1969, *The Theory of Social Structure*, Cohen and West, London.

O'Hanlon, Rosalind, 1985, *Caste, Conflict and Ideology: Mahatma Jotirao Phule and Low Caste protest in Nineteenth- Century Western India*, Orient Longman, New Delhi.

Omvedt, Gail, 1976, *Cultural Revolt in a Colonial Society: The Non-Brahman Movement in Western India, 1873 to 1930*, Scientific Socialist Education Trust, India.

Oommen, T.K., 2001, *Understanding the Indian Society: The Relevance of Perspective from Below*, Department of Sociology, University of Pune, Pune.

Parsons, T. 1961, 'The School Class as a Social System' in A.H. Halsey and J. Floud (eds.), *Education, Economy and Society*, The

Free Press, New York.

Parvathamma, C., 1978, 'The Remembered Village: A Brahminical Odyssey', *Contributions to Indian Sociology*, Vol. 12, No. 1, pp. 91-96.

Rao, Yagati Chinna, 2003, *Dalits' Struggle for Identity: Andhra and Hyderabad 1900-1950*, Kanishka Publishers, New Delhi.

Sarkar, Sumit, 2005, *Writing Social History*, Oxford University Press, New Delhi.

Scoville, James G., 1991, 'Towards a Model of Caste Economy' in James G. Scoville (ed.), *Status Influences in Third World Labour: Market, Caste, Gender and Custom*, De Gruyter, Berlin, New York.

Singh, Y., 1994, *Modernization of Indian Tradition*, Rawat Publications, New Delhi.

Valmiki, Omprakash, 2003, *Joothan: A Dalit's Life* (Translated from Hindi–*Joothan* by Arun Prabha Mukherjee), Samya, Kolkata.

Viswanathan, Gauri, 2001, *Outside the Fold: Conversion, Modernity, and Belief*, Oxford University Press, Delhi.

Wankhade, M.N., 1992, 'Friends, The Day of Irresponsible Writers is Over' in Arjun Dangle (ed.), *Poisoned Bread* (translated from the Modern Marathi Dalit Literature), Orient Longman, New Delhi.

Wallerstein, Immanuel, 1996, *The Gulbenkian Commission: The Restructuring of Social Sciences*, Stanford University Press, California, USA.

Zelliot, Elionar, 1970, 'Learning the Use of Political Means: The Mahars of Maharashtra' in Rajni Kothari (ed.), *Caste in Indian Politics*, Orient Longman, New Delhi.

———, 1992, *From Untouchable to Dalit*, Manohar, New Delhi.

11

The *'Coming Crisis'* of Social Science Education in India—Issues and Challenges

Avinash Kumar Singh

Many years ago, the American Scholar Alvin Gouldner wrote a book called *The Coming Crisis of Western Sociology*. Indian nationhood has been in 'crisis' at least since 15 August, 1947 and global capitalism has been in crisis at least since the middle decades of the nineteenth century. But in this case the term is well merited, for the 'crisis' of Indian social science is indeed upon us. (Guha 2008: 35)

The social science education in India suffers from multiple crises, in terms of its design, disciplinary practice and use by the stakeholders at large. The crises can be seen in terms of increasing social conflict and tensions, utter neglect of the disadvantaged and marginalised, and unemployability of social science graduates, etc. Although one cannot blame education alone for the current state of social affairs in the country, as it is merely a sub-system of the whole, it cannot be denied as well that there is the need to examine our education system entrusted with the task of preparing a social order imbued with justice, equality and fraternity. This paper attempts to present current and emerging issues affecting the social science education in India as the signal of a coming crisis[1] with the implications of restructuring and rejuvenation. The paper identifies gaps in the policy design and practice of social science education in the country. The cumulative crisis includes issues, such as, marginalisation of equity agenda, sub-ordination of the State to market forces, increasing withdrawal of State resources from education system in general and social science based university system in particular, and growing disenchantment among the educated towards the efficacy of their own thoughts and paradigms. The paper on the whole reflects upon the relationship between social problems and social science education in the country.

I. SOCIAL PROBLEMS IN INDIA

The nature and magnitude of the growing social problems currently faced by the country, such as, rape, murder, suicides, corruption, poverty, unemployment, etc is overwhelming and compels introspection. The prevailing condition is not simply an issue of anomie but a heightened form of social disorder. India which is in a state of social turmoil, political instability and economic uncertainty, showing symptoms of normlessness, needs a very well grounded scientific social inquiry. One wonders where more than one fourth of the population are illiterate and below poverty line, how education alone can be blamed for the sorry state of affairs. But if every second, when inhuman crimes like rape, murder and loot happen, one gets circumscribed to look into the way the children are raised in the family and taught in schools, and adults are seeking livelihood with or without education. As observed by Thorat (2013), the occurrences of discrimination based on caste, gender, race and religion are not disparate but a reflection of the ways in which our society works. And the existing education system, with its present curricula and pedagogy, has less to offer by way of civic learning and democratic engagement that shapes good citizens out of men and women.

So, the question arises, 'Do the social problems have any implication for the education system in general and social sciences in particular?' What is more fundamental in education, is the quality of education, as it determines the quality of the individual it brings out. In fact, the rising social problems are linked to the ineffective education system in the country. Although all levels and disciplines of education need systemic evaluation, the paper is limited to the nature and scope of social sciences only. There is the need to review the policy and practice of social science education in the country.

II. SOCIAL SCIENCE EDUCATION

In broad terms, the social sciences are those that aim for a rational and systematic understanding of human society. The social sciences comprise the application of scientific methods to the study of the human aspects of the world. At the school level, it is an integrated area of study covering contents drawn from the disciplines of history, geography, political science, economics and sociology, psychology, law, language, arts and so on. It differs from natural science education in a fundamental way. Besides academic, the social sciences have normative responsibility to instil right values in the students. The nature of the integration of contents becomes increasingly complex as we move from lower level to higher levels of education.

The discipline of social science has a close association with the university system, as it was the social scientists that were mainly responsible for the revival of the university systems in the nineteenth century[2] (Wallerstein 1996) The history of 'Social Science' as a body of knowledge also indicates that it grew where it was backed by reform agenda. Even in Europe where it originated, the seeds of seminal ideas were sown by the reformation and renaissance movements. The significance of teaching social sciences in schools is increasing day by day, as the human life is becoming increasingly complex and chaotic. In India, humanities and social sciences constitute more than half of the total higher education intake.[3]

The teaching of social sciences has been emphasised both at the school and higher education levels. The teaching of social sciences in post-independence India has been influenced by the goals of nation building, modernisation, and social justice as articulated in the Constitution and policy declarations. The Education Commission (1964-66) envisaged the role of social sciences in preparing the citizens of the Indian nation by raising the issue of evolving national standards for teaching of both natural and social sciences at different stages of school education. The curricular frameworks developed and prepared at the national levels are testimony to the processes incorporating national concerns and issues in the curriculum and textbooks. The theme of citizenship education has been a recurring theme of the social science textbooks since 1975 in all the curricular frameworks (1988, 2000 and 2005) with the aim of preparing a citizenry conscious of their rights and duties and committed to the principles embodied in the Constitution (NCERT, 2006)

At the higher education level, the history of the growth of social sciences in India indicates that the social science disciplines have had close association with the modern university system in the country linked with colonial encounters. The first three modern universities which were established during the British period in 1854, and the basic contents of the courses taught in the institutions were not changed for a long time (Chalam, 2012). The social science education in India did not get the backing of a reform agenda which the Europeans had. It is often alleged that the Indian education system has not been able to disengage from its colonial past of practising esoteric educational practices not linked to the land. The Indian education system has not engaged effectively with the prevailing issues. The basic ideological premises of social and economic development that evolved during the freedom struggle and got incorporated into the Constitution, are yet to be implemented effectively. The legal safeguards and protective measures embedded in the Constitutional provisions need to be coupled with strong civic learning professed by higher education institutions.

III. THE CRISIS OF SOCIAL SCIENCE EDUCATION

The crisis of social science education in India lies in the helplessness its academic disciplines to engage effectively with the subjects of their enquiry. Higher education in India today lacks the potential and capacity to promote cognitive knowledge, social skills, values and actions for civic learning and democratic engagement that are essential to build citizenship. (Thorat, 2013) The crisis can be seen in many forms, in terms of research and teaching. The Report of the ICSSR Review Committee (2007: 20) points out,

> While the scale and range of social science research in the country has been expanding, the nature, scope and quality of research output, as well as its contribution to better understanding of socio-economic processes and shaping public policy is widely perceived to have fallen short of expectations and is also not commensurate with the resources spent on them.

i) In India, universities and public-funded educational institutions are the main providers of social science education, in terms of teaching and research. However due to diminishing state support for academic research, the quality and scope of social science education have been on the decline and limited. According to Altbatch (2005), India's colleges and universities, with a few exceptions, have become large, underfunded and ungovernable institutions. Underinvestment in libraries, information technologies, laboratories and classrooms makes it very difficult to provide top quality instructions or engage in cutting edge research.

ii) In the post liberalisation and globalisation period, a number of non-governmental research organisations and private consultancy firms have come up to carry out specific goal oriented research, mainly in the forms of applied projects and policy oriented research programmes. These new actors and networks have a negative impact on the conventional research conducted in universities, as they wean the competent researchers away from the university system. The external brain drain problem, once restricted to the sciences and engineering, has also started affecting the humanities and social sciences (Guha 2008; Krishna and Krishna 2010)

iii) Social science educational institutions suffer from lack of freedom and autonomy. Major research projects on themes such as, religion, caste and ethnicity are vulnerable to political influences. The ideological rivalries are not much on intellectual and methodological grounds, but on political leanings. 'In such a situation, it becomes easy to pigeonhole individual scholars in ideological terms, as pro or anti *mandir*, pro or anti *mandal*, pro or anti market.' (Guha, 2008: 35) There is reluctance on the part of policy makers and academicians to have full scale inquiries of the social problems, currently faced by the society. Despite predominance of the caste system, there has been reluctance to conduct full scale caste census (Deshpande and Sundar, 1998).

iv) Low status to social sciences and marginalisation of the disadvantaged groups

It is to be noted that teaching of social science has close connection with equity issues in education. By equity issues in education, we mean issues related to education of the disadvantaged and marginalised who have remained deprived. Even after six decades of planned educational development, their participation in education at all levels of education has been limited. The participation is further skewed at higher education level, as they have to depend mainly on less demanded social science courses in public-funded universities and colleges. With diminishing government funds for universities and colleges, it is obvious that educational interests of the disadvantaged groups are getting compromised. The students from higher castes and classes are preferring science and engineering courses. In fact, at the very entry level in higher education, a large number of good students are lost to Science, Technology and MBA courses (Altbatch 2005)

v) Moreover in comparison to natural sciences, social sciences are also accorded lower status by the parents and community members who within the family set-up often select daughters or low performing sons for humanities and social science courses, keeping in mind the future returns on education. The policy makers and administrators treat these institutions and courses of lower priority, in terms of resource support and meant mainly for the disadvantaged groups, such as SCs, STs, and other backward groups. The social composition of students in higher education as reflected in Table 1 explains and illustrates how these disadvantaged groups are concentrated mainly in social science courses.

Table 1: Participation in Higher Education by Type of Course (%)

Courses	*ST*	*SC*	*OBC*	*Others*	*Total*
Arts	59.29	49.10	39.77	34.12	39.04
Science	5.70	11.12	12.37	10.19	10.95
Commerce	6.39	11.38	11.40	15.97	13.37
Medicine	0.00	0.32	2.21	3.54	2.51
Engineering	6.16	4.85	11.87	11.41	10.51
Agriculture	2.58	0.19	0.75	0.82	0.77
Law	0.10	0.26	0.50	0.74	0.56
Management	0.57	1.30	0.98	3.34	2.12
Education	4.45	2.17	2.80	1.72	2.26
CA	0.44	0.27	0.18	1.09	0.63
IT all levels	9.88	13.34	14.60	14.52	14.23
Vocational	4.44	5.71	2.58	2.52	3.04
Overall	**100.00**	**100.00**	**100.00**	**100.00**	**100.00**

(*Source*: NSSO, 64th Round, 2010)

So, social group-wise participation in disciplines indicates that students belonging to the disadvantaged groups depend largely on Arts, Humanities and Social Sciences. Keeping in mind the increasing costs of professional education, the distribution would be getting further skewed against the already marginalised.

vi) Marginalisation of 'Equity' as a Policy Concern: 'Equity' as a policy concern in education refers to education of the disadvantaged and marginalised who have remained excluded from the zone of education and development. They include groups, such as the SC, the ST, the Muslims, the OBC, etc. The nature of socio-economic composition of students in higher education institutions has increasingly become more heterogeneous and diverse. Now a large number of students from rural areas and from OBC, SC and ST categories are joining the university system. Although the nature of socio-economic composition of students in higher education institutions has increasingly become more heterogeneous and diverse, the civic learning is essential for dealing with diversity.

vii) The approach and policy of inclusion has been half hearted and less productive. If we add the numbers of all the disadvantaged and marginalised, together they would constitute more than half of the population in India, and the majority in many states, so much so that some of the states as whole entilities can be treated as excluded from the zone of education and development. So the issue is not 'inclusion' of a few groups of people, but the overall development of the society, and the design and process of education and development, adopted by the country as a whole, whereby the focus has been more on the peripheries, rather than holistic. Unfortunately, the target-based approach to education, without having proper thinking on 'relevant education' has not helped the disadvantaged.

viii) Although a large number of private institutions of higher education have started functioning, it is to be noted that the government is still the main provider of higher education especially social science education in the country (See Table 2). The students of the disadvantaged and marginalised groups

Table 2: Participation in Higher Education by Type of Institution

	Participation in Higher Education by Type of Institution (%)				
Types of Institutions	*ST*	*SC*	*OBC*	*Others*	*All*
Govt.	57.00	52.00	41.00	45.00	47.00
Local	2.00	1.00	1.00	1.00	1.00
Private aided	21.00	31.00	31.00	29.00	28.00
Private unaided	20.00	14.00	26.00	25.00	22.00
Not known	-	2.00	1.00	1.00	2.00
Overall	**100.00**	**100.00**	**100.00**	**100.00**	**100.00**

(Source: NSSO, 64th Round, 2010)

depend mainly on the government universities for education and their participation in social science education is higher in social science courses than in other technical and professional courses. At the higher education level, social science disciplines within the university system are getting marginalised, leading to further marginalisation of the deprived and marginalised, as reflected in the dwindling number of students opting for social science subjects at the graduate and post-graduate levels.

ix) Unemployment and Unemployability of the Social Science: The prime focus in school and higher education learning system in recent years has been mainly preparing for the job market. (Thorat, 2013). The government employment data (NSSO, 2014, 68th Round) clearly indicates the inverse relationship between education and employment. That is, the rate of unemployment rises with the level of education. In other words, unemployment rate is the highest at the highest level of education. Moreover, the problem seems insurmountable with increasing unemployment among the educated disadvantaged including SCs, STs and minorities. The incidence of educated unemployment is higher among the social science graduates than among the students of other disciplines (Singh, 2006). This clearly indicates that there is something wrong with the ongoing education system as a whole in terms of policy design and practice.

x) Higher education is getting privatised on a massive scale. The public institutions dependent on social science courses are facing resource constraints due to diminishing State financial support. A dilemmatic condition prevails, as higher education remains in animated suspension like *Trishanku* between the State and the market (Tilak, 2005; Kapur and Mehta, 2004). The issue is not only funding, but overall resource support and autonomy. International experience suggests that mere financial availability is not sufficient to develop social sciences. Study on ICSSR funding, too, in early 1970s noted that research output did not necessarily improve with increased funding. Clearly, other conditions are necessary for research funds to have the desired results. (Chatterjee, 2002).

IV. THEORETICAL CRISIS IN SOCIAL SCIENCE

According to Guha (2008), the current state of affairs in the social science education amounts to nothing less than a "crisis", comparable to the level of crisis articulated by Gouldner (1970). There is a feeling of helplessness not only among the policy makers and planners, but also among the academicians about the efficacy of theoretical ideals and conceptual tools. It seems that macrogeneralisations in the form of functional and conflict theories have been played out and are not offering critical insights in understanding the complex Indian social contexts. Higher education in India today lacks the potential and capacity to promote cognitive knowledge, social skills, values and actions for civic learning and democratic engagement that are essential to build citizenship. (Thorat, 2013). The ideological premises of socio-economic development which evolved during the independence movement got incorporated into the philosophy of socio-economic development after independence, have yet to yield satisfactory results. Although the Constitution of India provides for democracy, freedom, secularism, equality and social justice, in the form of Fundamental Rights and Directive Principles, untouchability and various other forms of social decimations based on traditional social structure are yet to be eradicated.

The process of indigenous knowledge creation in social science has been far from satisfactory. It suffered from western domination of knowledge, elitism, urban bias, and further due to disciplinary imbalance, lack of inter-disciplinarity and brain drain (Sharma 1992). There is dominance of western knowledge over the productivity ambience of the Indian social science education. The colonial legacy of modern formal education has left an indelible impact on theoretical perspectives deployed by the Indian social scientists who often seek credence in the Euro-American knowledge base. However, it is also true that concepts derived from the western paradigm of knowledge will not be of much help in developing a proper understanding of problems rooted in the Indian context. According to Bagchi (1996), contemporary social science displays many tensions between specialisation and efforts at integration, between borrowing from other disciplines and 'sticking to one's last', and between recognition of the specific disciplinary demands of cognate disciplines and overweening ambition to impose one specific method on the discussion of all questions in social science disciplines.

Concluding Remarks

The social science education in India is facing a deep disciplinary crisis, to prove its efficacy. The depth of the crisis lies more in its nature than in its degree. The contemporary disciplinary scene of social science education is described as a sea of mediocrity with tiny islands of excellence. It is often said that the first phase of social science education which took roots in western enlightments during the nineteenth century and got nurtured in public institutions, had constructive engagements with Indian freedom struggle and post-independence Constitutional reforms and development. The status and effectiveness of the disciplines has been on decline and worsened in recent years. With increasing domination of the market over the State, university education system which once nurtured social science disciplines, is facing aggressive privatisation and commercialisation, throwing equity agenda out of gear. 'Privatisation in education has resulted from a breakdown of the state system and the exit of Indian elites from public institutions, to both private sector institutions within the country as well as abroad' (Kapur and Mehta, 2004:2). Consequently the social science courses within the university system have become a refuge or parking slots for the underperforming students drawn mainly from disadvantaged and marginalised, who otherwise cannot afford costly quality technical and professional courses in private institutions. Consequently, the nature, quality and scope of social science education in education both in terms of research and teaching have fallen short of expectations (ICSSR, 2007; Guha, 2008). *The World Social Science Report-2010* remark that "Social Science is least developed where it is most needed" applies to India, keeping in mind the rising social problems and declining standard of social science education in the country.

NOTES

1. The phrase 'Coming Crisis' has been used in this chapter, with insights drawn from Alvin Gouldner's (1971) *The Coming Crisis of Western Sociology*, in which the author has discussed the eroding base of macrotheoretical generalisation advocated by the western thinkers. The current and emerging problems of the social sciences in India not only indicate the lack of resources, but also the lack of theoretical ideas to take up the challenge.
2. Between 1850 and 1945, a series of disciplines came to be defined as constituting an arena of knowledge to which the name 'social science' was accorded... done by the establishing universities first chairs, offering degrees in the disciplines, research, association of scholars on disciplinary lines, the creation of library collections catalogued by disciplines (Wallerstein, 1996)
Wallerstein, I 1997: 'Euro-centrism and its Avatars: The Dilemmas of Social Science', *Sociological Bulletin*, 46 (1): 21-39.
Wallerstein, I et al. (1996): *Open the Social Sciences: Report of the Gulbenkian Commission on the Restructuring of the Social Sciences*, Vistaar Publications, New Delhi.
3. According to Wallerstein, 1966. Social Science is the enterprise of the modern world to develop systematic, secular knowledge about reality that is validated empirically.

REFERENCES

Altbatch, P. 2005. 'Higher Education in India', *The Hindu*, 12 April, 2005, Tuesday (www.hindu.com/2005/04/12/stories).

Bagchi, Amiya Kumar. 1996. 'Contextual Social Science: or Crossing Boundaries', *Economic and Political Weekly*, Vol. 31, No. 43, (October 26), pp. 2875-2882.

Chalam, D.S. 2002. 'Rethinking Social Sciences' *Economic and Political Weekly*, Vol. 37, No. 10 (March, 9-15) pp. 921-922.

Chatterjee, Partha. 2002. 'Institutional Context of Social Research in South Asia', *Economic and Political Weekly*, Vol. XXXVII, No. 35, August 31- September 6, pp. 3602-3612.

Despande, Satish and Sundar, Nandini. 1998. Caste and the Census: Implications for Society and the Social Sciences, *Economic and Political Weekly*, Vol. 33, No. 32 (August, 8-14) pp. 2157-2159.

Gouldner, Alvin W. 1970. *The Coming Crists of Western Sociology*, Basic Books Inc. Publishers, New York.

Government of India. 1966. *Education and National Development - Report of the Education Commission (1964-66)*, Ministry of Education, New Delhi.

Guha, Ramachandra. 2008. 'Autonomy and Ideology', *Economic and Political Weekly*, Vol. 43, No. 5, pp. 33-35.

Indian Council of Social Science Research (ICSSR). 2007. *Restructuring the Indian Council of Social Science Research - Report of the Fourth Review Committee*, ICSSR, New Delhi.

Kapur, Devesh and Mehta, Pratap Bhanu. 2004. 'India Higher Education Reform: From Half Baked Socialism to Half Baked Capitalism', CID Working Paper-108, Centre for International Development, Harvard University, Massachussets.

Krishna, Venni V. and Usha Krishna. 2010. 'Social Science in South Asia' in UNESCO *'World Social Science Report - Knowledge Divides'*, UNESCO-ISSC, Paris, pp. 77-81.

Mahatma Gandhi University. *Village Sustainable Development: KRPLLD Project Report*, School of Social Sciences, Kottayam.

MHHDC (Mahbubul Haq Human Development Centre). 2004. *Human Development in South Asia: The Employment Challenge*, Karachi: Oxford University Press.

Mukherji, P.N. and Sengupta, C. (eds) 2004. *Indigeneity and Universality in Social Science: A South Asian Response*, Sage Publications, New Delhi.

NCERT. 2006. *Position Paper-National Focus Group on Teaching of Social Sciences*, NCERT, New Delhi.

National Sample Survey Organisation. 2010. *Education in India 2007-08: Participation and Expenditure*, Report No. 532 (64/25.2/1), New Delhi

National Sample Survey Organisation. 2014. *Employment and Unemployment Situation in India, 2011-12*, Report No. 554(68/10/1), New Delhi.

Singh, Avinash Kumar. 2006. 'Degree Devaluation in Higher Education', *Journal of Educational Planning and Administration,* Vol. XX No. 4, October, pp. 411-428.

Thorat, Sukhdeo. 2013. 'Unlearning Undemocratic Values', *The Hindu,* 26 December, Thursday.

Tilak, J.B.G. 2005. 'Higher Education in 'Trishanku': Hanging Between State and Market' *Economic and Political Weekly,* Vol. XL, No. 37, September 10, pp. 4029-4037.

UNESCO. 2010. *World Social Science Report—Knowledge Divides,* UNESCO-ISSC, Paris.

Wallerstein, I. 1997. 'Euro-centrism and its Avatars: The Dilemmas of Social Science', *Sociological Bulletin,* 46 (1): 21-39.

Wallerstein, I., et al. 1996. *Open the Social Sciences: Report of the Gulbenkian Commission on the Restructuring of the Social Sciences,* Vistaar Publications, New Delhi.

About the Contributors

Prashant Bansode is Associate Professor and in-charge of the Center for Study of Social Exclusion and Inclusive Policy at Gokhale Institute of Politics and Economics, Pune. His areas of interest are Sociology of Agrarian Society, Sociology of Development, Social Movements and Marginalized Groups. He has also taught at the Department of Sociology, University of Mumbai and University of Pune. His doctoral work is on Dalit Assertion for Land in Maharashtra. His recent research focus has been on Social Exclusion and Inclusive Policy for Dalits, Adivasis, Labour, and Sugarcane Cutters and Domestic workers. He has published several papers in these areas in various journals. Currently he is working on to understand the social inclusiveness of Maharashtra Agricultural Competitiveness Project (MACP) as Social Development expert besides on the issue of indebtedness and faremrs' suicides in Maharashtra.

Vaishali Kolhe is currently working as Associate Professor and Chairperson of the Centre for Disability Studies and Action, School of Social work at the Tata Institute of Social Sciences (TISS). She is primarily engaged in teaching, training, research and consultation in the field of rehabilitation and disability in context of health, mental health, early intervention, family, education, livelihood and accessibility. She is also instrumental in initiating first field action project, 'I Access Rights Mission: TISS Initiative for Inclusion' at the Centre for Disability Studies & Action. This works with students with disability and peers on emerging issues of students with disability at university level and works with stakeholders like teachers, staff, peers to facilitate the process of deconstructing stereotypes and initiating inclusion processes at classroom level with peer support. The project works at conducting access audits of university and conducts sensitization programmes using art, creative expression and theater to create an inclusive culture.

Vivek Kumar is Professor of Sociology at the Center for the Study of Social Systems, School of Social Sciences, Jawaharlal Nehru University where he earned his M Phil and Ph D and a recipient of Fulbright Teachers' Fellowship. Professor Kumar was visiting Associate Professor in the Department of Sociology, Columbia university and also he has been visiting fellow at Humboldt University, Berlin under the DAAD-UGC programme. He also taught at the Tata Institute of Social Sciences, Universities of Pune and Jammu. His publications include *Caste and Democracy in India* and edited a volume *Dynamics of Change and Continuity in the Age of Globalization: Voices from the Margins, India's Roaring Revolution and Dalit Leadership in India*. He has published several articles and papers in journals and books besides he completed a research project on Indian college students jointly with a professor from university of British Columbia. His specialization includes Methodology of Social Sciences, Social Stratification, Social Movements and Dalit Studies.

Renu Nanda, Professor of Education, is currently Head, Postgraduate Department of Education, University of Jammu, Jammu & Kashmir (J&K). She has earned PhD Degree in Education from Department of Education, University of Jammu. She is member Governing Body: Sarva Shiksha Abhiyan, State Literacy Mission Authority for Implementation of Female Literacy, Rashtriya Madhyamik Shiksha Abhiyan, J&K State and member, Review Board, J&K State Prisons, State Core Group for Programmes of NUEPA, Advisor, Sahara School, Jammu (for differently abled children). Prof. Nanda has research experience on issues related to educational technology, primary education, higher education, gender, non formal education and governance and three major research projects (ICSSR, BS&G, NCERT). She has experience of extension and field work in education, social work and reach out for the last 25 years. She has authored 34 research papers, two books, one monograph. Recipient of National Values

Award for promoting and inculcating values among rural, and under privileged children in the border villages of J&K, Eni Management, Milan, Italy for Children's Education Programme on Energy, Efficiency Campaign, Petroleum Geology and Global Warming in India in 2009 and Uprashtrapati Award as Ranger Leader for J&K State in 2003.

Gaurav J Pathania, a trained sociologist and research scholar at the Zakir Husain Centre for Educational Studies at Jawaharlal Nehru University (JNU). He has been researching student activism in India since 2010. His MPhil, dissertation explores the emergence of caste based student activism and identity assertion at JNU. The research findings of this study have been presented at the University of Oxford. His doctoral thesis is on ethnographic study of the student movement at Osmania University for Telangana Statehood. His writings on student activism have been published in national and international journals including Sage and Cambridge Scholars Publishing. He has also reviewed the latest published account on Telangana which appeared in *South Asia Research*. His upcoming publications include Regionalism in Democracy (in an edited volume on Democracy by CSDS); and Ethnography of Caste on Campus. His future work will explore issues of identity and social justice among lower caste youth and students in India.

Ivan Reid, Ph D, CertEd, CertPS, FCollP, FGCYDCA, FRSA is the Chancellor of Share World Open University, Malawi, Emeritus Professor of Education at Loughborough University and a Visiting Professor at York St. John University and the University of Bradford University [all UK]. Although a trained butcher and history teacher, nearly all of his career has been almost exclusively in teacher education and training, though he regards himself as a sociologist and this is reflected in his publications. He has taught, researched and managed at Edge Hill College of Education and the Universities of Liverpool, Bradford, Leeds and Loughborough. He has published extensively – some 14 books, 30 contributions to books, over a hundred academic journal papers and an even larger number of reports and monographs - in the fields of his research and scholarly activity, primarily on British social inequalities and educational opportunity, the sociology of education, teacher education and the evaluation of local and national education policy initiatives. He has acted as a consultant, visiting academic or external examiner in some ten countries worldwide. He served over 30 years as the Executive Editor of *Research in Education* and a Founder Executive Editor of the *British Journal of Sociology of Education*. He served twice as Vice Chair of the Universities' Council for the Education of Teachers [UCET], and is Emeritus Board member of the International Council on the Education of Teachers [ICET].He has supervised a considerable number of higher degrees across a broad spectrum of approaches—from ethnographic to the analysis of official data—a number of disciplines - mainly sociology, psychology, social psychology and history - and sited in a range of situations, including most educational and some para-medical, familial and voluntary institutional ones and spanning several countries.

Pradeep Shinde, Assistant Professor of Sociology, Centre for Informal Sector and Labour Studies, School of Social Sciences, Jawaharlal Nehru University, New Delhi. Pradeep has been a recipient of numerous fellowships/awards for his research in anthropology/sociology. Some of these are: a doctoral fellowship from the Ford foundation International Fellowships Programme 2002-2005, LSE's Doctoral thesis writing awards for three consecutive years, a DAAD Teaching fellowship under the India Passage programme in 2011 by Kassel University, Germany, and the IGK Work and Human Lifecycle in Global History fellowship by the Centre re:work, Humboldt University, Berlin in 2012-13. He obtained a PhD from the London School of Economics and Political Science in Social Anthropology in 2011. During the same year, he, as a post-doctoral fellow, taught at the International Centre for Development and Decent Work and researched in the following year at the Centre re:work, Humboldt University, Berlin. He has published on the categories of work and caste in the informal sector in national and international journals. He continues to engage with these along with concepts of mobility, labour, and Denotified tribe in his research. Prior to this, he also taught sociology at the University of Pune for a year. Along with teaching sociology at CISLS, Pradeep is currently involved in ethnographic research on informal sector workers in Mumbai and the National Capital Region.

Avinash Kumar Singh, currently working as Professor and Head of the Department of Educational Policy, National University of Educational Planning and Administration, New Delhi. Previously served as Associate Professor at Tata Institute of Social Sciences, Mumbai. Has completed several large scale research studies and published research papers and articles in national and international journals and books in the field of tribal education, decentralized educational governance, alternative schooling, etc. His recent publications include, *Education and Empowerment in India: Policies and Practices.*

Smriti Singh is a trained elementary school teacher and currently a doctoral student at Zakir Husain Centre for Educational Studies, School of Social Sciences, Jawaharlal Nehru University (JNU), New Delhi. Her Doctoral research is on "Middle Classness, Education and Cultural Practices among the Gated Communities of Gurgaon". She is currently a Nehru-Fulbright Doctoral Fellow and is visiting University of Michigan at Ann Arbor, Michigan as a fellow. She had completed her M Phil from JNU in 2012 on "Teacher Agency, Subjectivity and Classroom Pedagogy: An Exploratory Study" She has also taught for brief periods at Undergraduate Courses at Delhi University, and Azim Premji University. She has been contributing articles in edited volumes for IGNOU courses.

Jandhyala B.G. Tilak, Professor and an economist of education, is currently Vice Chanellor, National University of Educational Planning and Administration, New Delhi. He has earned PhD in Economics from the Delhi School of Economics (University of Delhi). He had taught in the Indian Institute of Education, the University of Delhi, Sri Sathya Sai Institute of Higher Learning, the Hiroshima University, and the University of Virginia. Dr Tilak was also on the research staff of the World Bank, Washington D.C., and has authored/edited a dozen books and more than 250 research papers. Recipient of the Swami Pranavananda Saraswati UGC National Award of the UGC in Education, Malcolm Adiseshiah Award, Inspirational Teacher of the Year Global Education award and Dewang Mehta National Education Award for outstanding contribution to education. Professor Tilak is the Editor of the *Journal of Educational Planning and Administration*, and is on the boards of several national and international journals. Prof Tilak is also a member of several official committees on education of the Government of India and also served the Comparative Education Society of India as its President. He also had a distinct privilege of lecturing in a meeting of the Nobel Laureates in Barcelona, in 2005.

Govardhan Wankhede, is former Professor and Dean, School of Education, Tata Institute of Social Sciences, Mumbai and has been engaged in research and teaching for more than three decades. His major areas of interest have been education of the Scheduled castes; particularly higher education and the Reservation Policy in India. Professor Wankhede has completed several major research projects for the Government of India including two international and published books and articles/papers in journals and books. He has been on several committees/boards of the Government of India at policy and planning level. He also participated and presented papers in many national and international seminars and conferences. He has been a recipient of faculty exchange fellowship of DAAD Germany, France and the UK.